D0166463

# New Proclamation
# Year A 2011

## Easter through Christ the King
## April 24, 2011—November 24, 2011

Nancy Claire Pittman

Richard I. Pervo

S. D. Giere

Shauna K. Hannan

David B. Lott, Editor

Fortress Press

Minneapolis

NEW PROCLAMATION
Year A 2011
Easter through Christ the King
April 24, 2011—November 24, 2011

Copyright © 2010 Fortress Press, an imprint of Augsburg Fortress. All rights reserved. Except for brief quotations in critical articles or reviews, no part of this book may be reproduced in any manner without prior written permission from the publisher. Visit augsburgfortress.org/copyrights/contact.asp or write to Permissions, Augsburg Fortress, Box 1209, Minneapolis, MN 55440.

Unless otherwise noted, scripture quotations are the author's own translation or from the New Revised Standard Version Bible, copyright © 1989 by the Division of Christian Education of the National Council of Churches of Christ in the USA, and are used with permission.

Illustrations: Joel Nickel, Peggy Adams Parker, Robyn Sand Anderson, Meg Bussey, and Paula Wiggins, © 2010 Augsburg Fortress
Cover design: Laurie Ingram
Book design: Sharon Martin

**Library of Congress Cataloging-in-Publication Data**
The Library of Congress has catalogued this series as follows.
New Proclamation: Year A, 2010–2011 Easter through Christ the King.
     p. cm.
  Includes bibliographical references.
  ISBN 978-0-8066-9631-7
     1. Church year.
  BV30 .N48 2001
  2511.6dc21 2001023746

*Library of Congress Cataloging-in-Publication Data*
ISBN 978-0-8066-9631-7

The paper used in this publication meets the minimum requirements of American National Standard for Information Sciences—Permanence of Paper for Printed Library Materials, ANSI Z329.48-1984.

Manufactured in the U.S.A.

| 13 | 12 | 11 | 10 | 1 | 2 | 3 | 4 | 5 | 6 | 7 | 8 |
|----|----|----|----|---|---|---|---|---|---|---|---|

# NEW PROCLAMATION

# Contents

## Time after Pentecost / Ordinary Time
## Proper 15 through Proper 22
## S. D. Giere

# Time after Pentecost / Ordinary Time
## Proper 23 through Christ the King plus Thanksgiving
### Shauna K. Hannan

# Preface

For nearly four decades Fortress Press has offered an ecumenical preaching resource built around the three-year lectionary cycle, a tradition that this latest edition of *New Proclamation* continues. *New Proclamation* is grounded in the belief that a deeper understanding of the biblical pericopes in both their historical and liturgical contexts is the best means to inform and inspire preachers to deliver engaging and effective sermons. For this reason, the most capable North American biblical scholars and homileticians are invited to contribute to *New Proclamation*.

New Proclamation* has always distinguished itself from most other lectionary resources by offering brand-new editions each year, each dated according to the church year in which it will first be used, and featuring a fresh set of authors. Yet each edition is planned as a timeless resource that preachers will want to keep on their bookshelves for future reference for years to come. In addition, *New Proclamation*, true to its ecumenical scope, has traditionally offered commentary on all of the major lectionary traditions. Now, reflecting changes in practices among the mainline Protestant denominations, those number just two: the Revised Common Lectionary (RCL) and the Roman Catholic Lectionary for Mass (LFM).

New Proclamation* is published in two volumes per year. The first volume, published earlier this year, covers all the Sunday lections and major festivals from Advent through Easter Vigil. This second volume begins with commentary on the Easter feast and covers the remaining Sunday lections and major festivals through Christ the King Sunday as well as Thanksgiving Day. For those churches that celebrate minor feast days and solemnities, including saints' days and the Feast of the Transfiguration (August 6), denominational days such as Reformation (October 31), and national days and topical celebrations, a separate volume covering the texts for those days is available: *New Proclamation Commentary on Feasts, Holy Days, and Other Celebrations* (ed. David B. Lott; Fortress Press, 2007).

Longtime users of *New Proclamation* will note that this latest edition adopts a fresh look, which ties the series in visually with Augsburg Fortress's popular worship resource *Sundays and Seasons*. We hope that this change not only makes the text more readable and accessible, but also encourages readers to use these fine resources in tandem with each other. We also invite you to visit this volume's companion Web site, www.NewProclamation.com, which offers access not only to this book's contents, but also to commentary from earlier editions, up-to-the-minute thoughts on the connection between texts and current events, user forums, and other resources to help you develop your sermons and enhance your preaching.

What has not changed with this edition is the high quality of the content that *New Proclamation* provides to preachers and those interested in studying the lectionary texts. Each writer offers an introduction to her or his commentary that provides insights into the background and spiritual significance of that season (or portion thereof), as well as ideas for planning one's preaching during that time. In addition, the application of biblical texts to contemporary situations is an important concern of each contributor. Exegetical work is concise, and thoughts on how the texts address today's world, congregational issues, and personal situations have a prominent role.

The writers in this volume not only come from different denominations and academic disciplines, but also are at different stages of their professions. Nancy Claire Pittman brings a wealth of experience in New Testament, practical theology, and spiritual direction to the Easter texts. Richard Pervo contributed several times previously to this resource's predecessor series, *Proclamation*, and is author of numerous acclaimed Fortress Press publications in New Testament studies. Samuel Giere and Shauna Hannan, who make their Fortress Press debuts with this volume, are both Lutheran homiletics professors who have just recently commenced their teaching careers; their promise shines through in their contributions. All four breathe new life into the lectionary texts and will help preachers do the same as they proclaim the gospel within the congregations they serve. We are grateful to each of these contributors for their insights and their commitment to effective Christian preaching, and are confident that you will find in this volume ideas, stimulation, and encouragement for your ministry of proclamation.

David B. Lott

# Easter
## Nancy Claire Pittman

The disciples hover in an in-between space in the Gospel readings for the season of Eastertide. The doorway between life before Jesus' death and life afterward has been opened by the resurrection. But they are not sure how to walk through into a life wholly different from anything they had known before. How to move from disciple to apostle. How to leave behind the familiar rituals of a static band of followers for the ever-expanding, always-changing new community of believers that we now call church. They stand on a threshold—looking backward, perhaps with longing, into a room full of memory of the beloved teacher, and looking forward, with trepidation by all accounts, into a room so brightly lit by resurrection glory that they cannot discern even the outlines of the furniture.

Anthropologists talk of liminality in human life, the in-between time when people change from one social role into another. It is a time that is marked by ambiguity, indeterminacy, and openness in terms of identity and status. Thus, persons who change status leave one "territory," in a metaphorical sense, to cross the threshold into a new territory, a new location of existence. Arnold van Gennep explained a century ago that to leave one place and enter another consists of three kinds of rites: "the rites of separation from a previous world, *preliminal rites*, those executed during the transitional stage, *liminal (or threshold) rites*, and the ceremonies of incorporation into the new world, *post-liminal rites*" (italics his).[1]

Unfortunately, the disciples had no time to invent such rites to help them move from preresurrection to postresurrection life, but they still experienced separation, transition, and incorporation. They had to find ways to separate from the previous social, political, and religious order, to make a transition into a new understanding of God's activity in the world, and at last to become incorporated into a new community of faith. While their words, experiences, and rituals, recorded in the Gospels and the book of Acts, cannot be so neatly divided into three stages, the drives to separate, to make a change, to become a new community are strongly present in these readings.

So in Eastertide we review the memories of these first followers as they struggled to find the right words to describe what exactly had happened to them in the death and resurrection of Jesus. We walk with them as they look for ways to express their newness not simply in terms of personal identity but in social stance toward the dominant culture. We hear how they were transformed into witnesses to God's extraordinary involvement in the life of Jesus, their own lives, and the lives of all to come after them. But only at the end of the season are they at last empowered by the Spirit to proclaim the gospel and to form an enduring ecclesial community.

Our task as preachers is to hold the door open between Jesus' resurrection and our own new life during this season. Too quickly we move from the alleluia-high of Easter to the long, liturgical green season after Pentecost. What if instead we invite our people to stand on the threshold with the disciples for the few weeks of Eastertide? What if we refuse the easy closure of "Jesus arose, appeared to a couple of people, moved on, and that's that," and instead with our congregations hover in the doorway with the disciples as they to figure out what it all means? The North American earth changes from winter browns and whites to summer greens; couldn't we stay around to watch the fits and starts of both scraggly weeds that must be pulled and colorful blooms that must be nourished? Our cultural climate is changing just as fast and with it our churches; couldn't we hang out for a long moment and think about how the resurrected Christ works in all these shifting times? Then we might give ourselves a chance to figure out what it all means for us right now. We might discover the ways the Holy Spirit is shaping us into a new community of faith. And we might gather the courage and the faith we need to go out into the world to witness to the abundant life God offers in Christ Jesus.

We have as resources for this work the Gospel readings in Year A of Eastertide. These are comprised of the resurrection accounts from all the Gospels except Mark and readings from the Gospel of John, which includes Jesus' instructions for the new community of friends given in the Farewell Discourse. As in every cycle of both lectionaries, the first readings of Eastertide are primarily taken from the Acts of the Apostles. In the RCL there are only three readings from the Hebrew Bible; two appear on Easter day and the other on Pentecost. There are no Hebrew Bible texts in the LFM.

The paucity of texts from the Hebrew Bible during Eastertide helps us guard against the temptation to interpret them through a postresurrection lens or the kinds of anti-Judaism and supercessionism that has so often characterized Christian preaching. However, Acts itself (not to mention Luke and John) is rife with this danger for two reasons. First, Luke used pieces of the Hebrew Scriptures in ways that seem random to our modern sensibilities to flesh out the meaning of Jesus' death and resurrection. He and his audience were not interested in original context or other canons of modern biblical scholarship and had their own rules of interpretation of the only sacred scriptures at their disposal to make sense of their experience of Jesus. Second, in the stories and speeches of Acts is much vitriolic finger pointing against the Jewish leaders who were accused of crucifying Jesus. These words, in turn, have been among the tools used historically by Christians to incite violent anti Semitism, often in Eastertide. We now have the obligation to do everything we can in our pulpits to speak honestly about problematic portions of the Christian Scriptures that have led to slanders and persecutions perpetrated against Jews, even today.[2]

As always, the psalms are selected to respond to the first readings; in this case, they highlight the proclamation of good news in the Acts texts. All of them in this season are joyous thanksgivings to God for escape from death, for abundance of life, for blessings beyond measure. The second readings in both lectionaries mainly consist of a semicontinuous reading of 1 Peter. However, on Sundays on which a particular theme predominates, the second reading is chosen from other epistles, or Acts, to harmonize with the Gospel lection.

## Notes

1. Arnold van Gennep, *The Rites of Passage*, trans. Monika B. Vizedom and Gabrielle L. Caffee (Chicago: University of Chicago Press, 1960), 21.
2. For more on how to avoid anti-Judaism when preaching from John's Gospel and other texts, see, among others: Ronald J. Allen and Clark Williamson, *Preaching the Gospel without Blaming the Jews: A Lectionary Commentary* (Louisville: Westminster John Knox, 2004); Marilyn J. Salmon, *Preaching without Contempt: Overcoming Unintended Anti-Judaism*, Fortress Resources for Preaching (Minneapolis: Fortress Press, 2006); *Anti-Judaism and the Fourth Gospel*, ed. Reimund Bieringer, Didier Pollefeyt, and Frederique Vandecasteele-Vanneuville (Louisville: Westminster John Knox, 2001).

# April 24, 2011
## Resurrection of Our Lord / Easter Day

**Revised Common Lectionary (RCL)**

Acts 10:34-43 or Jeremiah 31:1-6
Psalm 118:1-2, 14-24
Colossians 3:1-4 or Acts 10:34-43

John 20:1-18 or Matthew 28:1-10

**Lectionary for Mass (LFM)**

Acts 10:34a, 37-43
Psalm 118:1-2, 16-17, 22-23
Colossians 3:1-4 or
    1 Corinthians 5:6b-8
John 20:1-9

The colorful baskets are prepared, loaded with trinkets, candy, and chocolate bunnies, and tucked away in a corner of the closet. The plastic and the dyed eggs have been sorted and hidden in age-appropriate levels of difficulty. The new clothes are all laid out on the backs of chairs. The ham sits in the refrigerator between the green bean casserole and the deviled eggs. In the sanctuary the white lilies line the steps of the chancel. The candles wait unlit on the altar. It is Easter morning, before the children have awakened, before the most faithful attenders have arrived for the sunrise service, before the trumpets have been tuned, the choir warmed up, the baptistery filled. Not a single alleluia has been shouted or chocolate bunny consumed. The congregation has not sung "Jesus Christ Is Risen Today." The pastor has not jokingly welcomed the "E and C" (Easter and Christmas) members.

In this stillness is found the moment of resurrection. In the dim light before dawn, in the moment before the birds begin to sing, something quiet happens. Unnoticed and unwitnessed by human eyes and ears. Just a stone rolling away from the opening of a cave; a breath of wind stirring in a cemetery. Jesus lives. And with him we live. Alleluia.

But how do we witness to this instant of unseen glory? How do we testify to this cosmic reversal that occurs in the space between one breath and another? How do we give voice to this wordless happening? Responding to these challenges is the preacher's Easter task, and what we have as resources to meet this task are the texts of the day— themselves efforts by the earliest Christians to bear witness to the ineffable. The texts selected from the Gospels and the Acts of the Apostles contain reports of the events of the first Easter morning and the testimony that Jesus somehow lives. The epistle readings are early confessions about the significance of Jesus' resurrection. Even the Jeremiah and Psalms texts are chosen for the way they express faith in God's enduring work of bringing new life in the midst of death.

# First Reading
## Acts 10:34-43 (RCL)
## Acts 10:34a, 37-43 (LFM)

This passage, which consists of Peter's response to the visions that brought him and the centurion Cornelius together, serves as one of several summaries of the salvific features of Jesus' life and death. Although the speech is occasioned by Peter's new understanding that God is not partial to one nation over another, that theme is muted in this text's appearance at Easter. This is especially apparent in the LFM, which omits Peter's opening statement concerning God's inclusion of all people in the scope of God's grace (vv. 34b-36). What is central to this text's placement today is the confession that God has acted in Jesus of Nazareth, in his life in Galilee and Judea, in his death in Jerusalem, and in his resurrection.

Furthermore, the speech emphasizes the significance of witness to God's work in Jesus for his followers. Four times, in verses 39-43, Peter uses a noun or verb form of the root *martureo*—to bear witness—in his description of what God has accomplished in Jesus. He reminds his hearers that the disciples were witnesses to what Jesus did in Judea and Jerusalem and to his death. They were chosen by God as witnesses to his resurrection appearances; and they were commanded to witness to the assertion that Jesus is now judge of the living and the dead. And as a final argument, Peter claims that even the prophets bear witness "about him that everyone who believes in him receives forgiveness of sins through his name" (v. 43). Saving claims made about Jesus are bound up with the believers' responsibility for witnessing to them. A central piece of that witness is the assertion that God offers forgiveness and shalom to all people, regardless of status or nationality, through Christ Jesus.

## Jeremiah 31:1-6 (RCL alt.)

To the dispirited Judean exiles, Jeremiah speaks of a hope for restoration to the ancestral land and for renewal of the covenant between God and the chosen people. He also proclaims that God's enduring love will one day restore Israel and Judah in a new and redemptive partnership. A key source of this hope is a cluster of metaphors drawn from memories of God's activity with the ancestors of the exiles. This small passage concludes with yet another promise of restoration. From the hills of Ephraim, a part of the lost Northern Kingdom of Israel, shall come a shout for all to go to Zion, the capital of the also-lost Southern Kingdom of Judah. Thus, the whole faithful community, "all the families of Israel," shall know the blessings of restored covenant with God. When the people recognize this, the only appropriate response will be praise and thanksgiving—as it is for the restoration promised in the Easter event.

## Psalmody
### Psalm 118:1-2, 14-24 (RCL)
### Psalm 118:1-2, 16-17, 22-23 (LFM)

This psalm belongs in an Easter morning celebration not only because the psalmist speaks of the goodness of God in victory, but also because he sings, "I shall not die, but I shall live, and recount the deeds of the Lord" (v. 17). As in the Acts passage, we see the theme of witness bound to God's life-giving action. The psalmist repeatedly summons worshipers to give thanks for what God has done for them in granting strength, might, and steadfast love. Further, he speaks of reversal, "The stone that the builders rejected has become the chief cornerstone" (v. 23), another theme associated with Christian understandings of Jesus' ministry and resurrection (see Matt. 21:42; Acts 4:11; Eph. 2:20; 1 Peter 2:7). What once seemed useless and used up is now the centerpiece of human salvation.

## Second Reading
### Colossians 3:1-4 (RCL, LFM)

The author of this epistle, probably not Paul but one of his disciples, looks at Jesus, the church, and the individual believer from a cosmic vantage point. He stands on tiptoe, looking over the horizon of the mundane and casual, and sees that a crucifixion of a Galilean Jew has significance for all creation. In fact, the resurrection of this Jew places him on the very throne of God. Those who have faith in him are raised with him and live now with more than one foot in heaven. Their minds and hearts are now located "among the things that are above" even if their bodies are not quite there yet. And someday, in the future that is beyond a simple tomorrow, the One who was crucified and resurrected shall be fully revealed as the Christ, whose life will fill all those who have faith in him.

Lest this sound too abstract, we would do well to remember the real-world consequences of this faith in the exalted Christ. When the earliest readers of this letter claimed that through his resurrection Jesus now sits on the heavenly throne, they were specifically rejecting any idea that the Roman emperor had any kind of cosmic authority and relativizing the power of any earthly potentate in light of Christ's ultimate supremacy. Such a claim was anathema to the Romans, who made their own absolutist claims about the emperor and the Roman state. Thus, when early Christians gave witness to the cosmic Christ and spurned all other declarations about imperial power, they faced at the very least the possibility of economic persecution and at the most death.

### 1 Corinthians 5:6b-8 (LFM alt.)

For commentary on this text, please see the second reading on Easter evening, below.

## Acts 10:34-43 (RCL alt.)

For commentary on this text, please see the first reading, above.

# Gospel
## John 20:1-18 (RCL)
## John 20:1-9 (LFM)

In John's account of what happened after the stone had been rolled away from the mouth of Jesus' tomb, three of his close friends become models for believers' testimony. Mary Magdalene serves as the first witness—the one who first sees the stone removed, the one who first encounters Jesus without recognizing him, and the one to whom Jesus first reveals his identity. Simon Peter serves as the first witness not to comprehend fully what has happened. When he arrives at the tomb after the disciple who loved Jesus, he enters it and sees the wrappings of the corpse, but can't make sense of what has happened. The unnamed "other disciple" serves as the first witness to understand the significance of the empty tomb and make the appropriate response: "Then the other disciple, who reached the tomb first, also went in, and he saw and believed; for as yet they did not understand the scripture, that he must rise from the dead" (vv. 8-9).

Mary, thus, is the perseverant one who arrives first and stays late; the beloved is the trusting one who needs no further information to believe. Peter doesn't come off so well, joining in the race to the tomb but giving up too quickly when he can't figure out what has happened. Just as in other parts of the Fourth Gospel, he is a model of cluelessness. While other characters in the Gospel often misunderstand Jesus' words and actions, Peter seems to do it even more frequently and with more dramatic consequences. Historians have pointed to this depiction of Peter as evidence of some sort of struggle between the early Christian communities that valued the testimony of the "beloved disciple," dubbed John well after the Fourth Gospel was produced, and those that valued the primacy of Peter. In terms of a reader-response approach, however, the contrast between the beloved and Peter serve as various ways readers come to an understanding of the resurrection of Jesus.

Jesus himself doesn't make an appearance until verse 14, after Mary Magdalene has returned to the tomb and spoken to the two angels. It is he who provides both consolation and explanation, such as it is. The two angels, with whom Mary speaks before she mistakes Jesus as the gardener, only ask a question about her grief; they provide no information or help. And, as is typical in the Gospel of John, Jesus isn't recognized by Mary. The motif of misunderstanding that is so prominent throughout the Gospel reaches a climax here. Now it is not merely Jesus' words and actions that are misconstrued; it is his very presence. And again typically, Jesus reacts to Mary with puzzling words, "Do not hold on to me, because I have not yet ascended to the Father. But go to my brothers and say to them, 'I am ascending to my Father and your Father, to my God and your God'" (v. 17). In this state, he cannot be grasped;

he cannot even be fully comprehended. Nonetheless, Mary returns to the disciples and announces the news that she has seen Jesus. Her role as first witness is thereby consummated and confirmed.

## Matthew 28:1-10 (RCL alt.)

In Matthew's first reporting of events following Jesus' death, the supernatural makes a stronger appearance. When two Marys, not just Magdalene but also "the other Mary," go to the tomb after the Sabbath had ended, an earthquake occurs, the result of an angel from heaven rolling back the stone that guarded the mouth of the tomb. This is the same stone that had been sealed on Pilate's orders to prevent anyone from stealing the body and claiming that Jesus had been raised from the dead.

The responses of the humans who witness this earthquake are again instructive to readers. On the one hand, the two women are told by the angel not to be afraid. He continues, "I know that you are looking for Jesus who was crucified. He is not here; for he has been raised, as he said. Come, see the place where he lay. Then go quickly and tell his disciples, 'He has been raised from the dead'" (vv. 5-7). The women obey the angel, fearful but also filled with joy. On the way back, they meet Jesus, whom they apparently immediately recognize, and they worship him—even taking hold of his feet (note the contrast between this description of the first encounter with Jesus and John's description). Jesus repeats the instructions of the angel. On the other hand, the soldiers who have been placed at the tomb by Pilate "shook and became like dead men" (v. 4). Some of them must have roused themselves, because, says Matthew, some of the guard return to Jerusalem, report what had happened to the chief priests, and accept a bribe to say that the disciples came and stole the body.

Readers are thus given opposing reactions to imitate. They can join the women in both genuine fear at this overturning of the normal course of events and great joy at the inference that Jesus is alive, or they can follow the guard into apparent death and then deceit.

. . . . . . . . .

On Easter morning, preachers have the responsibility to answer to some degree the question raised at the beginning of this discussion: How do we witness to this instant of unseen glory? These texts are bound together by the theme of witness, whether as witness to saving events that occurred long ago, as in the Jeremiah text and the psalm, witness to the activity of God in the resurrection of Jesus, as in the Gospels, or witness to the continuing implications of the resurrection for believers, as in Acts and the epistle readings. But how shall we bear witness today?

We would do well not to fall into the trap of trying to prove our witness with appeals to rationalist explanations of Jesus' resurrection. All the evangelists are careful to avoid even giving the appearance that someone saw the actual moment when Jesus was raised to life. Any attempts to prove resurrection in a rational or scientific way fall into the fallacy that all truth is of the same kind and order—demonstrable and verifiable.

We must avoid such language, not because it is impossible to explain the Easter events with it, although it is, but because it in no way conveys the mystery of these events. Such mystery can better be expressed in story, poem, and song. So, like the evangelists, we can only tell stories that hint at what it might be like to find something we expected to be full of death—that is, a tomb—now empty of everything, including death. And then we might speak of what it is like to hang around fearful and weeping at the loss of the corpse—because at least a dead body is something to hold on to—or to shrug and leave quickly without realizing what has happened, or to look at the empty place, smile inside, and believe.

Perhaps the only complete witness to the resurrection is the life of an individual or a community lived faithfully and well—full of daily witness to what God continues to do in the cycles of the seasons, in the sequences of human living, in the phases of a church. If Jesus lives, then we live, right now, ready to sing praises to the God who does not ever abandon us even to death. Ready to speak truth about the Christ who saves us from fear, from sin, from all the things that cause us to collapse in upon ourselves. Ready to act toward others because Jesus really does live among us—guiding us toward righteousness and peace. Ready to wait with hope and joy for whatever God will offer next.

# April 24, 2011
## Resurrection of Our Lord / Easter Evening

**Revised Common Lectionary (RCL)**
Isaiah 25:6-9
Psalm 114
1 Corinthians 5:6b-8

Luke 24:13-49

**Lectionary for Mass (LFM)**
Acts 10:34a, 37-43
Psalm 118:1-2, 16-17, 22-23
Colossians 3:1-4 or
    1 Corinthians 5-6b-8
Luke 24:13-35

Between Easter morning and Easter evening, we move quickly from the very climax of the Gospel, the resurrection of Jesus Christ, to anticlimax. It is very easy for us to sing the alleluias on Easter morning and then take our Easter lilies and go home to overeat and take a nap, disregarding the fact that something has occurred that changes our lives, our churches, even our world. The readings for this afternoon insist that we continue to reflect on what has happened and allow it to make a difference in the ways we relate to one another and to those beyond the boundaries of community. Thus, we heard this morning that in Easter dawn Jesus has been encountered by a precious few; now we hear how he begins to appear to others. No character in the Gospel readings this morning fully understood what to make of the resurrection; it is in the Gospel and epistle readings for this evening that we get a glimpse of the significance of the Easter event and its claim on our actions. This claim is wrapped in the Easter tones of celebration for what God continues to do in the first and responsive readings.

## First Reading
### Isaiah 25:6-9 (RCL)

"All peoples" will be included in this feast upon the mountain of the Lord, surely a reference to Mt. Zion. Note the universalist strains here in the depiction of a great festal gathering in which only the best is served: rich meats filled with marrow and well-aged wines. In verses 7 and 8 we hear how God will destroy everything that brings death to the peoples of the earth. These verses, says Gene Tucker, "express the deepest human hopes for an end to mourning ('the shroud that is cast over all peoples'), to death itself, and to all grief ('wipe away the tears from all faces'), and they do so in highly evocative images and poetic cadences."[1] This short reading ends with an anticipatory call to praise and joy: "It will be said on that day, Lo, this is our God; we have waited for him, so that he might save us. This is the LORD for whom we have waited; let us be glad and rejoice in his salvation" (v. 9).

Without the Christian setting that the lectionary gives these verses, we hear of a yearning for a time when suffering and death hold no power over a people too accustomed to loss and tragedy. We also hear of a God who is unlike the Canaanite gods of the Israelites' neighbors. For one thing, the God of Isaiah brings salvation to all people, not just some. And for another, this God is God alone; there is no understanding here of multiple gods or a personification of death as in Canaanite religion. In fact, the god Mot (Death) in Canaanite mythology is the one who swallowed all things, not God, who in this passage swallows death itself.

Placed at this point in the Christian lectionary, the text reminds us of the eschatological dimensions of the resurrection. After all, Isaiah is dreaming of a time beyond time in which the natural order is wholly upturned, when all peoples join together on the mountain of God to enjoy the best food in the company of one another and of God. A time when no one knows death or grief. A time when all people will rejoice in God's salvation. And note well that this is a onetime event, not the annual cycle of rebirth and renewal that was a part not only of Canaanite religion, but also of Greco-Roman religions of the first century C.E.

It is from this passage, and similar texts in the Hebrew Bible, that early Christians like Paul were able to build an understanding of the resurrection as a sign of the arrival of the new age, even if the old one hasn't yet vanished. Paul paraphrases this passage in 1 Corinthians 15:26 and quotes it in 15:54-55 in his extended discussion of the significance of Jesus' resurrection for all believers. In this context, we can see how this reading helps us celebrate what God has begun for us and for all people on Easter.

## Acts 10:34a, 37-43 (LFM)

For commentary on this text, please see the first reading for Easter Day, above.

# Psalmody
## Psalm 114 (RCL)

This psalm, because it is traditionally associated with Passover, serves as a reminder that our Easter celebrations are grounded in an ancient Jewish observance of the cosmic victory of God in the exodus events. When the Israelite people escaped from Egypt, the psalmist sings, creation itself responded—the sea fled, the hills and mountains skipped and gamboled like sheep. For Christians, the triumph of God, so visible in the victory over the Egyptians, is just as visible in the deliverance from the death dealt out by the Romans—and just as cosmic. It has significance for the whole world, not just a man in ancient Judea or a ragtag group of people in ancient Egypt.

### Psalm 118:1-2, 16-17, 22-23 (LFM)

For commentary on this text, please see the Psalmody for Easter Day, above.

## Second Reading
### 1 Corinthians 5:6b-8 (RCL, LFM alt.)

In the midst of resurrection glory, the real world comes crashing in. Paul has some strong and irate words in this passage for a community that believes in the resurrection of Jesus and yet tolerates misbehavior. His anger is directed not so much at the man who is living with his father's wife, mentioned at the beginning of chapter 5, but at the church that would allow this incest to continue without challenge. How could these Christians be so cavalier about one another's actions? How could they condone such unrighteous behavior by letting the man remain in fellowship with them?[2]

Two paschal metaphors shape his argument as it appears in this brief reading this afternoon. First, the yeast of immorality, like the old leaven used in baking bread for non-Passover days, must be cleaned out, so that the church may be as pure and new as the unleavened bread of the holy feast. Second, the One who brings this church together, Christ Jesus, is himself the paschal lamb who has been sacrificed for the feast. "Therefore, let us celebrate the festival, not with the old yeast, the yeast of malice and evil, but with the unleavened bread of sincerity and truth" (v. 8).

## Gospel
### Luke 24:13-49 (RCL)
### Luke 24:13-35 (LFM)

Two people are walking down a road and talking animatedly in the opening scene of this Gospel's extended account of Jesus' first postresurrection appearance. It takes place later on the same day in which the women found the tomb vacant, and their companions found their news about this empty tomb idle. Peter had also already seen the linen cloths lying in the tomb. One of these people, says Luke, is named Cleopas; the other is unnamed. Brandon Scott says that in other ancient literature if a man with another person is named but the accompanying person is not, she is a woman. Maybe we have here a married couple.[3]

The two are discussing all the things that have happened in the last few days, when one whom they take to be a stranger approaches them. They tell him all about Jesus of Nazareth, "who was a prophet mighty in deed and word before God and all the people" (v. 19), and how they had hoped that he would be the one to redeem Israel (v. 21). They tell of his death. They tell of how the women claimed that the body was not in the tomb and that they had seen angels saying something about Jesus being alive. And they admit that they don't understand any of it. Their eyes have been blinded, just as the eyes of the chief priests and leaders in Jerusalem had been blinded.

The stranger rebukes this couple for their blindness in harsh language: "You are stupid and slow of heart!" And then he begins to explain the Scriptures, exclaiming, "Was it not necessary that the Messiah should suffer these things and then enter into his glory?" (v. 26). But how could these two grieving people know such a thing? There are precious few references to a suffering Messiah in the Law and the Prophets, only the Suffering Servant in Isaiah. And yet there are models: the prophets of God are rejected more often than not. Their presence is not welcome because they are always pointing out just how limited is the power of kings, emperors, presidents, prime ministers. Such power is limited by God, they preach, and by God's intention for justice and mercy for all people.

But that's not all that our couple on the way to Emmaus is missing. They are not getting the claim that the stranger is trying to convey that only through suffering does the Messiah enter into glory. We might note that of course they couldn't comprehend this matter; such a claim is not really clearly made in the Hebrew Bible. But there's a deeper reason for their blindness on this point: Who would want to find such an ironic declaration in Holy Scripture and then hold fast to such a truth? To the couple on that first Easter day, and to us, it seems patently obvious that the God who *can* make all things good happen *ought* to make all things good happen, including messianic glory—and without too much fuss, bother, or pain. We might concede a little pain for the purpose of getting our attention, but certainly not pain all the way to death. But in this passage, Jesus is making just this point: the one who wants to attain the glory that only God offers does so by rejecting all earthly glories even if it means agony and death. Furthermore, as we will see in subsequent Sundays, this claim applies not only to Jesus but to all who follow him.

But our couple will not have to remain in blindness. In fact, in spite of their blindness, the two travelers still have the good sense to invite the stranger to dinner. Maybe that display of hospitality is the first step toward the ability to recognize the resurrected Jesus. And the second step comes in the actual sharing of the meal: "When he was at the table with them, he took bread, blessed and broke it, and gave it to them" (v. 30). Jesus' four actions here—taking, blessing, breaking, and giving bread—mirror his actions at the feeding of the five thousand and the Last Supper.[4] Their eyes are opened fully; they see and know Jesus. And they leap up from the table, run back to Jerusalem, and tell the others what they have seen and what they now know.

The second half of the Gospel reading for the RCL, Luke 24:36-49, recounts Jesus' second resurrection appearance in this Gospel. On the evening of the same day, after Cleopas and his companion had rushed back to Jerusalem and were telling the "eleven and their companions" all about what had happened in Emmaus, Jesus appears. As before, the basic theme of fulfillment of scriptural promise is reiterated. This time, however, the quality of Jesus' postresurrected presence becomes a central issue. He is not a ghost, he says, as he invites the group to touch him and then eats broiled fish. In telling these details, Luke presents the most physical understanding of the resurrection that we find in the New Testament. Nonetheless, as Brandon Scott says,

"Yet even for Luke the physical body of the risen Jesus is not like an ordinary physical body since the couple on the road to Emmaus does not recognize Jesus and Jesus suddenly appears among the eleven."[5]

Three very important inferences can be drawn from these stories. First, we should note that Luke is not so much proof-texting the Scriptures as he is following the interpretation standards of his own day drawn from Jewish midrashic practice. Robert Tannehill says it like this: "Thus we may guess that Jesus in verse 27 is interpreting scripture by pointing to a pattern of prophetic destiny revealed in the lives of Moses and the prophets, as well as in the words of the prophets and psalmists."[6] Second, early Christians discerned the presence of their risen Lord when they gathered together and shared in a communal meal that had both eucharistic and secular overtones. In fact, it may be most accurate to say that the earliest followers of Jesus did not make distinctions between sacred and secular. What mattered is that they shared food with one another in memory of the One who was always sharing food with them (see discussion of Acts 2:42-47 on the Fourth Sunday of Easter, below). Finally, it is not enough to see Jesus at the meal, say to one another, "Well, how wonderful," and leave it there. The appropriate response is to get up and go tell someone about it. The two people in the first half of the reading were so excited that they couldn't wait to announce what they had seen and heard, to be witnesses. As for the group in the second half? They, too, will have ample opportunity to give witness to what has happened in their lives.

. . . . . . . . .

Anticlimax or not, the community that celebrates Jesus' resurrection has work to do on this Easter evening. Even as we rest in the faith that God indeed triumphs over death and the powers that bring death to the earth, we are called to give voice to that faith. To wait hopefully with Isaiah for the invitation to God's feast of plenty for all; to sing joyfully with the psalmist of God's cosmic triumph; to speak strongly of the ethical blemishes in our churches that besmirch the Easter festival; and to arise willingly and go tell everyone we encounter about this good news—these are the tasks we are given tonight and throughout Eastertide.

## Notes

1. Gene M. Tucker, "The Book of Isaiah 1–39," in *The New Interpreter's Bible* (Nashville: Abingdon, 2001), 6:217.
2. Richard A. Horsley, *1 Corinthians*, Abingdon New Testament Commentaries (Nashville: Abingdon, 1998), 79.
3. Bernard Brandon Scott, *The Trouble with Resurrection* (Salem, Ore.: Polebridge, forthcoming 2010).
4. Robert C. Tannehill, *Luke*, Abingdon New Testament Commentaries (Nashville: Abingdon, 1996), 357.
5. Scott, *Trouble with Resurrection.*
6. Tannehill, *Luke,* 356.

# May 1, 2011
## Second Sunday of Easter

**Revised Common Lectionary (RCL)**
Acts 2:14a, 22-32
Psalm 16
1 Peter 1:3-9
John 20:19-31

**Lectionary for Mass (LFM)**
Acts 2:42-47
Psalm 118:2-4, 13-15, 22-24
1 Peter 1:3-9
John 20:19-31

The day after any major celebration in both secular and ecclesial life is always a letdown—and the Second Sunday of Easter is no exception. On this Sunday in most churches, worship services are almost as badly attended as they are on the Sunday after Christmas. After all the hoopla of Easter, we generally think we deserve a little rest. And perhaps we do—but the Scriptures of the day will have none of it. In Acts, Peter must explain what has happened, the fourth evangelist must deal with the persistent problem of doubt within a community, and the author of 1 Peter has a few things to say about the blessings of faith in Jesus. Meanwhile, the psalmists celebrate and call us to join in the praise for a God who brings life out of death.

## First Reading
### Acts 2:14a, 22-32 (RCL)

After the extraordinary events of Acts 2:1-13, which are read on Pentecost, Peter stands up to explain it all. This is the first of four speeches Peter makes in Acts. On this Sunday the RCL gives us only the statement that Peter addressed the crowd before it skips verses 14b-21, which, like the first part of the chapter, are not read until Pentecost. This reading then takes up again at verse 22. The speech itself is a response to what has happened to the followers of Jesus in the opening days of the early Christian community's existence. In point of fact, the entire chapter of Acts 2 is the beginning of the fulfillment of a prophecy Jesus uttered just before he ascended: "But you will receive power when the Holy Spirit has come upon you; and you will be my witnesses in Jerusalem, in all Judea and Samaria, and to the ends of the earth"

(Acts 1:8; for a full treatment of this text see the first reading for Ascension Day, below). This prophecy-fulfillment motif is one of Luke's most familiar techniques for organizing the story that he is telling, giving his account weight and credibility. He is using the very words of Jesus to set out the program that the disciples will follow in the remainder of the book.

Because almost all of Acts 2 is read in both the RCL and the LFM for the next three weeks and Pentecost, it may be useful to look at the structure and general themes here as a context for the parts that are taken up in successive Sundays. One way of charting the chapter, somewhat in accordance with the way in which the LFM and the RCL break it up, looks like this:

Acts 2:1-4: the coming of the Holy Spirit;
Acts 2:5-13: the response of the people who heard the sound of the disciples speaking in various languages;
Acts 2:14-21: the introduction to the first speech in which Peter attempts to gain authority for what he has to say by quoting the prophet Joel so that he might show how this Scripture is being fulfilled today;
Acts 2:22-36: the remainder of the speech (discussed below);
Acts 2:37-41: response to Peter's speech by the first converts;
Acts 2:42-47: daily life in the early Christian community.

Acts 2:22-36, which contains today's RCL reading and next week's LFM reading, is the Lukan Peter's explication of God's purpose for the world in Jesus' life, death, and resurrection. First, Peter recites the salient incidents of Jesus' life and death, including a barbed reminder that "you," the men of Judea, crucified and killed him (see the introduction to Eastertide, above). But death could not hold Jesus in its grip. Peter then quotes another Scripture, Psalm 16:8-11, to make a connection between David's words in the psalm and the raising of Jesus from the dead. Just in case his listeners miss this point, Peter explains that although David died, he knew that God would keep the promise of placing one of his descendants on the throne and so spoke of a resurrection of the messiah. Notice how the Lukan Peter implicitly redefines the Jewish idea of a messiah from the anointed one who would lead the people of Israel in a sociopolitical sense to the One who would be seated at the right hand of God as ruler of the cosmos. The speech concludes with yet another scriptural quotation from Psalm 110 and a ringing announcement that God has made Jesus "Lord" and "Messiah."

In composing this speech, Luke uses midrashic techniques to place the story of Jesus within the larger story of God's interaction with all humanity that is told in the Hebrew Scriptures. Such stringing together of seemingly unrelated texts is somewhat jarring to interpreters more accustomed to historical-critical approaches to Scripture.[1] What is important to keep in mind here is Luke's primary point: Jesus' messiahship and exaltation are the fulfillment of God's designs throughout the history of the Jews.

But those designs do not end with Jesus; they are continued in the life and work of the Christian community as it receives the outpouring of the Spirit.

## Acts 2:42-47 (LFM)

For commentary on this text, please see the first reading for the Fourth Sunday of Easter, below.

# Psalmody
## Psalm 16 (RCL)

Because it is quoted in the first reading, Psalm 16 is placed here as the responsive reading in the RCL. Luke places it on Peter's lips as a support for his understanding of the resurrection. After all, the psalmist speaks of not being given up to Sheol, translated as "Hades" in the Septuagint, the version used in Acts. For Luke, the psalmist is David, who foresees Jesus' rescue from death and corruption of the flesh. The psalm as a whole is a song of confidence in the God who protects the psalmist, gives him counsel, does not abandon him to Sheol, and shows him the way of life. In return, the psalmist lives among the holy ones, forsakes pagan rituals, chooses what God offers, and blesses God constantly. All in all, this is an appropriate psalm for Eastertide in its joyful celebration of the blessings of life lived in the presence of God.

## Psalm II8:2-4, I3-I5, 22-24 (LFM)

Portions of this psalm appear in the LFM on Easter Day, Easter Evening, and today. The only significant difference in today's selection is the inclusion of verses 13-15 in place of verses 16-17, but even this difference does not change the overall tone of praise and thanksgiving in the use of this psalm. In today's verses the psalmist speaks of being pushed hard to the point of falling, but the Lord rescued him. Indeed, God is strength and might; God is salvation. Let everyone join in "glad songs of victory."

# Second Reading
## I Peter I:3-9 (RCL, LFM)

With this reading both lectionaries introduce a series of continuous texts taken from 1 Peter—the only time this epistle appears in either lectionary in a major way. Although it bears the name of the apostle Peter, it was probably produced later, probably between 80 and 100 C.E., and pseudonymously by a follower who drew on the authority of the Petrine name to speak words of encouragement and challenge to the Christian communities of Asia Minor.[2] In this opening passage, the author offers a lengthy one-sentence blessing of God (which actually extends through verse 12), which has been cut up into smaller sentences in translation. "Blessed be the God and Father of our Lord Jesus Christ!" he opens in traditional Jewish fashion and then chants support for the praise.[3] Great mercy, new birth, imperishable, undefiled, and unfading inheritance kept in heaven—all reasons to stop whatever we are doing and bless God.

Notice that the work of God for 1 Peter extends through vistas of time and space. The author challenges his audience to situate their sufferings and trials within God's grand scheme, one in which salvation is not a here-and-now kind of feeling but a work of God that may be begun here yet will only be completed in a heavenly future. That is to say, this author not only sees the personal results of "new birth into a living hope" for each believer. He sees spatial and eschatological dimensions opened up by the resurrection of Jesus. This work of God, as particular as it might be for each one in his audience, has effects that reverberate across the cosmos.

And notice a theme that will appear again in the Gospel reading of the day—that of believing without seeing Jesus. The writer of 1 Peter praises his audience in their love for the Christ, even though they did not know him in the past and do not see him now: "Although you have not seen him, you love him; and even though you do not see him now, you believe in him, and rejoice with an indescribable and glorious joy" (v. 8).

## Gospel
### John 20:19-31 (RCL, LFM)

Perhaps one of the reasons church attendance is so low on the Sunday following Easter is that people know they will hear again a sermon on "Doubting Thomas," based on this story! After all, these verses appear in both lectionaries every year at this point. And so we preachers will rehearse yet again the story of how Jesus on the evening of the resurrection appeared to all the disciples except Thomas (and Judas, of course, but he has completely dropped out of the narrative at this point) and showed them his pierced hands and side. Then we will talk about how Thomas insisted that he could not believe unless he saw for himself—which he gets the opportunity to do just a week later. Poor Thomas, we will cluck. He just couldn't believe in the resurrection of Jesus without proof.

To make this point we have to forget conveniently that the other disciples couldn't believe without proof either. They just got their proof a week earlier! There they are huddled behind locked doors for fear of the Jews even though Mary had already told them she had seen the Lord. Their joy only actually began when *they* saw the Lord with *their* own eyes (20:20b). And Mary herself is no paragon of faith; she was herself weeping hopelessly in the garden only hours before because *she* hadn't seen Jesus. In fact, even when she saw him she didn't recognize him. It is only when she hears his voice speak her name that she identifies him correctly. So it appears that almost everyone in John's account is harboring their own doubts until they have the opportunity to see the Resurrected One for themselves. In fact, we might say that the Scripture today isn't a story about a singular doubting Thomas but the climax of a story about a whole gang of doubters.

But doubt concerning the resurrected Jesus is not really the most pernicious disbelief in John's version of the events that took place after Easter morning. What seems to be even more dangerous is the lack of faith in one another's witness that is displayed throughout these events. Communal distrust pervades this account like a noxious gas. The disciples don't believe Mary, and Thomas doesn't believe the disciples. All of them must think that the reporter is either a bald-faced liar or a raving lunatic or both. No wonder that in verse 29 Jesus stands up on tiptoe to look over the heads of all those disbelieving disciples and straight into our eyes, saying, "Blessed are those who have not seen and yet have come to believe." This connects all the faithful hearers outside the Gospel with the one person within it who does not see Jesus but believes anyway—the unnamed beloved disciple (20:8).

So it turns out that all of us Christians who have never had the luxury of poking and prodding the resurrected body of Jesus for ourselves are included in this blessing. For we believe enough to show up to church on the Sunday after Easter. And what we believe is the testimony of the beloved and of all those who have come with us and before us who haven't seen Jesus with their own eyes either. We are people who can sing with Thomas the climactic confession of the Fourth Gospel, "My Lord and my God!" without ever once thrusting our hands into Jesus' side. But we are also the same people who can distrust one another as easily and quickly as those first disciples did. We, too, can turn on one another in a heartbeat with our ever-present cynicism and ready skepticism that covers our own anxieties and fears. Maybe our only hope is this: in spite of all this doubt, Jesus still comes and stands in our midst, breathes peace on us, and offers blessing when we notice his presence.

It is this theme of trust in the witness of others so prominent in the Gospel reading that captures my attention for this Eastertide. North American society has been infected with a deep mistrust that has spread through every institution. We find ourselves disbelieving information and truth-claims based not so much on what is said and the reasons given for it but on who says it. This lack of trust seems to be breaking us into ever-smaller enclaves of like-mindedness in which we repetitiously reinforce our own views and opinions without ever subjecting them to challenge or question. It's bad enough that such mistrust is rampant in our politics and civil life, but it has also contaminated our communal life as Christians. We may not argue so much anymore across the divisions of doctrine, but we continue to lob verbal grenades over matters of church order and practice as well as issues of morality and ethics. As we load and reload our weapons, we turn to those who agree with us and laugh about how well we have aimed our barbs, how effectively we have shot our arrows. In the midst of all this, Jesus says, "Blessed are those who believe without seeing"—those who believe the witness of those who have spoken and continue to speak of resurrection. Blessed are those who can trust the basic faith of others even while disagreeing about particulars. Blessed are those who can live in community with one another even while allowing safe space to speak and to listen from their own perspectives.

## Notes

1.  See Robert W. Wall, "The Acts of the Apostles," in *The New Interpreter's Bible* (Nashville: Abingdon, 2002), 10:65–66.
2.  For a summary of the evidence see Nancy Claire Pittman, "The Epistolary Tradition: The Letters of James, 1–2 Peter, 1–3 John, and Jude," in *The Chalice Introduction to the New Testament,* ed. Dennis E. Smith (St. Louis: Chalice, 2004), 263–64.
3.  Fred B. Craddock, *First and Second Peter and Jude,* Westminster Bible Companion (Louisville: Westminster John Knox, 1995), 22–23.

# May 8, 2011
## Third Sunday of Easter

**Revised Common Lectionary (RCL)**
Acts 2:14a, 36-41
Psalm 116:1-4, 12-19
1 Peter 1:17-23
Luke 24:13-35

**Lectionary for Mass (LFM)**
Acts 2:14, 22-33
Psalm 16:1-2a + 5, 7-8, 9-10, 11
1 Peter 1:17-21
Luke 24:13-35

By this Sunday, Easter is becoming a dim memory and we are launched full-tilt into the activities that characterize a North American month of May: graduations and Mother's Day. Rightly or wrongly, however, the lectionaries of Eastertide are not shaped by these concerns, but continue along the trajectory of lections begun on the previous Sunday. In the Gospel reading we hear of the resurrected Jesus' encounter with the two travelers on the road to Emmaus and their recognition of him in the breaking of bread. In the lesson from Acts, which continues Peter's first speech to all the people who had come to Jerusalem on the festival of Pentecost, we hear of the simple demands of the gospel: repent, be baptized, receive the gifts of the Holy Spirit. In 1 Peter the stringency of these same demands is beginning to be exposed.

These readings from Acts and 1 Peter have generated over the centuries conversations about the meanings of baptism in the Christian faith, not surprisingly since Eastertide has been for many churches a time of preparation for baptism.[1] In Acts, Peter links baptism with repentance—the primary significance of John the Baptist's practice as described in the Synoptic Gospels. But an additional connotation appears in Peter's response to the people who ask him what they should do now that they have been "cut to the heart." As James Wall says, "Baptism, then, is initiation into a community that lives within the powerful realm of God's Spirit."[2] All those who come to confess Jesus in Acts are baptized; there appears to be no one in the community who has not participated in this ritual.

Some scholars have suggested that at least the first section of 1 Peter is an extended meditation on the meaning of baptism for the churches in Asia Minor.

While this theory has been largely repudiated in recent decades, Christians throughout the centuries have used this epistle for training for and reflection upon the act of baptism. After all, persons enter the exilic status of being Christian in a non-Christian world, an identity that is central to this epistle, through the rite of baptism. So we hear exhortations to prepare, to understand implications of belief for action, to love one another.

# First Reading
## Acts 2:14a, 36-41 (RCL)

Lest we forget the literary context for this reading, both the RCL and the LFM (which takes up this text next Sunday) include again verse 14a: "But Peter, standing with the eleven, raised his voice and addressed them. . . ." Then they skip to verse 36, Peter's conclusion: "Therefore let the entire house of Israel know with certainty that God has made him both Lord and Messiah, this Jesus whom you crucified." In this statement, Peter summarizes the central theme of his speech. God has acted in the life, crucifixion, and exaltation of Jesus as the fulfillment of God's plan for all people.

Verses 37-41 narrate the response of the listeners to Peter's words, a response that balances the earlier questions of the crowd in verses 5-13. After hearing Peter's explanation of the strange events of the morning, they are "cut to the heart." The text is unclear about exactly what touches them so deeply. Perhaps they are convicted by their own guilt in the death of Jesus that Peter kept mentioning throughout the speech. Perhaps they are convinced of the truth of his understanding of God's saving action in Jesus for the nation of Israel. Whatever the cause, they ask what they must do now. And Peter responds with three actions: repent, be baptized so that their sins may be forgiven, and thus receive the gift of the Holy Spirit. He then reminds them that the promise God has made and fulfilled in Jesus is not only for them but for their children and for those far away, probably a reference to the Gentiles. Luke reports that three thousand people were welcomed into the community through baptism. Here the meaning of this action is enlarged beyond the understanding of John the Baptist's ritual of repentance. Now it is also a rite of initiation into the community of believers. And once people are included in the community, they are commissioned for the work of witness.[3]

## Acts 2:14, 22-33 (LFM)

For commentary on this text, please see the first reading for the Second Sunday of Easter, above.

# Psalmody
## Psalm 116:1-4, 12-19 (RCL)

God's surprising and gracious rescue from the snares of death (v. 3) prompts actions that overflow with complete and utter gratitude in this profoundly personal psalm of thanksgiving. Just as Peter in the Acts reading details what God had done through Jesus for the throngs in Jerusalem, so the psalmist names (without much specificity) how God has saved him from distress and anguish. And just as Peter tells the people how they might respond to God's offer of salvation for them, so the psalmist lists the three things he will do in return. He will lift the "cup of salvation," a reference to the drink offering that followed the burnt offering (see Num. 28:7); he will pay "vows to the LORD in the presence of all his people" (vv. 14 and 18), promises that signify the psalmist's commitment to the ways of God; and he will make a thanksgiving offering (v. 17), his own sacrifice that makes his inner sense of gratitude real and evident.[4]

## Psalm 16:1-2a + 5, 7-8, 9-10, 11 (LFM)

For commentary on this text, please see the Psalmody for the Second Sunday of Easter, above.

# Second Reading
## 1 Peter 1:17-23 (RCL)
## 1 Peter 1:17-21 (LFM)

For a variety of reasons, this epistle can be difficult to understand and interpret in a twenty-first-century context. The language, which was originally a lovely and well-enunciated Greek, is dense even in English. The religious symbolic world, largely drawn from Leviticus, is distant. And the social setting of the first readers is very different from our own. Many of us find its meanings opaque and somewhat irrelevant to the busyness of our lives. But there are treasures here for the building of our faith if we take the time to look for them.

It may be particularly useful to remember who those first readers were before we explore the selection for today. The Christians of Asia Minor who received this letter would have been a tiny minority group in the exotic reaches of the Roman Empire. All of the regions listed in 1 Peter 1:1 were Roman provinces, a reminder that the power of the empire now encompassed places far from the city of Rome. And the provinces themselves contained a diverse population of people native to the region, Roman citizens, and Jews of the diaspora. In fact, says Leonhard Goppelt, "in Asia Minor numerous ethnic groups and cultures experienced mutual assimilation. Therefore, this region became the classical land of Hellenism, and cross-regional migrant peoples of the time found a home there."[5] Goppelt also tells us that the majority of Christians in these churches were most likely Gentiles; there are none of the concerns about Jewish and Gentile relations within the Christian community in this letter that are so common in the earlier Pauline epistles.

The minority status of these ancient Christians is extremely important for understanding this letter. These were people who had turned away from the traditions and obligations of their own families to form new communities whose ties were not based on blood relationship. They had willingly given up their identity as denizens of

Pontus, Galatians, Cappadocians, Asians, and Bithynians, including the very strong social, political, and religious ties that defined who they were for others. They had deliberately chosen to remove themselves from full participation in the larger cultural life with its supporting rituals of obeisance to multiple deities, its deeply engrained patterns of reverence for family gods, and, of course, the emperor worship that the Romans encouraged in the Asia Minor society, which was already prone to deify its own rulers. So when the author of 1 Peter calls them "exiles of the Dispersion" (1:1) and refers to their life lived "during a time of exile" (1:17), they surely resonated with the fresh realization that they were indeed now strangers in their own homes.

One way to comprehend more fully their situation and the meaning that a term like *exile* might have had for them is to recall that many Christians in the twenty-first century also live as a minority enclave in countries in which the majority practice another religion. When my husband and I served on the faculty of a Christian seminary in Taiwan, we became more aware of what it means to live in a minority religious community. The Christians with whom we worked had often been called upon to sacrifice familial bonds and more lucrative employment because of their commitments to Christ and the church. On occasion, we heard of families who refused to speak again to one of its members who had been baptized or rejected the marriage of one of its own to a Christian. Furthermore, Christian affiliation often had political ramifications as well. Many Taiwanese Christians suffered at the hands of the Chinese group who fled to Taiwan with Chiang Kai-shek after the communist revolution on the Chinese mainland because they spoke up for justice for the Taiwanese people. Although such repression has since abated in Taiwan, these Christians are still quite cognizant of the fact that they live in the shadow of the modern Chinese empire and may be called upon to speak again for the wholeness and peace for all people for which Jesus died.

Of course, the term *exile* also has a theological dimension. The author of 1 Peter not only draws upon a sociological experience of exile; he also draws upon the ancient Israelite experience of living in a foreign land, first in Egypt and later in the dispersion caused by the Babylonian conquest. The people of God had mourned the loss of a homeland of their own and had felt keenly the sharp pain of distance from the places and the people they had once loved. Although 1 Peter transposes this longing for a physical land of one's own into a yearning for a heavenly abode in which God is fully present, the same painful emotional reaction to foreignness is captured here. Just as the Israelites were not truly home in the Babylonian Empire, so the Christians of Asia Minor were not home in these earthly cities.

And just as the law codes in Leviticus and the ancient prophetic literature urged the Israelites to cling to holiness even in exile, so does 1 Peter. The verses immediately before today's reading exhort the Christian exiles to turn away from the desires of their former lives and set their hearts and minds on Jesus. They can do this by speaking and acting with care and reverence. In support of the exhortation, Leviticus 19:2 is quoted: "You shall be holy, for I am holy."

In this literary context is embedded today's reading. Verse 17 speaks of the impartiality of God who judges people not according to family ties or political affiliation but according to their deeds. If this is true, then the Christian exiles should ensure that their deeds are worthy and pure so that they might be judged favorably. After all, they have been ransomed by "the precious blood of Christ, like that of a lamb without defect or blemish" (v. 19), a conflation of imagery drawn from at least two metaphorical spheres. First, behind the reference to the blood is yet another theme in Leviticus, the sacrifice of well-being in which the animal must be perfect in order for the act to be efficacious (Lev. 22:21).[6] Second, a ransom is a purchase of a slave from a master in the ancient Near Eastern world. The author speaks here of the pure and spotless nature of the one who has freed his readers from slavery to the emptiness of the lives of their ancestors. This action frees Christians to respond both with hope in the grace offered by Jesus (see 1:13) and with the same purity of action that Jesus has demonstrated toward one another and, as we will see in subsequent readings, toward the society in which they live. The RCL strengthens this message with the inclusion of verses 22 and 23, which emphasize the mutual love among this newly constituted family of Christians.

# Gospel
## Luke 24:13-35 (RCL, LFM)

For commentary on this text, please see the Gospel for Easter Evening, above.

. . . . . . . . .

What do we do to receive the gifts of God, and how do we respond to these gifts? These are the questions today's texts encourage us to ask for ourselves. For centuries Christians have struggled to answer by developing rituals, speaking creedal formulations, instituting polities and hierarchies, offices and orders. We do all this in an attempt to understand, claim, and make our own what is finally only mystery. God acts through Jesus' death and resurrection; that is what the Peter of Acts and the writer of 1 Peter tell us. And that action matters to us, saves us somehow from all that chokes life out of us—be it blinding tradition, binding empire, or shattered relationship. We cannot face all that deals out death by ourselves; we can only call on God who answers, and answers, and answers with steadfast graciousness yet again, as the psalmist attests. And then with the whole baptized Christian community we can witness to God's answer. Cleopas and his companion leap up from the table when they recognize Jesus and run out the door to tell others. They model for us a way of taking what we share at the eucharistic table to people outside who are just as hungry as we are.

## Notes

1. J. D. C. Fisher, "Baptism," in *The New Westminster Dictionary of Liturgy and Worship* (Philadelphia: Westminster, 1986), 55–56.
2. Robert W. Wall, "The Acts of the Apostles," in *The New Interpreter's Bible* (Nashville: Abingdon, 2002), 10:67.
3. Ibid.
4. Robert Davidson, *The Vitality of Worship: A Commentary on the Book of Psalms* (Grand Rapids: Eerdmans, 1998), 381.
5. Leonhard Goppelt, *A Commentary on 1 Peter*, trans. and augmented John E. Alsup (Grand Rapids: Eerdmans, 1993), 6.
6. David L. Bartlett, "The First Letter of Peter," in *The New Interpreter's Bible* (Nashville: Abingdon, 1998), 12:258.

# May 15, 2011
## Fourth Sunday of Easter

| **Revised Common Lectionary (RCL)** | **Lectionary for Mass (LFM)** |
|---|---|
| Acts 2:42-47 | Acts 2:14a, 36-41 |
| Psalm 23 | Psalm 23:1-3a, 3b-4, 5, 6 |
| 1 Peter 2:19-25 | 1 Peter 2:20b-25 |
| John 10:1-10 | John 10:1-10 |

I confess that I tune out sermons in which the preacher talks about the stupidity of sheep based upon her or his conversations with modern shepherds. The comparison of congregations with obtuse sheep grates on me and I'm never sure who is being more slandered: the sheep or the people in the pews! Opportunities to preach these sermons are legion because pastoral imagery abounds in the Hebrew Bible and the Christian Scriptures. So every time prophetic texts like Ezekiel 34, or a psalm like the Twenty-third, or the Synoptic parables dealing with lost sheep, or John 10 shows up in the lectionary, chances are too high that one of us preachers will stand up and begin again to speak about how foolish sheep are and how much we are like them. The Fourth Sunday of Easter provides one of these occasions because a portion of John 10 is included in every cycle of both lectionaries under discussion. In this particular year, the risk is even greater because John 10:1-10 appears with Psalm 23. Yet the texts from Acts and 1 Peter may mitigate the need for silly sheep as may fresh readings of this ancient pastoral imagery.

# First Reading
## Acts 2:42-47 (RCL)

This reading begins with the subject "they," which might refer to the first converts described in Acts 2:37-41 or, as both the RCL and the LFM presuppose, the entire Christian community, which now includes the three thousand who were welcomed by the 120 believers who had waited for Jesus' promise to be fulfilled in Jerusalem (see 1:15). Regardless of who "they" are, Luke presents an idealized portrait of the earliest assembly of believers, one that is devoted to one another and to God. They are also devoted to the teaching of "the apostles," here a technical term that implies commission as those who are sent by Jesus and thus possessing authority and leadership.

Two components of this ideal snapshot should be mentioned here. First, the teaching, fellowship, breaking of bread, and prayers—the four activities of verse 42—are often assumed to be liturgical acts akin to coming together in worship, preaching, praying, and celebrating the Lord's Supper. But Hans Conzelmann argues that "the character of the summary, the concepts themselves, and their sequence all argue against this interpretation."[1] Luke has no clear dividing line between the activities of daily life and those of liturgical life. Rather, he sees all the routines of human living as a unity, including the act of eating bread in remembrance of Jesus and of eating bread as an ordinary meal.

Second, one of the divine signs accomplished by the apostles may well be the *koinonia* that resulted among all these people drawn "from every nation under heaven."[2] Neither kinship nor common nationality nor language brought them together; only their common belief in a God who had fulfilled God's promise to the Jewish people in Jesus Christ held them. Further, this *koinonia* manifested itself concretely in the sharing of all possessions and goods that each individually owned. Not only did they trust God; they trusted one another and the apostles to take care of them and to take care of their sisters and brothers in Christ. This kind of trusting *koinonia* is a gift from the Spirit and a sign that God's new age had actually begun in this radical reordering of social patterns and relationships. Thus, the real wonder is not that people held things in common; similar practices were maintained through extended families and patron-client systems all over the Greco-Roman world. What is significant in Luke's portrayal is that people are sharing their material goods outside of familial relationships. A wholly new family, with all attendant rights and responsibilities yet not bound by blood or patronage, has been formed.

### Acts 2:14a, 36-41 (LFM)

For commentary on this text, please see the first reading for the Third Sunday of Easter, above.

## Psalmody
### Psalm 23 (RCL)
### Psalm 23:1-3a, 3b-4, 5, 6 (LFM)

A student in one of my preaching classes once remarked on how unsettling it has become for her to hear this psalm read outside a funeral. In her mind it is firmly associated with consolation offered in death; indeed, we all know that mourners will frequently ask for this text to be read at their loved ones' funerals—it is so familiar and so comforting. Yet here it appears in the middle of Eastertide, a season for celebrating new life. If we shake it loose from its funeral moorings, we can hear affirmations of life right here and now in its well-known phrases.

In the first two-thirds of Psalm 23, God takes on the trappings of a shepherd. God offers rest in green pastures and guidance beside still waters; God's rod and staff, a shepherd's equipment, provide protection. But the metaphor shifts in the last two verses. God suddenly becomes a generous host, preparing a table and anointing the psalmist's head with oil, things a shepherd would never do for a sheep. Nor would a shepherd allow the sheep to dwell in his house. Taken together, the two constellations of images could point to the royalty of God. Just as the human king of ancient Judah and Israel served as shepherd and host of his people, so God does in this psalm.[3] Right away then we should note the extreme faith statement of the first verse: God is the psalmist's shepherd, not the king, not the government or the nation, not anyone else.

Lurking within these familiar images is a theme of trust—the psalmist trusts God to protect, prepare, provide, not in some afterlife, but now. The psalmist needs no one else and certainly needs no other thing. He is dependent solely on the God who walks with him through deep valleys, who provides food and rest, who offers guidance in right paths. These words are just as appropriate to worshipers today. As J. Clinton McCann Jr. says, "In a consumer-oriented society, it is extremely difficult to hear the simple but radical message of Psalm 23: God is the only necessity of life!"[4]

## Second Reading
1 Peter 2:19-25 (RCL)
1 Peter 2:20b-25 (LFM)

Both lectionaries sidestep a difficult issue by cutting off the opening verse of this reading, which begins a series of instructions directed at persons in various "stations" within the Christian household.[5] The first station to be addressed is that of slaves: "Slaves, accept the authority of your masters with all deference, not only those who are kind and gentle, but also those who are harsh" (2:18). The RCL reading opens at verse 19, in which the direct address, "you" (plural), obscures the fact that the author is talking to actual slaves. The LFM passage doesn't open until verse 20b, thereby also eliminating the somewhat embarrassing reference to the endurance of undeserved beatings found in verses 19 and 20a. By cutting off this material in one way or another, the lectionaries implicitly convey a sense that these words are general exhortations for the whole community and not for a subset.[6]

What may be more important for preachers to consider on this particular Sunday is the christological meanings of these verses—which accounts for why, again in both lectionaries, these verses are taken out of order and placed before next week's epistle reading, 1 Peter 2:2-10 (RCL) and 1 Peter 2:4-9 (LFM). Slaves are exhorted to endure whatever comes their way, justly or unjustly, because Jesus himself suffered. Once again the author appeals to Hebrew Scripture to make sense of Jesus' passion as he draws upon the image of the Suffering Servant in Isaiah 53 in the remainder of the reading. Like the Suffering Servant, Jesus was sinless, refused to return abuse for abuse, bore human sinfulness in his crucifixion, and by his wounds healed the faithful community. The author concludes the exhortation to slaves with this: "For you were going astray like sheep, but now you have returned to the shepherd and guardian of your souls" (v. 25). Here is found the connection to both the responsive and the Gospel readings about the good shepherd that mandated the inclusion of this passage from 1 Peter on this Sunday.

We might consider at least one more idea from this reading in preparation for the sermon. The command to submit to authority that characterizes this entire section of 1 Peter is not only rooted in Jesus' own submission but represents for the author the appropriate, maybe even necessary, stance for all the faithful—not just Christians who are slaves. David Bartlett explains that there is a paradox in the Christian life described here that can serve as challenge and possibility; "No one can take my freedom from me; but because I am God's slave, I am free not to resist violence with violence, not to fight fire with fire or to oppose the lies of the oppressive with my own list of persuasive exaggerations and caricatures."[7] Nonetheless, while Bartlett's words make this text a bit more palatable for us Western Christians, to accept naïvely these words from 1 Peter is quite problematic in light of other Christian values we hold dear.

## Gospel
### John 10:1-10 (RCL, LFM)

When we hear Jesus' claims about himself in John 10, which contains one of the several "I am" speeches that characterize the Fourth Gospel, in tandem with Psalm 23, we begin to hear just how radical they are. Drawing upon Psalm 23 as well as Ezekiel 34, the Johannine Jesus arrogates to himself the attributes of God that are described in these selections of the Hebrew Scriptures. No wonder the Pharisees in this Gospel are so put off by everything Jesus says and does! Of course, we will miss some of this radicality because of the way both lectionaries cut up John 10, giving a portion of it to each Fourth Sunday of Easter in the cycle: 10:1-10 in Year A; 10:11-18 in Year B; 10:22-30 in Year C.

John 10:1-5 is a parabolic response to the events told in John 9, which begin with the healing of the blind man and end with his being thrown out of the synagogue. Note that in 9:41 Jesus addresses himself directly to the Pharisees who have just asked, "Surely we are not blind, are we?" In the "figure of speech" that comprises Jesus' answer, understandings of the faithful community and Jesus himself are implicitly offered. Dennis E. Smith explains that the verb for being thrown out of the synagogue in chapter 9 is the same Greek verb of the phrase translated in 10:4 as "when he has brought out all his own," and related to the verb in the phrase of 10:3, "and leads them out." Smith continues, "When the two stories [in John 9 and 10:1-5] are placed side by side, they describe the same experience from two different perspectives. The pilgrimage of the community of John out of the synagogue is not only a 'turning out,' but also a 'calling out.' . . . In both stories, it should be noted, the path of true faith requires movement into an unknown future."[8]

But they do not move alone into that future. In 10:1-5 we hear of a shepherd who calls the sheep by name and who leads them into the safety of the sheepfold. The identity of the shepherd is not fully revealed until 10:11, but we readers are already aware that Jesus is talking about himself. First, however, we hear him saying, "I am the gate for the sheep." The image functions in two ways. On the one hand, the gate that is Jesus is a doorway to safety and a place of protection away from the thieves and the bandits.[9] On the other, the gate is an entry into the community of those who believe. Says Gail R. O'Day, "When Jesus identifies himself as the gate for the sheep (v. 7), he points to the ways in which one's place in the sheepfold, and hence one's identity as a member of the flock, is determined exclusively by one's relationship to Jesus as the gate."[10] Both functions combine to provide a picture of Jesus as the one who gives security and membership into the group. Taken together they offer life itself (v. 10).

One other word about this passage. We can too easily allegorize other characters in the text. The gatekeeper of verse 3 might reasonably be identified as the Spirit, consonant with John's understanding of the Spirit as advocate and confirmer of truth (see below, Sixth Sunday of Easter). And the thieves and bandits of verses 1, 8, and 10? Because the narrative context is Jesus' response to the Pharisees of John 9, we might be tempted to follow much of the history of Christian tradition and identify them as the Jewish leaders of the first century (not to mention the many Jewish leaders of subsequent centuries who have been persecuted on the basis of this and other Johannine texts). And in fact that may well be one of the identifications that the author of this Gospel intended his readers to make. But it is not the only one. We might also see other pretenders to leadership in both political and ecclesial communities. We might see the pretensions to faith and the attractions of various forms of apostasy that get in the way of our hearing the voice of Jesus. In any case, my prayer is that we avoid perpetuating stereotypes of Jews, ancient or modern.

. . . . . . . . .

In the lections for today we have an idealized portrait of the early Christian community in Acts; we have an idealization of the suffering of slaves, and indeed all Christians, that is connected to the suffering of Jesus; and we have an ideal Christ and church working together as shepherd and sheep. Peter W. Marty, in a short article titled "The Poetry of Sheep," offers yet another ideal picture of the church: "Metaphorically speaking, it's like a jumble of words coming together to form an unexplainably rich poem." His inspiration comes from a sheep farm in England in which a writer spray-painted a single word on each sheep in the flock and then set them loose. As the sheep wandered around, the words took on constantly shifting poetic forms. Marty says, "We in the church would do well to think of God as writing

poetry with our lives. You can't write a poem with one word. It takes a whole flock. . . .
[A]lways God is trying to figure out how to get us to be this unexplainably rich poem
we're capable of being."[11]

## Notes

1.   Hans Conzelmann, *Acts of the Apostles*, Hermeneia (Philadelphia: Fortress Press, 1987), 23.
2.   William H. Willimon, *Acts*, Interpretation: A Bible Commentary for Teaching and Preaching
     (Atlanta: John Knox, 1988), 40.
3.   Robert Davidson, *The Vitality of Worship: A Commentary on the Psalms* (Grand Rapids: Eerdmans,
     1998), 83.
4.   J. Clinton McCann Jr., "The Book of Psalms," in *The New Interpreter's Bible* (Nashville: Abingdon,
     1996), 4:769.
5.   Leonhard Goppelt, *A Commentary on 1 Peter*, trans. and augmented John E. Alsup (Grand Rapids:
     Eerdmans, 1993), 162ff. These instructions to various stations found in 1 Peter 2:18—3:7 are also
     referred to as household codes in scholarly literature.
6.   See Shelly Cochran, *The Pastor's Underground Guide to the Revised Common Lectionary, Year A* (St.
     Louis: Chalice, 1995), 156–57.
7.   David L. Bartlett, "The First Letter of Peter," in *The New Interpreter's Bible* (Nashville: Abingdon,
     1998), 12:286.
8.   Dennis E. Smith and Michael E. Williams, eds., *The Storyteller's Companion to the Bible*, vol. 10,
     *John* (Nashville: Abingdon, 1996), 102.
9.   Ibid., 103.
10.  Gail R. O'Day, "The Gospel of John," in *The New Interpreter's Bible* (Nashville: Abingdon, 1995),
     9:669.
11.  Peter W. Marty, "The Poetry of Sheep," *Christian Century* (September 9, 2008), 10.

# May 22, 2011
## Fifth Sunday of Easter

| Revised Common Lectionary (RCL) | Lectionary for Mass (LFM) |
|---|---|
| Acts 7:55-60 | Acts 6:1-7 |
| Psalm 31:1-5, 15-16 | Psalm 33:1-2, 4-5, 18-19 |
| 1 Peter 2:2-10 | 1 Peter 2:4-9 |
| John 14:1-14 | John 14:1-12 |

The word *martyr* in English is basically a transliteration of the Greek word for "witness." Its original connotations had nothing to do with death as it does today. A martyr in the ancient Near Eastern world was simply one who stood in a courtroom to testify to eyewitness events or who stood in the marketplace to speak his own understanding of truth, be it verifiable or not. The accretion of connotations of death to the word did not appear until the second and third centuries C.E.

All of the readings for today speak in one form or another about being a martyr—a witness—even if such activities lead to death. From the Acts of the Apostles we hear of the stoning of Stephen in the RCL; the LFM reading witnesses to a successful resolution of potential conflict. The psalms witness to the constant care of God for believers. First Peter urges us to proclaim good news, and in the Gospel reading we hear again the Johannine confession about the nature of Jesus and thus his community. Bear witness to the goodness of God, regardless of cost; speak of the work of Jesus; invite everyone to join in.

## First Reading
### Acts 7:55-60 (RCL)

Stephen, one of the seven chosen to serve the community in Acts 6, makes a lengthy defense of the Jerusalem community's newfound faith (7:2-53), enrages the crowd and its leaders (7:54), and is promptly taken out and stoned to death. He is the first witness to Jesus to die, but by no means the last. Luke shapes the story along the contours of Jesus' own death: both deaths occur outside the city and Stephen speaks similar pleas for his spirit to be received and for forgiveness for those who are killing him. Nonetheless, the fact that he is stoned and not crucified emphasizes a significant difference between the two deaths, in Luke's view. One is salvific for the whole world; the other is a sign of true faith in the first death.

This story serves as a narrative turning point in the broad sweep of Acts. Stephen's stoning ignites a general persecution in Jerusalem (8:1), impelling the witness to the saving acts of Jesus to move beyond the boundaries of its birthplace toward Rome. From now on little of the action will take place in Jerusalem. Also, a new character in the drama arrives on the scene—the zealous Saul participating in the persecution of these early Christians. And we all know what happens to him.

### Acts 6:1-7 (LFM)

How did the early community described in Acts handle conflict? In this familiar part of the story, the Hellenists were complaining against the Hebrews "because their widows were being neglected in the daily distribution of food" (6:1). While the identity of both parties is a bit unclear since neither group has put in an appearance thus far in Luke's story, the method is sure. Take people's concerns seriously and respond helpfully by bringing new people into leadership so that the needs of all people can be met. Which is just what the Twelve did. They appointed seven "deacons," ordained them by laying hands on them, and gave them a job to do. And so, concludes Luke, "the number of the disciples increased greatly in Jerusalem" (v. 7). Even the priests of the temple were so impressed that they joined the fledgling group![1]

## Psalmody
### Psalm 31:1-5, 15-16 (RCL)

As a response to the stoning of Stephen, the RCL lectionary authors have chosen this hymn of prayer for deliverance from enemies. The psalmist prays to the God who is a rock of refuge and a fortress for rescue from all who would shame him. But not only does he petition God; he offers numerous expressions of trust: "You have redeemed me, O LORD, faithful God" (v. 5b); "My times are in your hands" (v. 15). This psalm also contains the line uttered first by Jesus and then by Stephen: "Into your hand I commit my spirit" (v. 5a).

### Psalm 33:1-2, 4-5, 18-19 (LFM)

Steadfast love and trust also characterize this psalm, although there are few petitions in it and none in the portions chosen for reading in worship. This song of praise redounds with joy in the God who makes creation beautiful with the divine presence, loves righteousness and justice, and delivers the faithful from famine and death. Making melody, singing, and shouting are the only appropriate responses to such a gracious Creator.

## Second Reading
### 1 Peter 2:2-10 (RCL)
### 1 Peter 2:4-9 (LFM)

The interweaving of Christology with ecclesiology that has characterized earlier readings from 1 Peter continues throughout this reading. Here the key link between Christ and church is the metaphor of stone. It is introduced in verse 4 when Christ is alluded to through a clash of imagery as a "living stone." This jarring sense is amplified when the community is referred to also as "living stones." How can stones live? Any attempts to explain away the clash through appeals to natural phenomena or uncut stone miss the point. The stone, says the author of 1 Peter, can be understood in the pastiche of quotations from the Hebrew Bible (Isa. 28:16; Ps. 118:22; Isa. 8:14). For him these scriptures point to Christ, the foundation, the One who was rejected, and the One who causes the disobedient to stumble. Yet this otherwise inert and nonliving rock is alive through the resurrecting power of God. This same power gives life to the faithful community and forms its own living stones into a "spiritual house" (v. 4), not, of course, unlike the temple in Jerusalem (long since destroyed if this epistle was written between 80 and 100 C.E.). The author continues in the same symbolic world of the temple, reminding them that their purpose is "to be a holy priesthood, to offer spiritual sacrifices acceptable to God through Jesus Christ" (v. 5).

At this point we would do well to remember that the audience being addressed here is Gentile. This means that these very Jewish images are being applied to a community that understands itself as true heirs to the worship practices of the ancient temple. This same constellation of stone and temple imagery was also used in the Qumran community for a very different purpose. In Qumran the intent is to restrict it to the faithful few; in 1 Peter the intent is to extend imagery for the ancient Jewish community to the new Christian (and Gentile) community.[2]

But the overall goal of this text is made clear in the ringing and oft-quoted affirmation of 1 Peter 2:9: "But you are a chosen race, a royal priesthood, a holy nation, God's own people, in order that you may proclaim the mighty acts of him who called you out of darkness into his marvelous light." (The RCL adds verse 10 as a conclusion, a conflation of Hosea 1:9 and 2:23.) It is not enough for our churches to be made of people as firm and strong as stone, even if we are stones that breathe the very life of Jesus. We are made to witness to all these things, to proclaim the call of Jesus, not just for our own sake, but for the sake of everyone else.

## Gospel
### John 14:1-14 (RCL)
### John 14:1-12 (LFM)

Two disciples, Thomas (whom we encountered on the First Sunday of Easter) and Philip, stand out in this conversation with Jesus. Its narrative setting is the Farewell Discourse in the Fourth Gospel in which Jesus offers his disciples fairly lengthy instruction immediately before his passion. As in other parts of this Gospel, Jesus speaks here metaphorically and spiritually while his listeners interpret everything he says literally. Thomas, Philip, and the other disciples just don't seem to get Jesus' message as they struggle to comprehend him, here or practically anywhere else. Of course, as characters in the story they don't know what is going to happen after Jesus finishes this speech.[3] Further, what Jesus does have to say that they understand is unsettling, even offensive! But the readers, ancient and modern, are well aware of what occurs subsequently and can hear Jesus explaining the meaning of his passion, death, and resurrection for their communities of faith, especially as they live into a future without his physical presence.

In 14:1 Jesus admonishes the disciples not to be troubled, using the same verb that the evangelist used in the account of Lazarus's raising to describe Jesus' emotion when he saw Mary (11:33). Though he was distressed at Lazarus's gravesite, perhaps by the thought of his own death, he now exhorts his followers not to be disturbed, but to believe. He then makes an implicit promise: "In my Father's house there are many dwelling places. If it were not so, would I have told you that I go to prepare a place for you? And if I go and prepare a place for you, I will come again and will take you to myself, so that where I am, there you may be also" (14:2-3). This language of place denotes intimacy and togetherness, not spatial location, as is so often assumed in modern Christianity. The Greek word for "dwelling place" has the same root as the word translated "abide," which almost always refers to a close connection, a "being-with" Jesus.[4] Thus, wherever Jesus is, so are those who believe in him; and, as we will see in the next section of this text, there also is the Father.

Thomas, a representative of all the disciples here, misunderstands, giving Jesus opportunity to make himself clearer. "I am the way, and the truth, and the life," he says (v. 6). Here John draws upon two already familiar christological concepts, life and truth. We only have to think back to the prologue in which these themes are set out and, again, to Jesus' encounter with Mary at Lazarus's tomb in which he says, "I am the resurrection and the life" (11:25). The phrase "the way" is not so common in this Gospel, although it appears in Acts as a denotation of the Christian movement, not as a christological title. Behind both usages is probably the metaphoric understanding of "way" as rule of life or practice common in the ancient Hellenistic world.[5] In Chinese Bibles the Greek word is often translated "tao," meaning literally "road" or "way" as in ancient Greek. This is also the word used in Chinese language systems to denote religion.

Further, Jesus says he is not "*a* way, *a* truth, and *a* life," but "*the* way, *the* truth, and *the* life." He continues, "No one comes to the Father except through me," thereby effectively cutting off other possibilities for getting to the intimacy and union he is presenting here. As abstruse as such claims are, they are also unsettling, if not disturbing. How could a person be the only way to the Father? And even if true, how could these Jewish disciples forsake all that they had once thought of as means for coming into the presence of God, things like the law and temple practice and synagogue association?

Many of us may be as unsettled as those first followers by the exclusivism expressed here. It eases our discomfort (albeit only slightly) to remember that this Gospel's historical context is one of conflict among Jews, some of whom believed these claims about Jesus and some of whom did not. Thus, the language these groups threw at one another was polemical and sharp. We might also consider that this community was making a confession of faith about what it knew to be true without necessarily carefully pondering its opposite. For those ancient Christian believers to speak of Christ as the way and the truth is to speak of their profound transformative experience with him, not an intellectual proposition to which everyone must assent.[6]

At 14:8 Philip's misunderstanding comes to the fore. It rests in the fact that he does not comprehend how he could possibly have seen or known the Father up to this point in the action. The problem is not that he doesn't understand that Jesus is talking about God when he uses parental language. It is that he doesn't realize Jesus' unity with the Father; in fact, so intimate are the two that they can barely be distinguished in this text and throughout the Gospel. And no wonder Philip and the others don't understand! Jesus' claim that the Father can be seen through him is outrageous, asserted as it is against a background of stories from the Hebrew Scriptures that affirm that God cannot be seen in any way by human eyes.

The RCL adds verses 13-14 to the LFM reading, which contain two promises: first, the believer will perform even greater works than Jesus, and second, whatever the believer asks in the name of Jesus will be done. These promises underscore the connection between Jesus and the believing community and between his actions and theirs. As a matter of fact, "their works in reality are Jesus' works."[7] Thus, what was begun in the ministry of Jesus continues into the ministry of the church.

John 14:1-12 in many ways encapsulates the message of the entire Gospel: Jesus is the way to the Father and all who believe in Jesus can be assured of finding that way. Yet this message, offered to comfort believers who encounter throughout life the difficulty of living faithfully without the physical presence of Jesus, is so often used as a weapon against those who do not believe. We use it against those who have faith commitments outside of Christianity, and we use it against those who do not believe as we do. The challenge is to hear and preach this message of assurance, so critical to that first Jewish-Christian community who read these words, and at the same time refuse to allow it to become adamantine walls behind which we cower, popping up occasionally to hurl spitballs at those outside our own belief systems.[8]

## Notes

1. For a modern-day take on how to take complaints seriously and respond usefully, see Robert Kegan and Lisa Laskow Lahey, *How the Ways We Talk Can Change the Ways We Work: Seven Languages for Transformation* (San Francisco: Jossey-Bass, 2002).

2. See Pheme Perkins, *First and Second Peter, James and Jude,* Interpretation: A Bible Commentary for Teaching and Preaching (Louisville: John Knox, 1995), 43; and Leonhard Goppelt, *A Commentary on 1 Peter,* trans. and augmented John E. Alsup (Grand Rapids: Eerdmans, 1993), 135–36.

3. For a delightful retelling of this theme of misunderstanding in a narrative context, see Dennis E. Smith and Michael E. Williams, eds., *The Storyteller's Companion to the Bible,* vol. 10, *John* (Nashville: Abingdon, 1996), 133–35.

4. Gail R. O'Day, "The Gospel of John," in *The New Interpreter's Bible* (Nashville: Abingdon, 1995), 9:740.

5. D. Moody Smith Jr., *John,* Abingdon Bible Commentaries (Nashville: Abingdon, 1999), 268.

6. In another approach to the problems raised by John 14:6, James H. Charlesworth argues that v. 6b, "No one comes to the Father except through me," is a later redaction. See James H. Charlesworth, "The Gospel of John: Exclusivism Caused by a Social Setting Different from That of Jesus (John 11:54 and 14:6)," in *Anti-Judaism and the Fourth Gospel,* ed. Reimund Bieringer, Didier Pollefeyt, and Frederique Vandecasteele-Vanneuville (Louisville: Westminster John Knox, 2001), 247–78.

7. O'Day, "Gospel of John," 746.

8. See ibid., 743–44.

# May 29, 2011
## Sixth Sunday of Easter

**Revised Common Lectionary (RCL)**
Acts 17:22-31
Psalm 66:8-20
1 Peter 3:13-22
John 14:15-21

**Lectionary for Mass (LFM)**
Acts 8:5-8, 14-17
Psalm 66:1-3, 4-5, 6-7, 16 + 20
1 Peter 3:15-18
John 14:15-21

The Holy Spirit comes to the fore in the Gospel reading for both the RCL and the LFM in which John depicts Jesus preparing the disciples to live faithfully without him. In the LFM the first reading is also centered on the Spirit, from Luke's viewpoint. The RCL, in the first reading, takes up Paul's speech to the Athenians. Both lectionaries select portions of Psalm 66 as response and offer another continuous reading from 1 Peter.

## First Reading
### Acts 17:22-31 (RCL)

The Saul whom we encountered in last week's RCL reading from Acts appears today as Paul, now a follower of Jesus and ready to offer his own defense of the gospel. Of course, by this time in Luke's story Paul is a seasoned preacher, and his skill shows throughout this speech as he makes his appeal to the Athenians through ideas and quotations found in their own remarkable culture. First, he flatters them on their consummate religiosity that the numerous altars and statues scattered throughout the city display (readers of this story, however, know how distressed Paul actually was by this city full of idols, 17:16). Then he makes common cause with them by referring to an altar of the unknown god, one whom he proceeds to make known to them. "The God who made the world and everything in it, he who is Lord of heaven and earth, does not live in shrines made by human hands, nor is he served by human hands, as though he needed anything, since he himself gives to all mortals life and breath and all things" (vv. 24-25). To buttress this claim, he quotes two Greek proverbs.

The tone of the speech shifts when he begins to speak of God's judgment, the need to repent, and the resurrection of the dead. Although he never mentions Jesus by name, he alludes to him as "a man whom [God] has appointed, and of this he has given assurance to all by raising him from the dead" (17:31). The reaction of the people listening, whom William Willimon calls the "cultured despisers," is mixed. As Willimon continues, "Christian proclamation is not to be judged merely by its success in winning an approving response. Where the Word is faithfully preached, some believe, some mock—for even the oratorical skill of Paul cannot remove the offense of the gospel, in fact it accentuates it."[1]

### Acts 8:5-8, 14-17 (LFM)

In the ministry of Philip, last seen in his appointment to the group of seven who would serve the community at the behest of the apostles, the gospel came to Samaria. And the people were eager to receive it, especially after they saw the signs and wonders that Philip was able to work among them. After skipping the conversion of a "certain man named Simon" (8:9-13), the lectionary resumes with the arrival of Peter and John, sent from Jerusalem to see what was going on in Samaria. In apparent approval, the apostles also prayed that this new band of Christians would receive the Holy Spirit. And they received it when the two laid hands upon them.

In the selection of this pericope from Acts, the LFM highlights the theme of the Spirit that is central to the Gospel reading today. It is important to Luke to note that Philip had not yet received the Spirit until John and Peter give it to him. At issue is not the act of laying hands on him; after all, the Spirit is imparted in several different ways in Acts. What matters here is that the central group of apostles serves as final arbiters of the new mission. Says Charles Talbert, "In Acts, the Twelve in Jerusalem represent the judges for a reconstituted Israel (Luke 22:29-30). As such they perform a supervisory role with reference to new developments in the Messianist mission."[2] Even the bestowal of the untamable Spirit is made through this rudimentary church order. In a somewhat different way than John allows in the Gospel reading, the Spirit signifies power and authority. This is underscored by the following episode, 8:18-24, which is also left out of the lectionary, in which the Simon whom Philip baptized tries to buy some of this power.

## Psalmody
### Psalm 66:8-20 (RCL)
### Psalm 66:1-3, 4-5, 6-7, 16 + 20 (LFM)

Both lectionaries use this psalm, although they cut it for worship in different ways. This joyful articulation of praise is full of exodus imagery, an event that the psalmist uses to illustrate God's good intentions for the whole world. But the psalmist does not simply exult in the cosmic dimensions of God's power. He also speaks personally, "Come and hear, all you who fear God, and I will tell what he has done for me" (v. 16).

Christians have traditionally associated this psalm with Easter. J. Clinton McCann Jr. sums up the psalm like this: "In the exodus (vv. 5-7), in recurring exoduses in new circumstances (vv. 8-12), and in individual experiences of deliverance (vv. 13-20), God is at work bringing life out of death."[3]

# Second Reading
## 1 Peter 3:13-22 (RCL)
## 1 Peter 3:15-18 (LFM)

"Always be ready to make your defense to anyone who demands from you an account for the hope that is in you; yet do it with gentleness and reverence" (1 Peter 3:15b-16a). The recurring theme of witness throughout Eastertide shows up again in this reading and is crystallized in these statements. Although it is possible that the author may have been speaking about some sort of formal, legal defense made by Christians who had been hauled before the courts on charges of atheism, it is equally likely that he had in mind a witness offered to anyone who asked about the believer's faith and lifestyle.[4] In fact, David Balch argues that these verses are closely related to the previous instructions to slaves, husbands, and wives (2:18—3:7), as the author urges believers to give a verbal explanation of the nonverbal conduct advocated in the directives.[5] Further, he encourages followers of Jesus to speak with gentleness; there is here no browbeating that is often associated with groups that are aggressive in their evangelism.

Note that this admonition is spoken in the midst of words of comfort for those who may be suffering unjustly—again a prominent issue in this epistle. We do not know exactly what kind of persecution or oppression these followers were experiencing at the time of writing. Were they singled out by their neighbors sporadically with cruel taunts and mean-spirited graffiti? Were they systematically arrested, tortured, or killed by government officials? Were they not allowed to buy or sell in the marketplace? Or were such activities only distant memories from other periods of persecution or constant threats that never materialized? Historians cannot say for certain. We do know that the author is not talking about just any kind of suffering, but suffering at the hands of others who are offended, if not outraged, by the readers' faithfulness to Jesus.

The appropriate Christian response in the face of this suffering is hope, a hope that is rooted in Jesus' own suffering. Fred Craddock says, "In the twenty centuries of Christian history, thousands of sermons, lectures, and books have probed the problem of the unjust suffering of God's people, but no response to the issue—philosophical, theological, or practical—has ministered to the victims quite like the reminder of the crucified Christ."[6] But the picture of Jesus presented in verses 19-22 (and left out of the LFM) has an odd feature. After his death he preaches to spirits who are in prison (v. 19), spirits whose identity is linked somehow with the time of Noah. Scholars generally agree that an allusion to the apocalyptic and noncanonical book of 1 Enoch is found here, but beyond that no one is certain about who these "spirits" are. The author interrupts his own train of thought about Jesus with words about the significance of baptism—a subject that may have come to his mind as he mentioned Noah. Then he returns to his primary subject with a more standard description of the exaltation of Christ at the right hand of God. Although references and meanings are obscure in these verses, what is clear is that the ministry of Jesus transcends earthly limitations. This is a Christ whose work has ramifications far beyond the lives of these ancient readers. It extends from the abode of spirits, whoever they may be, to the heavenly throne room.

## Gospel
### John 14:15-21 (RCL, LFM)

This reading is a continuation of last week's Gospel text and the Farewell Discourse that Jesus is giving to his disciples on the occasion of his final dinner with them before his arrest. As I said in last week's discussion, at issue is how the followers of Jesus will live faithfully once he is no longer with them. In today's lection Jesus promises an Advocate who will accompany the faithful community in its mission, even when it is treated with hostility and disregard.

The lectionaries mark off this passage with an inclusio. In verse 15 Jesus says, "If you love me, you will keep my commandments"; in verse 21, the same message is repeated—"Those who have my commandments and keep them are those who love me"—and then amplified to include the Father in this circle of love. The word *commandments* in this Gospel is often synonymous with the words of Jesus and point to the entirety of Jesus' teaching.[7] For John this is characterized by believing in Jesus and loving one another, but concrete examples or rules about these activities are never given. What is at stake is more fundamental than regulations: How will the disciples and indeed all those who believe in Jesus continue to love him even when he is no longer present? How can they, and we, live in unity with him when his physicality is not available for them, and us, to hold on to?[8]

In response to this dire problem Jesus promises "another Advocate" (v. 16). The use of "another" begs the question of who was the first Advocate; Jesus himself remains the best answer. This is the first time the word *Advocate* appears in the Fourth Gospel (an English translation of the original Greek is "Paraclete"), although we have already heard mention of the Spirit in the baptism of Jesus. Here the Advocate functions less like legal counsel, as in 15:26 and 16:7-11, and more like a comforter and a certifier both of the truth of God and of the continued presence of the resurrected Jesus. As Sandra M. Schneiders says, "The Spirit will be the interior presence of Jesus within his disciples maintaining their union with him, leading them moment by moment, as they are able to bear it, into all truth, and uniting them to the Father."[9] Moreover, it is this Spirit that will make possible the disciples' ongoing union with one another in the love that they are commanded to live out.

Love, commandments, abiding, Father, Spirit, Paraclete—all are familiar Johannine ideas, so simple to utter and so difficult to explain rationally. They chase each other in endless and seemingly closed circles throughout the Gospel and the Johannine epistles. The ineffable experience of this author and of his first audience can hardly be captured in ancient words, and we ourselves, centuries later, struggle to bring these concepts to life. Further, the Spirit in this Gospel doesn't manifest itself in the same way as it does in Paul's first letter to the Corinthians—gifts of ecstatic, incomprehensible speech—or in Acts—stormy fire that makes its presence known in all the languages of the world. Here we leap from pure conceptual Spirit, sent by the Father, to pure conceptual Love that abides among those who keep the Son's commandments, which turn out basically to be summed up in loving one another so that the Spirit might dwell among us. Maybe the only way to put clothes on these ideals is to ground them in our own very human relationships. In the ways that we love our spouses and life partners, fixing them food and cleaning their houses; in the ways that we love our friends with gifts of encouragement; in the ways that we love the people in our churches, visiting them in the hospital or laughing with them as we build habitats for humanity and offer food in soup kitchens—in these places the commandments of Jesus are fulfilled, the Spirit dwells among and within us, and God smiles.

## Notes

1. William H. Willimon, *Acts*, Interpretation: A Bible Commentary for Teaching and Preaching (Atlanta: John Knox, 1988), 144.
2. Charles Talbert, *Reading Acts: A Literary and Theological Commentary on the Acts of the Apostles* (New York: Crossroad, 1997), 86.
3. J. Clinton McCann Jr., "The Book of Psalms," in *The New Interpreter's Bible* (Nashville: Abingdon, 1996), 4:938.
4. David L. Bartlett, "The First Letter of Peter," in *The New Interpreter's Bible* (Nashville: Abingdon, 1998), 12:291.
5. David Balch, *Let Wives Be Submissive: The Domestic Code in 1 Peter* (Atlanta: Scholars, 1981), 90–93.
6. Fred B. Craddock, *First and Second Peter and Jude*, Westminster Bible Companion (Louisville: Westminster John Knox, 1995), 60.
7. Gail R. O'Day, "The Gospel of John," in *The New Interpreter's Bible* (Nashville: Abingdon, 1995), 9:746.
8. Rudolf Bultmann, *The Gospel of John: A Commentary*, trans. G. R. Beasley-Murray (Philadelphia: Westminster, 1971), 613.
9. Sandra M. Schneiders, *Written That You May Believe: Encountering Jesus in the Fourth Gospel*, rev. and exp. ed. (New York: Herder & Herder, 2003), 60.

# June 2, 2011
## Ascension of Our Lord
### (may be moved to Sunday, June 5)

**Revised Common Lectionary (RCL)**
Acts 1:1-11
Psalm 47 or Psalm 93
Ephesians 1:15-23
Luke 24:44-53

**Lectionary for Mass (LFM)**
Acts 1:1-11
Psalm 47:2-3, 6-7, 8-9
Ephesians 1:17-23
Matthew 28:16-20

Religious experience is notoriously difficult to put into words, especially words that others will understand and accept. The ascension of Christ is no exception. Whatever those first disciples saw and felt can hardly be contained by rational explanations or grossly physical depictions of Jesus hovering in between earth and heaven like a humanoid spaceship. So we must turn to the language of imagination and poetry to express what is at last as ineffable as our own most private moments of saying goodbye to someone we have loved. At such time, our inarticulate stutterings, our too-tight graspings, our heartfelt yearnings for more are sources for connection with the ancient goodbye stories of the ascension. The Jesus whom the disciples had known and loved is really, truly leaving. His absence almost overwhelms his last words.

## First Reading
### Acts 1:1-11 (RCL, LFM)

These first verses of the Acts of the Apostles not only recount the ascension of Jesus, hence their placement at this point in the lectionary, but also contain the Lukan Jesus' program or mission statement for the disciples after he ascends. They also mark a boundary line between the time in which these followers lived with their teacher, both as earthly and as resurrected body, and a time when they no longer experience his presence in any form. Further, this is their last conversation with him. In it Jesus promises that they will receive the Holy Spirit as presence and power.

The programmatic mission statement is a response to the disciples' continuing concern about a political return of the land of Judea to its former status as independent kingdom ("Lord, is this the time when you will restore the kingdom to Israel?" 1:6). After all this time with Jesus, after his death and resurrection, the disciples are still fixated on some kind of socially empirical change in the status quo of Roman rule. Jesus will not respond directly to this concern, deflecting it with words about not knowing the times of God. Rather than struggling for the autonomy of the land of Israel, Jesus offers another vision of their future work: "But you will receive power when the Holy Spirit has come upon you; and you will be my witnesses in Jerusalem, in all Judea and Samaria, and to the ends of the earth" (v. 8). Their task is not political rebellion against Rome; it is witness through proclamation. And this witness is not simply some private sharing of individual impressions of Jesus, but public and universal speech, from Jerusalem, the disciples' current home, to the ends of the earth.

No sooner has Jesus set out their mission to them than he disappears from their sight. Two men in white robes suddenly appear and verbally prod the disciples to get started: "Men of Galilee, why do you stand looking up toward heaven?" (v. 11a). But that is not all they say. "This Jesus, who has been taken up from you into heaven, will come in the same way as you saw him go into heaven" (v. 11b). These words add an eschatological overtone to the whole scene. Whatever the disciples might accomplish in the coming years will not be complete until Jesus returns.

## Psalmody
### Psalm 47 (RCL)
### Psalm 47:2-3, 6-7, 8-9 (LFM)

The order of the universe is secure, according to the words of this enthronement psalm. God is in charge; "God is king over the nations" (v. 8). This may not seem so obvious, we might think, as we turn on the television news or scroll through the morning updates on our computers. It was probably not any more obvious in the ancient world in which people were much less insulated from famine and war than we Americans. Walter Brueggemann says, "The Psalms of celebration . . . greatly overstate the case because they are essentially promissory. That is, they are not descriptions of what is evident, but they are renderings of what is surely promised and toward which the speaker is prepared to live."[1] They evoke a new, alternate reality that gives us a chance to envision and work toward a world in which all might live together peacefully with the realm of God. We sing praises now in anticipation and hope.

### Psalm 93 (RCL alt.)

This is also an enthronement psalm that proleptically celebrates the possibility of God's reign. Even the great floods lift up their voice and praise God. While it may seem absurd to make such a claim in the face of the natural disasters of our age, the psalmist calls us to cling to a vision of shalom for all creation.

## Second Reading
### Ephesians 1:15-23 (RCL)
### Ephesians 1:17-23 (LFM)

This portrait of the exalted Christ looms over this passage and the entire epistle to the Ephesians like a great golden and blue Byzantine mosaic. Christ now raised from the dead, seated at the right hand of God in a throne room that fills the starry sky, his feet resting on the edge of the earth—just above our heads, his luminous brown eyes gazing through us and beyond us, his right hand, with palm still stained with blood, lifted in blessing. This is Jesus ascended and glorified.

According to the author of this epistle, this reality, of which words and glittering mosaic stones are but poor imitations, is also the source of our hope and the object of our faith. He prays that we might know that the power of God is greater than any other power, including that of any empire that has come and gone, any political or economic system that has claimed human allegiance. He prays that we might develop the wisdom to see that nothing endures forever except the glory of God that is displayed in the paradox of a suffering, now-exalted Christ.

## Gospel
### Luke 24:44-53 (RCL)

Luke has a problem inherent in the way he has set up the story of Jesus and the community that he founded. It's a dramatic problem: How to get Jesus off the stage so the disciples can take center stage and thus propel the action forward? To be sure, he shares this problem with the other evangelists, but none of them attempt to narrate a second half of the story. They don't need to push Jesus off the stage quite so visibly and so finally. It is also a theological problem: somehow the mission that Jesus began must be placed firmly and squarely in the hands of his disciples and then handed on to the readers themselves. In other words, how does Luke get the followers of Jesus to take responsibility for the work that has begun while Jesus was present? Luke's way to solve both forms of this problem is to narrate the removal of Jesus from the center of action in terms so concrete as to be almost too corporeal. We only have to think of the countless paintings in the history of Christian art that have depicted a very physical Jesus, bathed in light and framed by fleecy clouds, hovering above the heads of open-mouthed disciples.

We should note here that Luke is somewhat careless about details between his Gospel and Acts as he tells of the ascension. In the Gospel the ascension takes place the very night after the morning of the resurrection—Easter Sunday night! In Acts Jesus ascends with the clouds forty days after the resurrection and ten days before Pentecost. There is no good way to resolve this anomaly in Luke's narrative except perhaps to note that the timing here is not Luke's primary concern.[2]

His major issue is basically demonstrated through the ways in which the two narrations of the ascension agree: a mission statement laid out by Jesus for his disciples before he ascends. In the Gospel the mission comes in the form of a promise and a task: the promise is the sending of the Holy Spirit (v. 49). Here Luke is uncharacteristically enigmatic, referring to the Spirit only as "what my Father promised." The enigma is quickly resolved in Acts 1:4-5 and then displayed in Acts 2. The task is the work entrusted to the disciples, to be witnesses to all that they have seen in the life of Jesus and to proclaim in the name of Jesus to all nations the forgiveness of sins.

As a buttress of support for this understanding of apostolic mission, Luke relates Jesus' correlation of his suffering, death, and resurrection with Hebrew Scripture. This is the third time in Luke 24 that the formula of Jesus' suffering, death, and resurrection makes some sort of appearance, perhaps as a threefold response to the three predictions of these events that Jesus made before his death (9:22, 44; 18:31-34). In the prepassion occurrences, the disciples do not understand what Jesus is talking about. But after the resurrection, the disciples' minds are opened and they at last grasp, in the light of Hebrew Scripture, what Jesus has been talking about all along. The passion and resurrection of Jesus not only fulfill the Law and the Prophets (and the psalms, which are included in this formula only here), but have saving significance for all humankind. A significance that points to repentance and the forgiveness of sins. A significance that is continued through the proclamation of the disciples.

The connection of the events of Jesus' life and death with Scripture is a particularly Lukan emphasis and becomes a major theme in the preaching of the apostles in Acts. It is almost as if the Hebrew Bible serves as an extended proof text for the events of the passion and resurrection. This is a result of Luke's real interest in showing how the early church's proclamation is in continuity with Jewish understandings of the promises and activity of God. Nonetheless, as modern preachers we must be careful not to obliterate the unique voices in the Hebrew Scriptures by a facile prophecy-fulfillment overlay that Christians often give to them.

## Matthew 28:16-20 (LFM)

The purpose of this commissioning scene that Matthew describes is similar to the ascension scene of Luke: to move responsibility for witness to the nations from Jesus to the disciples. Matthew is not as occupied as Luke with getting Jesus off stage so the disciples can get on with the mission, but there is an aroma of closure around the whole scene. At the same time we should note that this is the only time in the first Gospel that Jesus appears to his disciples. In fact, it's the first time he has seen them since they all ran away at his arrest. So here at this transitional moment, Jesus doesn't really say goodbye—although, again, absence lurks in the background—but offers words of encouragement even as he sends them out to the world to "make disciples of all nations, baptizing them in the name of the Father and of the Son and of the Holy Spirit, and teaching them to obey everything that I have commanded you" (vv. 19-20).

I am captivated by the apparently dropped-in phrase, "but some doubted," in verse 17. This issue of doubt after the resurrection is not unique to this Gospel; we have already heard of Thomas's problem in John's Gospel. And, according to M. Eugene Boring, the Greek phrase might better be translated "and they doubted," meaning the same group that worshiped Jesus when they saw him also weren't quite sure about this. After all, they had neither witnessed the resurrection (note that Matthew himself never describes the event itself) nor encountered Jesus immediately afterward. Boring explains the moment this way: "The latter translation represents Matthew's own theological understanding of the meaning of discipleship, which is always a matter of 'little faith,' faith that by its nature is not the same as cocksureness, but incorporates itself in the act of worship."[3]

This strikes me as very good news for modern Christians who are bombarded with all kinds of reasons not to believe, including one we share with those first disciples—resurrection makes no sense according to the laws of nature. Perhaps all of us harbor a certain amount of disbelief at various times, including during worship, simply because we cannot get our heads around a Jesus who returns from death and offers life to everyone, to the nations. Richard Rodriguez, in an essay entitled "Atheism Is Wasted on the Nonbeliever," says this: "It seems to me not inappropriate that I take my inner atheist with me to church every Sunday. The atheist within me is as noisy as my stomach, even when I am standing in the Communion line. . . . This is my prayer: *Dear God, I believe in you. Please strengthen my disbelief.*"[4] Amen.

· · · · · · · · ·

In the introduction to Eastertide I spoke of liminality, the state of being in between what was and what is to come. Luke's descriptions capture just such a moment of liminality—the ending of a Gospel, a life of Jesus, and the beginning of an Acts, a life of the faithful community. Whenever we say goodbye to people who are significant in our lives and wonder how we will construct our lives now that they are gone, we are caught in that moment. The task of separation, one of the phases of liminality, is complete. But we are standing in a doorway of transition, not quite ready to move forward, now certain we cannot go back. Incorporation into a new life has yet to occur. Many of our churches in North America seem to be in the same place. We cannot go back ever again to the glowing days of a previous era in which people flocked to worship and organized their lives around church programs. We've said goodbye to that. But we don't know what lies ahead for us. Neither did the disciples, and for now there is comfort in that fact.

## Notes

1. Walter Brueggemann, *Praying the Psalms* (Winona, Minn.: St. Mary's, 1984), 32.

2. Robert C. Tannehill, *Luke,* Abingdon New Testament Commentaries (Nashville: Abingdon, 1996), 362.

3. M. Eugene Boring, "The Gospel of Matthew," in *The New Interpreter's Bible* (Nashville: Abingdon, 1995), 7:502.

4. Richard Rodriguez, "Atheism Is Wasted on the Nonbeliever," in *The Best American Spiritual Writing 2008,* ed. Philip Zaleski (Boston: Houghton Mifflin, 2008), 157.

# June 5, 2011
## Seventh Sunday of Easter
### (if Ascension is not celebrated here)

| Revised Common Lectionary (RCL) | Lectionary for Mass (LFM) |
|---|---|
| Acts 1:6-14 | Acts 1:12-14 |
| Psalm 68:1-10, 32-35 | Psalm 27:1, 4, 7-8 |
| 1 Peter 4:12-14; 5:6-11 | 1 Peter 4:13-16 |
| John 17:1-11 | John 17:1-11a |

This Sunday's readings offer one more pause for reflection on what it means to be faithful to Jesus before the excitement of Pentecost. The disciples huddle behind closed doors in Jerusalem, perhaps reassuring one another with psalms. The author of 1 Peter ponders meanings of the suffering of those who stand up for Jesus and finds comfort in the affirmation of Jesus' own suffering and exaltation. And John remembers Jesus praying for unity among the disciples, Jesus, and the Father of us all.

## First Reading
### Acts 1:6-14 (RCL)

For commentary on this text, please see the first reading for the Ascension of Our Lord, above. Also note that discussion of the three additional verses, verses 12-14, not included in that material is found immediately below.

### Acts 1:12-14 (LFM)

In the RCL reading, the introduction to Acts and the scene at hand in verses 1-5 have been cut off and we are left with the account of the ascension of Jesus (discussed in the Ascension of Our Lord, above), the return to Jerusalem, and a listing of who is left among the group who followed him. The LFM reading, verses 12-14, consists only of the return and the listing. Neither lectionary includes the account of the election of Matthias at Eastertide. Nowhere in Luke's two-part narrative do the disciples go to Galilee as they do in Matthew and John, nor are they instructed to do so as in Mark. For Luke the epicenter of the initial action is Jerusalem.

The group returned to a room upstairs where they had been staying, according to Hans Conzelmann, "the place for prayer and conversation."[1] It includes eleven disciples minus Judas, the same ones listed in Luke 6:14-15 albeit in a different order; "certain women" (cf. Luke 8:1-3; 23:49-56; 24:1-12), as well as Mary the mother of Jesus; and the brothers of Jesus, blood relatives of Jesus not to be allegorized as members of the faithful community.[2] In other words, this is a typical Lukan recounting of the people who surrounded Jesus in his earthly life. What is most remarkable about the entire reading is the obedient and faithful response of these followers. Jesus told them to return to Jerusalem and wait for the coming of the Spirit—which is exactly what they did.

# Psalmody
## Psalm 68:1-10, 32-35 (RCL)

This psalm takes on a slightly pleading tone in its use of the subjunctive mood: let God rise up, let those who hate him flee, let the righteous be joyful. The psalmist expresses a confidence that is based in past events at Mt. Sinai, but his words are not as proleptically celebrative as they are in the enthronement psalms. He is too aware that there are orphans and widows still desolate and needing to be protected and prisoners still to be given homes and freedom. Nonetheless, he urges the people to sing with joy, to ascribe only to God majesty and power, to praise God for all that has been given to them.

## Psalm 27:1, 4, 7-8 (LFM)

It doesn't take too large a leap in imagination to hear the disciples chanting this psalm when they returned to the place of prayer and conversation after Jesus had left them. This psalm, particularly as it is divided in this lectionary, expresses mingled feelings—faith in a God who is light and salvation but also desolation in the cry for God to come and show God's face. In their uncertainty and anxiety, they say to one other, "For God will hide me in his shelter in the day of trouble." And they wait.

# Second Reading
## 1 Peter 4:12-14; 5:6-11 (RCL)
## 1 Peter 4:13-16 (LFM)

Suffering again. This author hammers away repeatedly, almost annoyingly on his theme of suffering as believers. Suffering at the hands of those who don't understand their faith in Jesus. Suffering as a sign of faithfulness to God. Suffering modeled on Jesus' own suffering. Suffering as a badge of glory. Suffering as a temporary doorway through which believers pass in order to reach heaven's bliss. Suffering on behalf of faith that seems on this spring day as far removed from life in these United States and Canada as ancient Rome was from ancient China. And still both lectionaries carefully pick and choose their way through these last chapters, avoiding other theological traps and incomprehensible yet disturbing assertions, concentrating all their energy on this kind of suffering.

What shall we say about this suffering in the modern Western world? Shall we shrug our shoulders and turn quickly to the Gospel readings of the season? Or shall we pause and wonder about those who have suffered and still suffer for Jesus' sake in places not so safe as ours? Shall we redefine suffering for Jesus into suffering for economic, religious, and racial justice, for mercy for those who are different, for compassion for those in pain? Shall we finally recognize that the American white experience of ease, comfort, and freedom, at least when it comes to religion, is not and has not been the norm for most Christians and thus stop defining truth or relevance in this foreign epistle by our own existence? Shall we listen for the challenge to define our lives according to the passion and death of Jesus—offering ourselves sacrificially when occasion demands (clearly a most difficult matter to discern) and looking for opportunities to give up prosperity in favor of a righteous sharing of all the gifts of life?

These are some of the questions 1 Peter poses. But even as we struggle with them, we might listen as well to the affirmations embedded in the entire epistle. The reign of Christ is attained through a narrow way defined not by a chariot of dominance but a cross of humiliation. In this claim the boasting of the mighty is turned upside down; no human person, group, or government has absolute authority through its own will to power. And the reign of Christ extends beyond the borders of this century and this continent into a future unbounded by fear and a realm of unlimited love.

# Gospel
## John 17:1-11 (RCL)
## John 17:1-11a (LFM)

Just as a priest or a minister ends a sermon with a prayer, so Jesus concludes the Farewell Discourse, parts of which were read on the Fifth and Sixth Sundays of Easter, with a lengthy appeal to God. Further, Jesus is following a pattern quite common in the Hebrew Bible and extracanonical books like *Jubilees* in which a patriarch or leader makes a final speech and concludes with a prayer, usually of blessing. The lection for today is comprised of the first half of that prayer, often dubbed "Jesus' High Priestly Prayer," because Jesus is now speaking to God and interceding on behalf of the disciples. In this reading, the themes of the Farewell Discourse and earlier speeches in the Gospel are reiterated. In fact, Gail O'Day tells us that this prayer is the "theological climax of the Fourth Gospel," situated as it is between the events of Jesus' life and his final instructions and the events of his death and resurrection.[3]

For our purposes we can divide today's reading into two parts. The first, verses 1-5, consists of Jesus' direct address to God and reminders of their unique relationship. The second, verses 6-11 (the LFM cuts off the last half of verse 11), is a prayer for the disciples, primarily that they might also be included in the unity that characterizes Jesus' bond with God. Again, we should keep in mind that the entire prayer is not included in either lectionary, leaving us with a somewhat distorted view of what is spoken here. (As a matter of fact, both lectionaries contain portions of John 17 on the Seventh Sunday of Easter in all three years in a pattern similar to that of the use of John 10 described above.)

At 17:1 Jesus looks up from the disciples and speaks to God. "Father, the hour has come; glorify your Son so that the Son may glorify you." It is important to note that when "glorification" is mentioned in this Gospel, it is embedded in an understanding of the incarnation to the point of human suffering. That is to say, Jesus is glorified through his willing passion on the cross.[4] This fact is especially pertinent in light of our discussion of the theme of suffering so prominent in 1 Peter. As Jesus continues in prayer, he speaks of the authority God has given him—authority to offer eternal life to the people God has given him. And that eternal life is knowledge of God. As D. Moody Smith explains, "The only true God is the God who has sent Jesus Christ, and true life is knowledge of that God through Jesus."[5] Moreover, says Smith, we should remember the constant hostility between Jesus and the Jewish leaders that revolves around questions not only of Jesus' identity but of God's identity. The Johannine answer is that God is most fully, if not only, known through the whole of Jesus' life, teachings, death, and resurrection.[6] In 17:5 Jesus asks, somewhat repetitiously, that God glorify him now in God's very presence.

Jesus' attention shifts in 17:6 to those who follow him: "I have made your name known to those whom you gave me from the world. They were yours, and you gave them to me, and they have kept your word." The Greek word in this verse for making God's name known is the word for "reveal." Here, at the theological climax, do we hear of the unique Johannine contribution to Christology—Jesus as heavenly revealer. He has shown his disciples God by showing them himself and he has passed on God's words (here synonymous with "commandments"). He then makes clear that he is not praying for those outside the Johannine community: "I am asking on their behalf; I am not asking on behalf of the world, but on behalf of those whom you gave me" (v. 9). The last phrase, "those whom you gave me," is a repetition of a phrase in 17:6, heightening the sense of what we now call predestination that pervades the Farewell Discourse.

Finally, we come to what Jesus is asking from God in this portion of the prayer—protection. "Holy Father, protect them in your name that you have given me" (v. 11). But the question is, protection from what? Possible answers may be found in the subsequent verses of the prayer not read today: protection from the hatred of the world (v. 14) or from the evil one (v. 15). But the second half of verse 11, "so that they may be one, as we are one," implies a slightly different answer. Jesus, at least in this part of the prayer, is asking God to protect his followers from the corrosive divisiveness that besets so many groups. In fact, Raymond Brown has taught us that the history of the Johannine church in the first century was marked by infighting, name calling, and disunity.[7]

And so at last we come to the rub for our own Christian faith as we continue to live out the scandal of Christian disunity. Just as the Father and the Son are one, so Jesus prays that we all might be one. Yet, twenty centuries later, we have yet to find a way to live in the circle of unity for which Jesus prays. Some of the things that divide us are extremely important; some are so petty as to be laughable if they weren't so tragic. Regardless, we have little hope of manifesting among ourselves—and I mean here all kinds of Christians—any kind of harmony.

Yet, after acknowledging this sad fact, perhaps we should try again, using the tools we've already been offered in the Gospel of John this Eastertide. We might begin with the love that Jesus commands us to keep. Not the love that is based on agreement and the happy, though occasional, accident that you and I might actually see eye to eye, but the love that is based on attention to one another. We might at least listen carefully—to understand, not to refute or to find tangential points of concord. We might notice sensitively our dissimilarities as well as our similarities. We might look for signs of the Spirit, that is, the presence of Jesus, in one another's communities, without condemning them as impossible or foreign. Garret Keizer remarks, "How little we see of our neighbors—and that for me, is as 'mystical' a realization as any. We are like tourists in Bethlehem, remarking that we might be better able to appreciate the spectacular star if it wasn't for some brat hollering in a stable."[8]

. . . . . . . . .

Today's texts, both in their setting in the church calendar and in their words, invite us to stop and attend to one another in all our outrageous particularities and in our unity with God. In a meditation on the spiritual discipline of attention, Frederic and Mary Ann Brussat remind us that "moments of grace, epiphanies, and great insights are lost to us because we are in too much of a hurry to notice them. Slow down or you'll miss the good stuff."[9] In our rush from one meeting to the next event, from one small task to the next major chore, from Easter to Pentecost, the lections of the day hold open a place for us to catch our breath, look around at our companions to find appreciation for their situations and compassion for their sufferings, and simply wait for whatever it is God wants for and from us.

## Notes

1. Hans Conzelmann, *Acts of the Apostles*, Hermeneia (Philadelphia: Fortress Press, 1987), 9.
2. Robert W. Wall, "The Acts of the Apostles," in *The New Interpreter's Bible* (Nashville: Abingdon, 2002), 10:44.
3. Gail R. O'Day, "The Gospel of John," in *The New Interpreter's Bible* (Nashville: Abingdon, 1995), 9:787.
4. For a succinct treatment of these issues see ibid., 790.
5. D. Moody Smith Jr., *John*, Abingdon Bible Commentaries (Nashville: Abingdon, 1999), 310.
6. Ibid., 310–11.
7. See Raymond E. Brown, *The Community of the Beloved Disciple* (New York: Paulist, 1979).

8.  Garret Keizer, *A Dresser of Sycamore Trees: The Finding of a Ministry* (New York: Viking, 1991), 144.
9.  Frederic and Mary Ann Brussat, *Spiritual Literacy: Reading the Sacred in Everyday Life* (New York: Simon & Schuster, 1996), 53.

# June 12, 2011
## Day of Pentecost

A surprise, in other words, is the sound of an old belief breaking," says Clay Shirky.[1] And we might add with the first disciples, it is the sound of fire and wind roaring through a community that is waiting for something to happen. Surprise, the Spirit has arrived! Surprise, we can no longer sit in our lounge chairs and watch the world go by! Surprise, we have words to speak and work to do! Surprise, we are together a people with a mission, a church! Pentecost is a day for surprises that we cannot control or manipulate any more than we can the fire of the Spirit. We can no longer hang around in nostalgia for some Norman Rockwell–tinged portrait of the good life. We have a future equipped both with a whole new set of tools, from Facebook to Twitter, and with the old means of face-to-face conversation and prayer—all of which we can use to connect with people inside the church and out with gospel love and hope. Connection, after all, is what Pentecost is all about.

## First Reading
### Acts 2:1-21 (RCL)
### Acts 2:1-11 (LFM)

When we left the followers of Jesus in the Acts reading last week, they were waiting in an upper room to receive something that Jesus had promised to them—they weren't sure what at that point. On the day of Pentecost, when they were all together, the promise was fulfilled through a roaring whoosh of wind and divided tongues of fire. The Holy Spirit had arrived. Luke depicts it through allusions to various manifestations of the divine in the Hebrew Scriptures. The Spirit comes suddenly like the wind that hovered over the waters of chaos in Genesis (Gen. 1:1) and the fire that led the Israelites out of Egypt (Exod. 13:21) or like the wind and fire that Elijah heard and saw on Mt. Horeb (1 Kings 19:11-12). Instantly, the group is empowered to proclaim the gospel in all kinds of human languages. The task of witness that Jesus commissioned them to perform at his ascension is given a new tool—the gift to communicate to everyone they encounter what God has done in Jesus.

Luke offers proof that they have truly received this gift in verses 5-13. Outside the place where the followers of Jesus had gathered were devout Jews from all over the Roman Empire who had come to Jerusalem to celebrate Pentecost, one of three annual festivals in which Jews journeyed to the holy city. To their amazement, these people understood what the followers of Jesus were saying in the many and various languages that they spoke. Some responded by wondering aloud how illiterate Galileans could communicate so well and so clearly in their own language and what such an astounding event might mean. But others reacted by sneering at the disciples and suggesting sarcastically that the followers of Jesus were drunk.

It is in response to all this amazement and scorn that the Lukan Peter opens his mouth and preaches his first sermon (vv. 14ff.), making use of the rules of Greco-Roman rhetoric prevalent in the first century. First, he addresses the crowd and the sneering. How could the followers of Jesus be drunk if it is only nine in the morning? He then immediately appeals to an authority held in common by all Jews, the prophetic writings. Through the extended quotation of Joel 3:1-5 (the Septuagint version; in the NRSV the quotation is Joel 2:28-32a), Peter begins to interpret the events as they had occurred so far. This particular citation was chosen because it links the coming of the Spirit with various manifestations of reversal of the status quo. All people, male and female, old and young, slave and free, will receive the outpouring of the Spirit; it is no longer reserved for the elite and the educated. And the entire cosmos is affected—the sun turned to darkness and the moon to blood. Further, at least one change that is made to the quotation highlights an early Christian theological interest. In the Hebrew and Septuagint version of Joel, the citation begins with the phrase "Then afterward"; but in Acts it is changed to "In the last days." In this change Luke firmly situates the events of Pentecost in the eschatological framework that is mentioned only later in the Joel citation (Joel 2:31; cf. Acts 2:20).

Because this is the primary text for Christian observances of Pentecost, preachers should pay close attention to what Luke is trying to convey in his narration of these events. First, the fact that the Spirit appears on the day of Pentecost has significance. Pentecost, also known as the Feast of Weeks, was a harvest festival that was celebrated fifty days after Passover. According to Charles Talbert, it was also associated with the covenant between God and the people established at Mt. Sinai and included a call to attend again to the law given to Moses and the people.[2] For Luke it would be natural to extend the observance of the coming of the law to a celebration of its fulfillment in the arrival of the Holy Spirit. This sense of fulfillment is underscored by Peter's quotation of the prophet Joel and his announcement that the things Joel prophesies are occurring right now in the midst of the people gathered in Jerusalem.

Second, the gift of the Spirit, in Luke's view, has purpose for the whole world. It is not enough for Christians to communicate with God for the edification of one another as Paul acknowledges in the Corinthian correspondence; the greater task is to speak intelligibly to the whole world. And the gift is available to all people. It is not restricted to whoever is considered to be the "in crowd," be they ancient priests of the temple in Jerusalem, pastors or other church leaders in modern church hierarchies, small groups of Christians who consider themselves special and set apart.

Third, Luke is concerned to show that the end of time as God has created it has actually begun in the events of Pentecost and that the awareness of this coming of God's end time should not produce despair, but precisely the opposite, hope. A hope that propels the Christian community forward into a mission of witness and proclamation. As Robert Wall says, "Simply put, Pentecost initiates Israel into a new epoch—'the last days'—of God's salvation history, when things said and done by Jesus' successors take on added urgency, not of an imminent apocalypse in the case of Acts but rather of a mission to restore God's kingdom to Israel."[3]

### Numbers 11:24-30 (RCL alt.)

The inclusion of this passage in the RCL strengthens the connection of the Pentecost events in Acts with the giving of the law to the Israelites. These verses also link spirit with prophecy—a factor in tempting us to impose upon this story a Lukan interpretation. That is, we might want to say the Spirit of God, as we understand it through Luke's eyes, gave these elders the charismatic power to prophesy. But what is actually meant by "spirit" in the Numbers text? It appears to be a divine bestowal that mostly belongs to Moses (11:17) and empowers him for leadership. And what is meant by "prophesy" here? Speaking in an ecstatic frenzy? Uttering a direct oracle from God? Predicting the future? In any case, it appears to be a temporary activity conducted only by the power of the uncontrollable and unpredictable spirit. And while this spirit grants authority to those who receive it, it also brings great responsibility (11:17). At the very least, we might learn from this passage that the spirit of God is not to be taken lightly and cannot in any way be channeled for our own human purposes.

## Psalmody
### Psalm 104:24-34, 35b (RCL)
### Psalm 104:1 + 24, 29-30, 31 + 34 (LFM)

The care of God for all creation is the sole theme of this psalm and the poetry is so beautiful that it defies attempts to analyze and break down into paraphrase or rational explanation. All we can do is say with the psalmist, "Bless the LORD, O my soul. You are clothed with honor and majesty" in your nurture of all the creatures of earth and sea. Or we can sing with St. Francis his "Canticle of the Sun" as it appears in many of our hymnals as "All Creatures of Our God and King." Or, for something more modern, we can wonder with Jaroslav J. Vajda about how all creatures praise God as he does in his hymn "God of the Sparrow, God of the Whale."

## Second Reading
### 1 Corinthians 12:3b-13 (RCL)
### 1 Corinthians 12:3b-7, 12-13 (LFM)

This selection from the Pauline corpus is inelegantly cut in both the RCL and the LFM, perhaps, as Shelly Cochran says, "to avoid what the lectionary considered an awkward reference to the Corinthians' spiritual roots in paganism."[4] Verse 3b, the starting point of this reading, actually occurs in midsentence; the ending, verse 13, abruptly cuts off the development of Paul's understanding of the church as a body. The LFM leaves out verses 8-11, an elaboration of the various manifestations of the gifts endowed by the Spirit to different members of the Christian community.

Taken in its lectionary form, the text begins with a very early creedal formulation, "Jesus is Lord," which, Paul explains, can only be uttered by one who speaks by the working of the Holy Spirit. This simple declaration forms the basis for the unity of believers and their various forms of gifts, services, and activities—as rhetorically delineated by Paul in verses 4-6 in a kind of proto-trinitarian flourish. After noting possibilities for differing charisms—that is, wisdom, knowledge, faith, healing, miracle working, prophecy, discernment, tongues, and interpretation of tongues—he returns to the theme of unity among all believers that is rooted in the presence and life of the Spirit.

Because the church-as-body imagery is so familiar to preachers and longtime Christians and because these verses appear relatively frequently in the lectionary, we can be lulled into disinterest as soon as the reading begins. But the claim Paul makes here is as radical as it was in the first century. That is, people who once belonged to different biological families, to distinctive racial and ethnic groups, to diverse nationalities—all with their own particular enmities, friendship pacts, and ways of doing and being in the world—now belong only to an organic and sufficient unity. Brought together by Christ and sustained by the Spirit, we now are a body, each equipped with her or his own gifts, each called to her or his own function, all serving the God we know through the lordship of Jesus.

### Acts 2:1-21 (RCL alt.)

For commentary on this text, please see the first reading above.

## Gospel
### John 20:19-23 (RCL, LFM)

This reading has already been discussed in the section on the Second Sunday of Easter (see above). It is included here in both lectionaries because Jesus, in his first resurrection appearance to the disciples as a group, breathes on them and invites them to receive the Holy Spirit. We might note that he does so without the fanfare of wind, fire, and multiple languages. Shelly Cochran says, "It is to the [RCL] lectionary's credit that it has linked this reading to the one in Acts and not hidden the differences between them. By doing so, the lectionary has invited both passages to speak to us and to each other. This dialogue not only gives us more than one view of the Holy Spirit, it also expands our understanding of both this passage and the passage from Acts."[5]

### John 7:37-39 (RCL alt.)

This alternate reading is given here because it mentions the Spirit, or better, the absence of the Spirit since it has not yet arrived. In John's view that could not happen until Jesus had been glorified, that is, been crucified and resurrected. In this case, John and Luke appear to agree in their incipient pneumatology—the Spirit can only appear and form the disparate band of disciples into a church when Jesus is no longer present. At the same time, we might note that Jesus speaks words about the living water of the Spirit in a situation of growing hostility. The leaders of the people are getting increasingly uneasy about Jesus' activity and the crowds' response to him and beginning to talk about arrest or murder. In their midst, Jesus cries out words of invitation, "Let anyone who is thirsty come to me" (v. 37). Or are they words of warning? It is difficult to say.

. . . . . . . . .

To my knowledge, no department store has yet to advertise a pre-Pentecostal red sale. Nor has anyone found a way to sell in the malls and superstores of our lives chocolate doves and hard-candy flames as trivial symbols of one of the great festivals of the liturgical year. Today Pentecost belongs wholly and completely to the church; the world has yet to discover how to make a buck out of it.

Which strikes me as particularly good news as we end our own lingering on the threshold with the disciples and move into the full-blown summer of the season of Pentecost. Without any external interpretations from the peanut galleries of the secular marketplace, we can leave this liminal stage in our own ways as we remember our incorporation into one of God's new creations—the community of the faithful. Many of our churches will roll out birthday cakes with red candles; others will pray for the Spirit to reignite our common passion for gospel salvation and gospel justice. My prayer is that we will continue to remember that the blessing we received at Easter, the gift of new life, will not be something we hoard behind closed doors. For it is our vocation not simply to be blessed, but to join with the psalmist of Psalm 104 in blessing God and blessing the world.

## Notes

1. Clay Shirky, *Cognitive Surplus: Creativity and Generosity in a Connected Age* (New York: Penguin, 2010), 100. Quoted by Pam McGrath in an ordination sermon, "Ministry: A Verb," preached at Southern Hills Christian Church, Edmond, Oklahoma, July 25, 2010.

2. Charles H. Talbert, *Reading Acts: A Literary and Theological Commentary on the Acts of the Apostles* (New York: Crossroad, 1997), 40.

3. Robert W. Wall, "The Acts of the Apostles," in *The New Interpreter's Bible* (Nashville: Abingdon, 2002), 10:64.

4. Shelly Cochran, *The Pastor's Underground Guide to the Revised Common Lectionary, Year A* (St. Louis: Chalice, 1995), 166.

5. Ibid., 167.

# Time after Pentecost / Ordinary Time
## Trinity Sunday through Proper 14

### Richard I. Pervo

The Christian calendar lacks a "Pentecost season." To early Christians the "Pentecost season" was the fifty days of Easter. Sundays subsequent to Eastertide may be designated as "the *N* Sunday *after* Pentecost," in contrast to Sundays *in* Lent or *of* Easter. The liturgical name for this period is "Ordinary Time." One cannot have a feast without a fast and vice versa, yet valid human existence is not a succession of bipolar flits between these extremes. Ordinary Time is necessary to mark both feast and fast as deviations from a standard.

"Ordinary Time" does not, however, mean business as usual. Ordinary Time is the sphere of Christian existence, life between Pentecost and Advent, the birth of the church and the final resolution. To say that believers live "between the times" is to locate us between Pentecost and parousia, that is, in ordinary time. This is not a holiday; it is time for growth. Festal and penitential times deal with big miracles. Ordinary Time points us toward the myriad of minor wonders abounding all around.

Exegetically oriented preachers look forward to Ordinary Time, as the readings allow one to engage consecutive texts. Place your favorite works on Romans and Matthew on handy shelves, knowing that they will be paying a long visit. The RCL extends this dimension by offering a series of passages from Genesis, while the alternate first readings follow the traditional practice of complementing the Gospel. An objection to this is that it makes the Old Testament an accessory to the New Testament; positively, this arrangement exhibits the unity of the Scriptures. The homiletic task of Ordinary Time is not the hunt for links between and among readings. Let those links find you—and others.

# June 19, 2011
## The Holy Trinity Sunday
### First Sunday after Pentecost

**Revised Common Lectionary (RCL)**
Genesis 1:1—2:4a
Psalm 8
2 Corinthians 13:11-13
Matthew 28:16-20

**Lectionary for Worship (LFM)**
Exodus 34:4b-6, 8-9
Daniel 3:52, 53, 54, 55
2 Corinthians 13:11-13
John 3:16-18

To make the transition from festal to ordinary time less bumpy—although, in fact, more so—comes the celebration of the Holy Trinity, originally introduced to wrap up the festal period by honoring all three persons. Celebration and worship of the triune God logically invite an explanation of that which Christians joyfully revere. Education is one of the preacher's charges, but few can expound the mysteries of the Godhead in a sermon of less than an hour. Two aspects of our creeds are worth affirming on this occasion. The first is that creeds do not define God; they define us, showing where the people of God fit into the scheme of things. Humans cannot describe God; we can say how God has been revealed to us and what God means for humankind. From this assertion flows the second: creeds are better sung than said.

This has nothing to do with aesthetics. Creeds are doxologies, hymns of praise. This fact can readily be glimpsed in the creedal canticles *Te Deum* ("You Are God") and *Gloria in Excelsis* ("Glory to God"), but it is part of the essence of creeds. As hymns, creeds are constant reminders that theology has much in common with poetry. As songs, creeds are corporate. They are not about how I feel today or your lack of appreciation for *homoousion* or *filioque*. These are the poems of a pilgrim people over millennia, with some images that seem inappropriate and others that are obscure. Not every woman would be flattered by "Your neck is like the tower of David, built in courses" (Song of Sol. 4:4), but the intent is clear. Creeds are magical because they waft us into a company of untold myriads, encircling the world and encompassing the ages.

The pastoral value of the Trinity is its affirmation of a God who is above and beyond us, yet beside us, sharing the journey of life, and, far from least, also within us. Trinitarian thought developed amid struggles to maintain the unity of the divine in the light of the experiences of the gift of the Spirit and the achievement of Christ's redemptive actions. Trinitarian belief is insufficiently monotheistic for some, while others note a lack of the clear merits of polytheism, which permits attribution of evil to the machinations of and conflicts between various deities. The trinitarian controversies of c. 250-450 C.E. were messy. Involvement with the world is messy, even for God.

# First Reading
## Genesis 1:1—2:4a (RCL)

The last time these words of the priestly (i.e., exilic) account of creation echoed in the churches was at the beginning of the Great Vigil of Easter. All trinitarian invocations are affirmations of the baptismal gift upon which that liturgy focuses. A not unimportant question is: Why did God create the universe? Life as a god would, by our lights, be far more enjoyable without the burden of the cosmos. That was precisely the view attributed to gods by Epicurus. Why be a god if one couldn't be detached? Ancient "Gnostics" focused on the problems of the material world. A real god could have done a better job. The crude mess we inhabit must be the handiwork of lesser or evil deities.

God's lights may be at variance with ours. Insofar as we know (cf. John 3:16), God created the world out of love. The apex of it all, in this unblushingly anthropocentric Genesis story, is the human race. The Almighty placed us in charge of the world and neglected to fill in the date, say the year 2000, on which this responsibility would end. An apparent advantage of the fervent belief that the end is near is relaxation of the responsibility for stewardship of creation. One difficulty with this posture is that God has not invited us creatures to fill in the blanks.

The creation story has experienced a fate kindred to that of the creed. Just as some would transform the creed into a description of and a set of rules for God, others would make Genesis 1 a scientific outline of how life came to be, an ancient venture into natural history. Like the creed, this carefully structured narrative is a summons to praise God as the source of all life and goodness. (This is not to say that creation is an "article" of the Israelite creed, which begins with the "wandering Aramean," Deut. 26:5-10.) Let the faithful savor its poetry and sublimity.

The text moves from chaos to rest. Ancients valued rest over motion (cf. the "unmoved mover"). This hierarchy of value does not come naturally to Americans. Resolution may be a more suitable concept for us than is rest. Chaos is creation out of whack, disorder in its various forms, including unfairness. To affirm God as Creator is to place God against all that is harmful for God's creatures. When creation is perceived to be out of joint, redemption and sanctification are likely to become engines of escapism.

The sword has two edges. God is more involved in the creation of humanity than with any other creature. We are special. With that privilege comes responsibility (1:27-28). Confession of God as Creator involves responsibility for creation. Just as the second article brings the redeemed into association with the Redeemer, the first links the creature *par excellence* to creation.

### Exodus 34:4b-6, 8-9 (LFM)

Timing, that is to say, context, is everything. The Israelites, not to mention Moses, have had better days. While Moses was closeted with God, receiving the covenant, the people became fed up with the notion of an aniconic deity—despite that God's successful leadership thus far—and opted for a god they could see and touch. The golden calf remains one of the most famous images of Western, at least, history. The essence of an idol is not its form or size or substance, but its character as an artifact, a god designed and manufactured by humans for our purposes. The covenant has been quite literally shattered. It is in the midst of apostasy on the journey that God's nature is encountered. "Almighty" is not a popular epithet in our narcissistic culture, since if God is all powerful, it is incomprehensible, indeed unforgivable, that God has not taken proper care of me. (Golden calves come in many forms, some of which are not iconic.) God is nonetheless mighty patient, even all-mighty patient. This text proclaims God in a trinity of qualities: "merciful and gracious, slow to anger and rich in kindness and fidelity" (v. 7, NAB). The revelation of God's name is central to the liturgical occasion. A name expresses the nature of the named and is thus power. "Stop in the name of the law!" is a dim reflection of the concept; "in the Name of the Father and of the Son and of the Holy Spirit" is more relevant. God's name means forgiveness; forgiveness is power. The forgiven and forgiving community can keep striving to keep its covenant.

## Psalmody
### Psalm 8 (RCL)

This psalm praises God for creation and also for placing the human race at its apex, despite our apparent insignificance in the face of the immensity of the universe. This is good commentary on Genesis 1. (Verse 5 is an interesting exception to this generalization in that it substitutes for the "image" of Genesis 1:27-28, a position slightly beneath the angels of the heavenly court. Most will not find much homiletic material there, but it is a good incentive for theological reflection.)

### Daniel 3:52, 53, 54, 55 (LFM)

This selection from the *Benedicite* (Song of the Three Young Men) is an apt response. Note that the first ascription refers to salvation history ("God of our fathers") and that the second evokes God's name (cf. Exod. 34:4-9).

# Second Reading
## 2 Corinthians 13:11-13 (RCL, LFM)

Canonical 2 Corinthians is a collection of letters and fragments assembled c. 100 C.E. This is probably the most difficult and the most engaging item in the Pauline corpus. This closing may originally have been associated with what scholars call the "the letter of reconciliation" (1:1—2:13; 7:5-16), although verse 11 suits the context. Readers are likely to read quickly through the closing verses of an epistle; they are so conventional and so similar. We do this to our loss, for these closings can indicate what the author wished to underline.

The background of conflict is apparent. One can understand the apostle to say that, if the four exhortations are heeded, the God of love and peace will be present. It is probably preferable to understand these words to mean that because love and peace are properties of God, the readers will be able to get it together, listen, and resolve conflict. Paul does not propose that if the community suppresses dissent and squashes conflict, it will enjoy peace. That sort of peace does not pass all understanding. The exhortation is for resolution, which now, no less than then, involves proper preparation, attention to authority, and a willingness to pursue a solution, even if it means not getting all that one wants.

Direction for the kiss indicates that the letter was read in a community assembly, presumably at worship. The peace is exchanged with those who are absent as well as those present. The final blessing, which could have been added by the editor, is more complex than usual. Its triadic form, in which God's love results in Christ's gift, which yields participation in the Holy Spirit, indicates the impulses that would give rise to more specific trinitarian definition. Even in its nascent stages, trinitarian thought focused upon what God does and means rather than what God is.

# Gospel
## Matthew 28:16-20 (RCL)

Matthew is the tidiest of Gospels, a quality that contributed to its long dominance of the lectionary. The conclusion of Matthew alone of the canonical Gospels has survived indisputably intact. Less tidy Gospels are more fashionable nowadays, but even the most fastidious must admire how much the evangelist has been able to pack into five short verses. This is the only resurrection appearance in Matthew in which Jesus communicates a detailed message. Among the functions of appearance stories are missionary commissions and church foundations. This passage includes both.

The opening is mysteriously untidy, for the narrator has said nothing about a specific Galilean mountain. This is the climactic association of Jesus with a mountain: 4:8 (temptation); 5:1 (sermon); 14:23; 15:29 (feeding, healing), 17:1 (transfiguration, with which the meticulous reader will find a number of parallels to this passage); 21:1 (entrance into Jerusalem); 24:3 (eschatological address); 26:30 (Gethsemane). A famous comparison is to Moses on Sinai. Mountains are ideal places for a theophany (in the background of which is the appearance of a storm god, thus the accompaniment of lightning, fire, cloud, and smoke, all demythologized). The best parallel is Isaiah 2:2-3. (Read it. No cheating!) In Matthew mountains are places for revelation and instruction, healing and temptation. A final notable comparison is Mt. Zion, site of the temple. Jesus replaces the temple; this mountain is Everymountain, nameless and ubiquitous, a mountain moved into place by faith wherever two or three gather. In place of the nations coming to the temple at Jerusalem are disciples going to the nations.

This final paragraph ties it all up with the liberal use of the word *all*. Among the themes that reach their apex, if you would, on this mountain are the authority of Jesus (cf. 7:28-29; 11:27; 21:23-27), the need for strong faith (cf. 8:10 etc.), Jesus as Emmanuel (1:23; 18:20; 26:29) and as authoritative teacher (4:23; 5:2; 5:19; etc.), a universal offer of salvation (cf. 2:1-12; 4:14-16; 5:13-14, etc.), transformation of Israel's hope, the mission of disciples, and the creation of the church through initiation and formation (e.g., 16:18). With Matthean thoroughness (and no lack of artistry), every leading strand is tucked into place. Two inclusions indicate completion. The second word of Matthew is "beginning" (*genesis*). At its close is "end" (*synteleia*). Verse 20 reverberates with 1:23: 'Look, the virgin shall conceive and bear a son, and they shall name him Emmanuel,' which means, 'God is with us.'"

For Matthew Galilee is associated with Gentiles. This, rather than conformity with Mark 16:7, explains the location. Their homage is an act of veneration (cf. 2:2; 28:9), indicating that the Risen One is a heavenly being. One expects verse 17 to say: "When they saw him, most believed, but some doubted." It does not. This illogic requires attention. Unlike Luke (positively) and John (negatively), Matthew makes no attempt to prove the resurrection. Doubt is not overcome by demonstration. It is just there. At the immediate level of Matthew this is, no *doubt*, the final reference to "little faith" (cf. 6:30; 8:26; 14:31; 16:8; 17:20). That refers to faith as something like moral courage, the God-given ability to stick it out, rather than to acceptance of a creed versus skepticism. Strong faith is empowering faith rather than being more dogmatically assertive than thou.

In a broader sense the text authorizes the continuing existence and acceptability of doubt. Neither Matthew nor, in this instance, the heavenly Christ worries about doubt per se. Paralysis is the problem. Many of those in church this Sunday may have doubts about smaller or larger portions of the creed. They still belong on the ship. Matthew worries about those who are not pulling their oars. Doubt some may, but they came in obedience to Christ's command.

Rather than comment upon his resurrection, Jesus goes straight to its results. Again, without proof, he claims to possess authority on earth and in heaven. Matthew 6:10 affirms that bringing these two realms into conformity is the principal divine goal. (For the meaning of this claim of authority, see Daniel 7:14.) The basis for the world mission—a church without national boundaries—is the exaltation of

Jesus as the eschatological world ruler. This authority also justifies the "repeal" of the limited mission (cf. 10:5-6) and of much of the Torah, including circumcision, which is replaced by baptism, and the commandments, now replaced by what Jesus has promulgated. The mission is to "make disciples," which has more to do with formation than with recruitment. Formation is mission and evangelism.

The implied baptismal formula surprises. One would expect baptism in the name of Jesus. Name is power. Matthew may have had reason for concern about the practice, which can have magical implications and be associated with a particular understanding of spiritual gifts that the evangelist found troublesome. The term "Father" establishes God as God, as creator and heavenly parent. Baptism does not only convey the power of Jesus' name; it places one into a relationship. The Spirit has no specific role. Christ is present. Unity characterizes this early trinitarian expression. There is but one "name." The persons are not distinct entities with different missions.

The abiding presence of Christ is essentially Jewish in that he is not present in the proclamation of the message, nor in spiritual power, nor through the body of the church, but in keeping his commandments, which is what it means to gather in his name. Finally, the narrator does not state that the disciples did as they were told. This is a good lesson for all who write or preach: it is desirable not to close with an unnecessary sentence. *Never* end with a dumb sentence.

## John 3:16-18 (LFM)

A few decades ago I regularly received telephone calls on Sunday afternoons with the query, "What is John 3:16?" Banners reading "John 3:16" were often displayed at football games. I learned to reply, "This is the text proving that God is a secular humanist." The virtue of this Gospel selection is that it does not look about for a reference to the three persons (as the inclusion of verses 1-15 would have accomplished), but focuses upon the *why* of the Holy Trinity: God's desire to deliver the human race because of God's love for us.

This is from the closing portion of Jesus' dialogue with Nicodemus (John 3:1-21).

Nicodemus is a sincere inquirer, but his categories, pious and traditional though they be, blind him from seeing a truth that does not follow a path congenial to his preconceptions. Nicodemus is a rather vulgar, even crude example, but his faults are not rare. The Fourth Gospel is a bit fonder of dividing humanity into two opposing groups than many of us find comfortable, but the method can be valid. For example, there are two kinds of people: those who acknowledge that they have a bit of Nicodemus within them, and liars.

John 3:1-21 represents a kind of conversation called "revelation dialogue." The dialogical element is attenuated. Nicodemus's dullness is not encouraging. By verse 12 Jesus has begun to speak in the second-person plural and Nicodemus is, to all intents and purposes, no longer present. Such infelicities are part of the wonder and exasperation of John. Challenges never end. The book has offered nothing thus far that adequately prepares the reader for these verses.

69

Two originally distinct christological models drive the text. One is the vertical descending (vv. 16-21) and ascending (vv. 14-15) Son of Man, the other the horizontal mission of the Son of God (e.g., v. 18). The evangelist juxtaposes them. "Pick your model," he seems to say; "Jesus fulfills it in accordance with God's will." The vertical links heaven to earth and guarantees the supernatural origin of the message. Through the horizontal people are confronted with one of their own—indeed, a very vulnerable example of one of their own—rather than with a voice from the sky.

Descent and mission have the same goal: salvation, defined as "eternal life." Eternal life is more than afterlife, more than enriched existence. It begins with baptism/conversion. Eternal life is, first and foremost, power, the power of God's love unleashed. The heart of Johannine "realized eschatology," manifest in verse 18, is the power of that love in the world now.

"World" is another difficult term in John. Dramatically, as the authorities become more hostile toward Jesus, the "world" acquires an increasingly negative connotation, becoming, in effect, the realm of opposition to God. (Historically one might note that this is the effect of a strongly sectarian stance, grounded in rejection.) Here the world is humanity distanced from but in quest of God. For most of the situations faced by readers of these words, that understanding of "world" will do well.

Another bonus of a present eschatology is that it removes ultimacy from time, a structure that humans can (and do) manipulate, and locates it in the convergence of the eternal into the temporal, in ordinary ecclesiastical language, into occasions of grace, that abundant new life breaking out, overflowing, and gushing from our God: Father, Son, and Holy Spirit.

# June 26, 2011
## Second Sunday after Pentecost
### Thirteenth Sunday in Ordinary Time / Proper 8

**Revised Common Lectionary (RCL)**
Genesis 22:1-14 or Jeremiah 28:5-9
Psalm 13 or 89:1-4, 15-18
Romans 6:12-23
Matthew 10:40-42

## First Reading
### Genesis 22:1-14

If this lesson is selected—it is free standing—it should not be read without some comment. This is a famous, beautiful, and moving story, appropriate to Holy Week. Modern hearers love the drama but may have difficulties with the motivation. Abraham's trust, which is better characterized as "fear," is viewed as admirable. One must do what God says, no matter what. We don't agree, frankly, for reasons good and otherwise. The good reasons are that we have had enough of people acting on divine orders and manifest healthy skepticism. The other side is that we have become a bit uppity. In short, the people of God have done some growing since this story first appeared. This passage has become much more challenging.

In the background was the promise, in Genesis 12:2, that a great people and ecumenical blessing would come from Abraham. The unlikely happens: a son in old age. Then God tells Papa to take out his kid. Abraham, who knows how to bargain (Genesis 18), accepts the demand in silence. Homely preparations ensue. The child has a question and learns that "God will see to a lamb." When the climax comes, no lamb drops down from heaven. Instead, there is a kid caught in thorns.

The promise is reaffirmed. Who has been tested? Abraham or God? Does God know the plot, or does verse 12 show that the patriarch's faith has led the Almighty to a change of plan? Questions abound. Faith involves understanding that even unconditional promises can be tough. "The Lord will see to a lamb" does not mean that providence is an endless bucket of bailouts. Abraham stayed alert and detected a *kid*. God writes straight with crooked lines. This is a bit more than an example of God's willingness to play Russian roulette. God's promises are wonderful. So are the promises of obedience we make in response. We shall never notice a kid in the thorns if we don't look; concomitantly, we have no right to presume that God must provide that kid.

### Jeremiah 28:5-9 (alt.)

This reading interacts with the Gospel, albeit not in a straightforward way or as "Old Testament background." The prophetic vocation is a tough one, not least for Jeremiah, who might have ended up with a life sentence if he decided to defend himself on a charge of driving ten miles per hour over the limit. The selection wisely ignores the context. Jeremiah was engaged in one of his acts of prophetic symbolism, wearing a yoke to symbolize the dominance of Nebuchadnezzar. His rival Hananiah broke that yoke and announced that God would soon smash the power of Babylon. He was wrong and died.

These two prophets supported parties with different approaches to the dominant power of the era. Nothing is cheaper than sonorous religious pronouncements about current events. Those who love to see a punitive god at work have many opportunities to exercise their sonority. Hananiah represented the optimistic opportunists. Babylon would have but fifteen minutes of imperial fame. Jeremiah envisaged a longer dominion. Both offered views that appealed to one political party and both agreed that God was in charge.

Some will chastise Jeremiah for seeing the glass as half empty. The glass is, in fact, always half empty and half full. Insofar as it is full, we hope and work for the best outcome. Emptiness motivates us always to be prepared for—not to expect—the worst. The overriding issue is criteria for true prophecy. Does one rely upon personal preferences and prejudices, quality of argument, or what?

Jeremiah's answer is as clear as it is irrefutable: true prophecies come true. This raises initial questions: Were people so naïve that they had to be told this? On second thought, all of us some of the time and some of us all of the time believe our political prophets of choice without regard to the verity, perhaps even the probability, of their predictions. Jeremiah notes that most prophets utter jeremiads. Forecasts of war, famine, and pestilence are well received. Insofar as future prediction goes, only time will tell. The more important question is: What message will be most helpful to the people of God?

Cheap shots and cheap consolation have nothing to do with genuine prophecy. Announcing that God is displeased with *X* region because it got hit with a hurricane or declaring that, since God likes us, tornadoes will strike some less-favored folk are only the grossest sort of examples. Prophecy includes calling to task when appropriate, praising where praise is due, weeping with those who weep, and rejoicing with celebrants. Those who will settle for nothing but predictions are likely to get the sort of prophet they deserve.

# Psalmody
## Psalm 13

This psalm suits the reading from Genesis. It is a lament that ends on a note of trust. This is useful because it gives voice to the disappointment in and anger with God that we often have difficulty acknowledging.

## Psalm 89:1-4, 15-18 (alt.)

This song of praise focuses upon the covenant, the understanding of which lies behind the debate depicted in Jeremiah. Is the covenant a one-way contract, with obligations upon God but none for the people? The answer is obvious. In its broader context this psalm is relevant to Jeremiah because it reflects a serious military defeat and its possible theological implications. (*Note*: Horn is a trope for the king, a synecdoche for power—a quality of large horned animals, especially the bull—applied by metonymy to the monarch.)

# Second Reading
## Romans 6:12-23

In preparation for the sequence of readings from Romans that follows, it will be helpful to read through the letter, preferably with the aid of a guide. If you have been longing to read a commentary or work on this book, make that a part of your weekly discipline.

This reading speaks clearly to the faithful with a message they can readily appreciate. The context is baptism (cf. vv. 3-11). Baptism frees believers from the domination of evil, but evil still exists. Paul views freedom *from* as the presupposition to freedom *for*. The term "bodies" in verse 12 is well understood as "selves," just as "members" in the subsequent verse means not physical limbs, but qualities and emotions also. The apostle is not setting up a body/soul or matter/spirit dualism. "Flesh" and "spirit" are modes of existence, not ontological categories.

In the context of a great treatise on freedom, slavery is jarring. The apostle asserts that, as the Israelites were once in bondage in Egypt, so all humans have been slaves to sin. That is reasonable enough. One might compare addiction and other forms of compulsion. The logic, no doubt ad hoc in the context of charges that he invites license, is that everyone is a slave to someone. That is unwelcome. Liberation from slavery to sin is excellent, but slavery to righteousness does not look like improvement. We want to be grown-ups, not dependents. Its logic for ancients was that God and Christ were addressed as "master," "owner" (*kyrios*). What the metaphor means is doing what righteousness summons us to do, "our bounden duty," or, for those who do not like Edwardian prose, "Be all that you can be."

The apostle does not reflect here upon sanctification as a process, upon personal and spiritual growth. This may be attributed to his eschatological orientation. He is much closer to the philosophy of "one day at a time." At other times he does speak of growth, individual and community, and understands edification as a work in process. It is preferable to allow each of these perspectives to stand in its own right, and it is certainly not desirable to read this passage from the orientation of growth.

## Gospel
### Matthew 10:40-42

If one of the virtues of the RCL is avoidance of bowdlerizing, it fails here, for the antecedent tradition began at verse 37. Paternalism will be with us always. Shortened or not, this pericope closes the second of Matthew's five thematic sermons. Mission is the general subject, but the evangelist devotes much attention to the proper stance in the face of persecution. In these final verses he returns to mission, with emphasis upon hospitality.

The generating aphorism, "Whoever receives me receives not me but the one who sent me," is very widely attested, with independent examples well into the second century. Comparison with one of these parallels, Mark 9:37-41, indicates that Matthew has added verse 41, thereby identifying four groups or categories: apostles (the dramatic audience of the speech), (Christian) prophets, the righteous, and "little ones." The first two categories receive attention in *Didache* 10–14, with which Matthew is often presumed to have affinities. It is tempting to view the "righteous" and the "little ones" along the lines of Paul's "strong" and "weak." The latter are certainly viewed as requiring protection (cf. 18:6, 10, 14). Be that as it may, the evangelist has expanded the discussion beyond the question of itinerant missionaries. The community is defined from without by persecution, from within by hospitality.

In nascent Christianity hospitality was essential to mission. Public lodgings were costly and of dubious moral and physical character. To withhold hospitality from a visiting coreligionist was to reject that visitor. Hospitality became a key weapon in the battles about proper doctrine (cf. 3 John). This gave an advantage to the relatively well off. By the time Matthew appeared, "welcoming" had acquired notions of doctrinal approval.

Three brief notes: "In the name of" is probably a Semitic idiom meaning "as such." In a dry climate a cup of cold water was quite welcome; even in a big city like Antioch, water was likely to be a bit less clear and cool than desirable, but the scope of the generosity should not be exaggerated. Small gifts are also welcome. Third, Matthew freely speaks of "reward." This does not mean that he advocates the idea of "loving Jesus so you'll go to heaven," but it does call for recognition, indeed for recognition of an egalitarian sort.

With summer at hand and travel multiplying, the theme of hospitality is highly welcome. The particular application is mission and hospitality, hospitality as mission. This is not to disparage hospitality as a missionary instrument, but Matthew urges us to look beyond that reward and to view hospitality as a form of the church's missionary vocation. In how many myriad ways does your church manifest hospitality? Which areas might be strengthened, what is being overlooked, what could be let go? My church, an urban cathedral, views its rather decrepit and inadequate parking lot as a failure of hospitality. The practice of welcoming visitors needs no mention. Are they perhaps being pressed a bit too hard? Not good hospitality.

The ancient Greeks laid strong obligations upon a host. Cautionary myths told of gods going about in disguise (cf. Acts 14:8-18; Heb. 13:2; note Gen. 18:1—19:29). We do not have to worry about the possibility of a god in mufti or some angels in disguise, because every visitor—a very broad category, including the poor and needy—is Christ. We do not entertain gods or angels unawares. The motive for our action is also its motor. God's acceptance of us through Christ makes our hospitality possible.

# June 26, 2011
# Solemnity of the Most Holy Body and Blood of Christ
# (Corpus Christi)

**Lectionary for Mass (LFM)**
Deuteronomy 8:2-3, 14b-16a
Psalm 147:12-13, 14-15, 19-20
1 Corinthians 10:16-17
John 6:51-58

Corpus Christi is analogous to the Feast of the Holy Cross (September 14), an opportunity outside of the unified drama of Holy Week to reflect upon particular features, in this instance the institution of the Holy Eucharist. This solemnity, which began in the thirteenth century (and because of which the church possesses the splendid communion hymns attributed to Thomas Aquinas), was once observed on the Thursday following Trinity Sunday (which was then the first "open" Thursday). Now it is observed on the Sunday. Real Presence is the overarching theme, to which point and from which flow such concepts as community created by shared nurture, food that conveys heavenly life, nourishment for life's journey. The needs and circumstances of various communities in their particular situations will help indicate which of these aspects invites special attention and reflection. The focus of the readings is not adoration. It is judgment.

## First Reading
### Deuteronomy 8:2-3, 14b-16a

Ech! Manna *again*! Familiarity breeds contempt; to coin a phrase, affluence nurtures complacency. Heavenly food and drink soon begin to cloy (cf. Num. 11:1-9). For the bored and complacent, the forty-year-long free lunch resulted in judgment. What the people viewed as a monotonous entitlement turned out to be a test. Heavenly food, as Paul well knows, cuts two ways. This truth intends to shake us out of our complacency rather than to paralyze us with fear.

Life, as this author knows, is a test and a trial in several senses of those words. The major test is whether we remember who is in charge. God is in charge here (v. 14). God is not only the boss; God is also our heavenly parent. Like a good mother, God knows what kind of food is best for us; as a good father he cares for his children in their experiments. To celebrate the most precious body and blood of our Lord Jesus Christ is to acknowledge that God does, after all, know best. Moreover—and this sentiment is easily misapplied and abused—God does this for our good, not to exact satisfying revenge upon puny creatures, but to reform them. With the right diet goes the right exercise.

That exercise takes the form of a journey. The Eucharist is food for pilgrims, *esca viatorum* in the words of the Latin hymn. That food is both corporate, building and shaping the church for its voyage through the centuries, and individual, individual nourishment for each journey of faith. At ease in Zion it is easy to forget that God feeds us on a journey rather than while dozing in earned indolence. Without this food this journey would be a fearful experience. With it the journey of life can be a grand adventure, an epic quest, as it were.

# Psalmody
## Psalm 147:12-13, 14-15, 19-20

This psalm of praise inspired one of St. Thomas's hymns: *Lauda Sion*. The culmination of the blessings in verses 13-14 is provision of the finest wheat. The symbolism needs no evocation. The four items—strong gates, children, internal peace, and wheat—interconnect. Without the wheat, peace, children, and strong walls could not exist.

# Second Reading
## 1 Corinthians 10:16-17

It will be helpful to read the context: verses 1-22. This is, in effect, a brief discourse on sacramental theology, opening with a reference to the exodus. Although Paul will grant in principle the freedom to eat meat sacrificed to idols (chap. 8), he will not condone participation in actual pagan worship. The experience of the wilderness generation shows that those liberated from bondage and subsequently fed with supernatural sustenance had no guarantee. The sacraments are not magical media that liberate recipients from the consequences of their behavior. They liberate and empower believers for love.

All at Corinth evidently agreed that the Eucharist is a community-creating act. Paul uses sacramental theology as a basis of ecclesiology. Communion benefits the individual, but it is not simply an act of individual piety and private edification. The body and blood of Christ form the body of Christ. For this reason the image of the single loaf as a sign of unity receives end stress. *Koinonia* (Lat. *communio*) is a rich word, including the senses of sharing and participation. The goal should not be to select the correct choice but to keep all of the possibilities in mind. The same term is used for the sharing of possessions in Acts 2–5. Some Corinthian believers were eager to partake of the divine world without any concern for those in need. Paul was the first person known to have played upon the two meanings of *corpus Christi*: church and sacrament.

## Gospel
### John 6:51-58

At times the fourth evangelist supplemented miracle stories with interpretive speeches, early sermons on the "text" of the stories. This activity shows that stories are to be interpreted, not just heard. The Bread of Life sermon runs from John 6:35-59. In verses 35-50 the eucharistic symbolism is sapiential. At verse 51 the reference shifts to crude realism, what is popularly called "in-your-face" talk. This section is not the earliest part of the Johannine tradition. The language is reminiscent of later writers, such as Ignatius of Antioch and Justin Martyr. The eschatology is unreservedly future; Christ is the agent of resurrection.

As in John 3 (cf. the Gospel for the previous week), the audience is unable to grasp the fundamental nature of religious language, which may be characterized as symbolic at the earthly level and realistic in heavenly terms. When we do not like revelation, we assign it to an easily dismissed category. Revelation tends not to fit our preconceptions, even if it must always be expressed in human action and language. Through this bold imagery Jesus crushes any dainty tendencies to imagine eternal life as the ingestion and assimilation of certain no doubt virtuous and useful notions. The wisdom we must swallow is the flesh and blood of the Son of Man, a life as human as any of ours, a life that met success and failure, setback and triumph, sorrow no less than joy, and more pain than glory. Eternal life does not begin at some as-yet-unspecified future date. This is not a postdated ticket for a free dinner. Eternal life is present no less than future and bodily no less than spiritual. Thus, we encounter it in the sacraments, earthly conveyors of heavenly reality, celestial vessels of terrestrial truth. The eternal life to which we are summoned in these unvarnished and initially unappetizing words is a life that can be extraordinary but is never fully free from all that is human. Without food and drink we cannot live, and this applies to eternal life as much as to simple biological survival.

Verses 56-58 supply comfort following the shock. The first of these utilizes the language of mutual indwelling, developed in John 15. Verse 57 shifts to the concept of the mission of God's Son (see the discussion of John 3 under Trinity Sunday, above). Christ will do for believers what the Father has done for him. The final words (v. 58) form an inclusio with verses 49-50. True heavenly bread is much better than that dull old manna, but the cost should not be neglected.

# July 3, 2011
## Third Sunday after Pentecost
### Fourteenth Sunday in Ordinary Time / Proper 9

| **Revised Common Lectionary (RCL)** | **Lectionary for Mass (LFM)** |
|---|---|
| Genesis 24:34-38, 42-49, 58-67 or Zechariah 9:9-12 | Zechariah 9:9-10 |
| Psalm 45 or Song of Solomon 2:8-13 or Psalm 145:8-14 | Psalm 145:1-2, 8-9, 10-11, 13-14 |
| Romans 7:15-25a | Romans 8:9, 11-13 |
| Matthew 11:16-19, 25-30 | Matthew 11:25-30 |

Few preachers will be so indifferent to what is happening in the life of the community as to ignore the national holiday. Movements exist to erode the tradition of separating church and state, generating a reaction that urges the government to be antireligious. The fiction that the founders intended to establish a "Christian nation"—in other words, an evangelical country—deserves refutation. Most of the founders came from Anglican and Protestant backgrounds that were then drifting away from traditional orthodoxy. The Mayflower Compact is a fine document, but less than 1 percent of Americans derive from its religious tradition. In the current political context, the question of the relation of God to one or another nation is more important than civic duty and the like. The prayers offer opportunity for relevant thanksgivings.

## First Reading
### Genesis 24:34-38, 42-49, 58-67 (RCL)

For preachers who intend to give this passage substantial attention, the entire story should be read (and reread). With the aborted offering of Isaac in chapter 22, the story of Abraham was essentially finished. Chapter 23 narrates Sarah's death. The overarching theme is the fulfillment of the promise to Abraham. God is the lead character in chapter 24, which illustrates the fulfillment of promises in unremarkable ways. The genre for such demonstrations of God's guiding hand resembles fiction.

Genesis 24 can be called a novella. Its charm includes suspense, humor, and the happy resolution, qualities that should not be ignored.

The structure includes four scenes:

1. Verses 1-9: Abraham and the servant
2. Verses 10-27: The servant and Rebekah
3. Verses 28-61: The servant and Rebekah's relatives
4. Verses 62-67: Isaac and Rebekah

Scenic duality prevails: two characters (which may be collective) are "onstage" in each scene. Transition and linkage are preserved through the retention of one character from the previous scene in each new section. The drama resides in the middle scenes, with a happy resolution at the close.

Because unmarried women generally did not leave the home, wells served as a kind of "singles' bar" in ancient villages, since girls did go to draw water (cf. Gen. 29:1-12 [and John 4, which plays on this theme]). Differences in courtship traditions spark interest—and horror. Many young men would not be comfortable having one of their father's slaves pick out a wife for them, and neither my mother nor yours would have approved of a daughter coming back from the well to announce that a strange man had put a ring in her nose and bracelets on her arms. The tradition of arranged marriages is still widespread; this tale makes it a part of our history.

Rebekah is not unlike Abraham, for she left her home in faith and hope of a new life. As in all romances, the themes of love, loyalty, and fidelity loom large here. These relate to God as well as to the human characters. The central theme for theological reflection is divine guidance, providence. The clouds do not hang low. Choruses of humming angels do not herald the epiphany of "the right girl" for Isaac. Speech about divine guidance includes two important subcategories: interpretation and human obedience. When everything is assigned to divine intervention, religion becomes selfish and oriented to trivia. Belief in providence means that no person or situation is utterly beyond redemption. Almost everything can be turned around. Fiction loves 180-degree turns, but even 45 degrees is a considerable improvement. Belief in providence means that we must labor to discern God's will. The second category is simple enough: The major question is not whether God is leading. It is whether we are following. Fiction satisfies because good and bad get their proper deserts. The life of faith is a bit more complex. Romance shows us how things should be. Faithful and obedient reflection helps us to labor to reduce the gap between what is and what ought to be.

For those who feel the tug of the national holiday, this lesson offers some good possibilities and dire pitfalls. The United States has received blessings, but it is not the beneficiary of peculiar and particular promises. God's guidance and leadership of nations are consistently associated with judgment of a frequently negative sort. In

Judaism Abraham is "our father." From him we might learn something about the role of founding fathers. Do we endorse all that they did? Certainly not! Is it incumbent upon us to discover and emulate their distinct and detailed views? Heavens, no! From their faith and vision we gather inspiration and hope. The alternate reading offers even more opportunities for this occasion.

## Zechariah 9:9-12 (RCL alt.)
## Zechariah 9:9-10 (LFM)

This reading comes from the collection of oracles concluding the Minor Prophets and does not belong to the writing that constitutes Zechariah 1–8. The passage is famous because of its citation in the Gospel stories of Palm Sunday. On this Sunday its purpose is to complement Matthew 11:25-30 by raising the question of the Messiah we think we want and the Messiah we shall get.

*Exegetical note:* Although the ass belongs to the tradition, it would already have seemed incongruous, if not ironic in the time of Jesus. Picture a president pedaling to his inauguration on a tricycle. For early Christians the arrival of a monarch was an image of present triumph and future promise. The entry of a ruler (Greek *parousia*, Latin *adventus*) into the capital was an event brimming with extravagant expectations.

The context utilizes the "divine warrior" metaphor for God, an image not popular in many Christian circles just now, as it is the great uncle of *jihad*. Holy war can look a bit different when waged against us. One branch of patriotic cerebration is willing to suggest that the Almighty has handed off the title and role of divine warrior to the United States of America, decently cloaked and modestly veiled as the notion may be. Those with their eye on the patriotic holiday will be authorized by this passage to note that God is the only divine warrior.

# Psalmody
## Psalm 45 (RCL)
## Psalm 145:8-14 (RCL alt.)
## Psalm 145:1-2, 8-9, 10-11, 13-14 (LFM)
## Song of Solomon 2:8-13 (RCL alt.)

The recommended psalm is 145:8-14 (RCL alt. and LFM). This acrostic hymn of praise has enjoyed devotional acclaim for millennia. Verse 2 has been taken into the *Te Deum*; verses 10, 15-16 are part of the traditional grace before meals. The other psalm choices call for comment as well. Psalm 45 is arguably secular in origin, a marriage song. Verses 2-9 address the groom. The selection begins with the address to the bride. In some ways wedding descriptions have not changed. There is attention to the gifts, to that dress to which the bride has said yes, to her trousseau, to the bridesmaids, and to the gifts. The sense of loneliness at leaving her home, implicit in Genesis, is clear. To this psalm belongs a rich and wondrous tradition of symbolic interpretation, but the interval between readings is not the best moment for a discourse on the history of exegesis. The same observations apply to the beautiful passage from the Song of

Solomon, although it will leave fewer people uncomfortable or angry than Psalm 45. Choral substitutes are another option, but this choice shifts the liturgy of the word decisively in the direction of romantic physical love, establishing long odds against Paul and Matthew.

## Second Reading
### Romans 7:15-25a (RCL)

Study should begin with verse 14. The Messiah, that is, king, in view here can be humble because God has done the heavy lifting. The concept of "power in weakness" does not make weakness a virtue to be pursued; it views weakness as an opportunity to acknowledge that God is in charge. Yet the manifestation of God's love in weakness does not mean that God is without power. It does mean that leaders can be humble because God is strong.

Romans is Paul's most diplomatic letter. He is trying to convince others that he is not the wild-haired propagator of libertinism that some of his opponents describe. Still, the apostle will not compromise on his view that the Torah in particular and law in general are not God's final answer to human problems and needs. This does not mean that they are wicked. Indeed, they are useful. Honesty leads Paul to paint himself into the occasional corner. We may disagree with his anthropology and find his understanding of psychology quite defective by modern standards, but we cannot deny that he refuses to settle for simple answers and attractive slogans. That lesson alone is worth a great deal.

In fact, the psychology of these verses resonates with all but those who have never failed to live up to some good intention. The apostle is working out a concept very much like what we call "conscience." Once again, it is important to stress that his opposing pairs, such as flesh and spirit, are not to be reduced to matter and spirit. The "flesh" that leads to sin is not an organ; it is most often an emotion. The first-person singular does not open a window into Pauline biography. Everyone, he assumes, is this "I." Additionally, the lectionary context invites preachers to remember that "yoke" is a metaphor for Torah as well as for wisdom. Reflection upon this passage in conjunction with Matthew 11:25-30 can bring quite fruitful results. Add Zechariah 9 to that mix. We should like a Messiah who would either make obedience to the law effortless or get rid of the whole business.

The "ordinary time" between Pentecost and Advent is life "between the times." No one understands that better than the apostle. Strengthened with eschatological gifts (baptism, chap. 6), believers can resist evil, but it is a constant struggle. Personal failure can also be identified as indwelling evil (v. 20). Paul does not authorize the view that "the devil made me do it." He says that our failures supply the devil with openings. Our problem is not particular issues with this or that law; it is our freedom to fail. Without that we cannot grow. Paul does not propose that we need to learn what sinful wretches we are so that we shall appreciate the gospel. He believes that the gospel can do something even with and for sinful wretches.

### Romans 8:9, 11-13 (LFM)

For comments on this text, please see the second readings for Propers 10 and 11, below.

## Gospel
### Matthew 11:16-19, 25-30 (RCL)
### Matthew 11:25-30 (LFM)

With chapter 11 Matthew marks the rise of growing opposition to the message of Jesus. Verses 2-30 constitute a unit that Matthew has generally constructed from Q. Comparisons between John the Baptizer and Jesus continue through verse 19, at which point Matthew inserts prophetic denunciations of Galilean towns. The early part of the story is read on Third Advent in Year A. This selection focuses on verses 25-30 (which alone are appointed in the LFM).

Reconstruction of the history of this Q material is a scholar's delight that cannot be pursued here. The underlying issue is the relation of John and Jesus to Wisdom, that is, Dame Wisdom, the personified divine power. The early tradition viewed them as "children of wisdom." This is explicit in Luke 7:35. The parallel in Matthew 11:19 reads "deeds." The significance of this emerges in Matthew 11:2 ("deeds of the Messiah"). The evangelist thus identifies Jesus with heavenly Wisdom, a direction in which Q seemed to have been moving. This step would have momentous implications for Christology. (In the Gospel of John, *Logos* [Word] is the equivalent of Wisdom.)

The background of the simile or parable in verses 16-17 is obscure. The setting is urban (*agora*). In the background may be a children's game or song. (Who knew what "Red Rover" was about? Children accept obscure rhymes.) The general sense is deprecation of those whom nothing can please. Verses 18-19a interpret the trope allegorically, in reverse (chiastic) order. John was ascetic and sought to get the people to repent. Boooring! Jesus took a drop or two from time to time and tried to get the people to recognize the presence of God's rule. He was written off for bad deeds and bad companions. Matthew 11:19b identifies Jesus and John as the children, Wisdom's children. Wisdom also preached in the marketplace: Proverbs 1:20. The effect of the passage is to minimize competition between John and Jesus—and the partisans of each. Both were rejected, both executed. This segment also illuminates—for those willing to go down the path—the language of verses 25-30.

Matthew 11:25-30 belongs to the list of passages over which proclaimers should paste the label "do no harm." If one can do no more than not stand in the way of these words, one has done well enough. Still, preachers do not just turn on the engine. We need to know how it works. The preceding verses have witnessed a denunciation of the Galilean towns in words like the oracles against great ancient city-states, such as Tyre and Sidon. Rejection is thus the Matthean context, quite unlike that of Luke 10:21-22. The section has three elements: the thanksgiving for revelation (vv. 25-26); an explanation of revelation's source (v. 27); and the invitation with promise (vv. 28-30). Verses 28-30 are peculiar to Matthew. The unit bears the form of the close of a wisdom speech, in which, after announcing her presence and Wisdom offers her message, invites people to accept it, with a promise for those who do (and sometimes threats for those who do not). For cogent examples see Sirach 6:24-30 and 51:23-27. In its original context the "father/son" terminology was sapiential, wisdom often presented in parent-child terms (Prov. 1:8, father; 31:2, mother; cf. also Wis. 2:17-18, 22). Already in Matthew this relationship views Jesus as the Son of God.

The language of verse 25 is like that of very early eucharistic prayers (cf. also the thanksgivings that open Paul's letters; e.g., 1 Cor. 1:4-9). God chose outsiders over insiders for reception of the message. "Hidden" versus "revealed" shows the divine purpose at work. In Matthew "these things" (v. 25) should be understood as messianic actions, via verse 2. The wise and learned are not only those with Ivy League credentials and official appointments. They are the authorities, whereas the "infants" lack status, power, and education. Since anti-intellectualism does well enough without homiletic endorsement, apt paraphrases on this occasion might be "hidden from Americans but revealed to Vietnamese" and the like. The apocalyptic determinism of these verses encourages the oppressed and lifts up the downtrodden; its flip side is unreflective self-righteousness. Because God is in charge, all of our self-confidences require qualification.

The threefold invitation ("come . . . take . . . learn") addresses all who feel the weight of burden and stress. Personified Wisdom(-Messiah) does not summon those identified as ignorant or lacking culture, but the wretched of the earth. (A good Fourth of July parallel is the inscription at the base of the Statue of Liberty.) The term *burden*, which forms an inclusio in verse 30, emerges in complaints against the Pharisees (whose demands for ritually approved products and for tithes raised prices and reduced income) that endured (cf. Luke 11:46; Matt. 23:4; Gal. 6:5; and, with the word *yoke*, Acts 15:10).

The content of the promise is "rest," a clear boon in its own right, and a theme that has enjoyed a diverse history in religious (Sabbath) and philosophical (rest as preferable to motion; cf. the comments on Genesis 1–2 for Trinity Sunday) thought. Rest is *the* eschatological goal: "Eternal rest grant unto them, O Lord." This is a term that requires volume after volume in the dictionary of life, with more definitions than any one person or group can articulate.

"Yoke" does not command much appeal in our culture nowadays. In the political sense (cf. Zechariah 9), yoke means domination. To "subjugate" is to place under a yoke. In a broader sense it refers to a system, school, method, or practice that allows one to "get a life." Some wish no more than a yoke and a goad. For others the yoke is a kind of primitive GPS, guidance when required. These dominical words come down against the heavy yoke containing rules for everything and harsh sanctions for deviation. Insofar as we do not find them comforting, we show our desire for a heavy yoke. Each of us has such desires from time to time.

One could call these promises the equivalent of the Beatitudes that open the Sermon on the Mount, in another form. Those attentive to their Greek can receive a fine reward, as Matthew would say: the word *gentle* (*praüs*) in verse 29 appears also in Zechariah 9:9, and thence in Matthew 21:5, but initially in Matthew 5:5. In these verses resides the Gospel of Matthew in a nutshell, and good news it is.

# July 10, 2011
## Fourth Sunday after Pentecost
### Fifteenth Sunday in Ordinary Time / Proper 10

| **Revised Common Lectionary (RCL)** | **Lectionary for Mass (LFM)** |
|---|---|
| Genesis 25:19-34 or Isaiah 55:10-13 | Isaiah 55:10-13 |
| Psalm 119:105-112 or 65:(1-8), 9-13 | Psalm 65:10, 11, 12-13, 14 |
| Romans 8:1-11 | Romans 8:18-23 |
| Matthew 13:1-9, 18-23 | Matthew 13:1-23 or 13:1-9 |

## First Reading
### Genesis 25:19-34 (RCL)

God writes straight with crooked lines. The promise has hovered over the narrative since chapter 12. The thread, it seems, is about to snap, for Isaac has failed to produce a son for two decades, and he is sixty. Rather than stretch out the suspense and underline the tension, the narrator has Rebekah pregnant within a verse, with due attention to prayer. The narrative abruptly implies a multiple conception and the resultant struggle. Everyone realizes that this presages future fraternal conflict. In despair Rebekah visits a shrine and receives an oracle that is both ominous and opaque. Conflict is in store. This is apparent when twins are born. The description of the birth seems comical, as are the names. Names were portentous in that world, but these seem to ridicule the tradition. ("Jacob" was evidently originally theophoric.) These are not idealized national heroes. For comparison one might tell how the young George Washington attempted to cut down a prized cherry tree but succeeded only in damaging both the tree and the axe. Primogeniture was never a part of the promise, but it dominated the culture. The heir believes that primogeniture and a dollar will get you a cup of coffee.

No tales of youthful prowess here. The narrator cuts straight to adulthood. The twins elect quite different career paths, Esau the old-fashioned life of the hunter, while Jacob embraces a pastoral vocation. Esau's ability to provide fresh game for the table wins his father's heart. Rebekah prefers Jacob. To us Papa seems a bit shortsighted; he is not rearing his son to be a patriarch. Mama's view raises the specter of a cabal in support of her favorite.

Feast and famine are part of the life of hunting cultures. Verses 29-34 are a short narrative flattering to neither of these patriarchs of sibling rivalry. Esau sells his birthright for a meal, while Jacob, the heel, exacts a heavy price for what brotherly love should have provided gratis. Esau the oaf wolfs down his dinner and leaves without further ado. A fairly crude pun—crudeness in puns is in the eye of the beholder— links the ruddy Esau, the red-hued stew, and the nation of Edom. One wonders why God let this character get out of the womb first.

The book of Genesis fluctuates between PG and R ratings. These stories of family travails retail raw emotion that must challenge any who would dismiss the Bible as psychologically naïve. God does not choose heirs on the basis of merit, nor does the status of successor call out the best in people. Mommy just may love Johnny more than she loves Nicky. Parents may love children but not rear them in helpful ways. One child may be good looking, another unattractive. Fair these things are not, but "What's fair got to do with it" is something we should know because the Bible tells us so.

For the outcome we must wait, despite cloudy intimations and ruthless amorality. Far down the spectrum of salvation history, one learns from this family saga (which will run through chapter 36 and occupy the RCL for a few more weeks) that we understand much less about God's ways than we imagine, that things are unpleasant and messy rather than tidily presentable on a PowerPoint graph. One thing that can always be learned from stories like this is the possibility of grace, that the real meaning of providence is not that God has a plan for your life, but that God has goals for the world, goals achieved by writing straight with crooked lines.

## Isaiah 55:10-13 (RCL alt., LFM)

This reading intersects with the Gospel in several intriguing and fruitful ways. This is the close of a "book," Deutero-Isaiah, and forms a bracket with its opening in chapter 40, which contrasts ephemeral grass to God's eternal word. Savor the tropes and figures used here, where musical mountains and applauding trees evoke the unity of creation and redemption under God's rule.

The most apparent intersection with Matthew 13 is in the comparison between God's word and agriculture. In Isaiah the comparison is explicit, taking the form of simile ("as . . . so"). Implicit comparison, like metaphor in narrative form, characterizes Matthew. The reader of Isaiah knows that God's word is not a form of precipitation. Auditors of Jesus' parables must first decide that Jesus is not just telling a boring story, next that he is not retailing agricultural advice, and, finally, wonder just what it may mean. Metaphor is more open and more prone to confusion. Preachers can spend some good effort, from time to time, reflecting about different forms of comparison.

The text also invites contemplation about the meaning of God's word. On the one hand it is effective (v. 11b); nonetheless, literal fulfillment is often wanting. This is not simply an admission that the hills were not alive with the sound of music, but that the return from exile was not a triumphal procession accompanied by miracles of nature. God's word is sure and permanent; it is also poetic. Everyone happily endorses sure and permanent, but all of us have problems with the poetic some of the time, and some of us all of the time. The history of revelation is the story of faithful believers who struggled with the concreteness of some revelations and the vagueness of others. The promise is certain; the how and when of fulfillment are not. Word puts us to work.

# Psalmody
## Psalm 119:105-112 (RCL)

Psalm 119 displays an engaging tension. Its external organization is formally elegant and complex; internally it can seem utterly disorganized. The overriding theme is praise of Torah. To us this mixture of promise, paranoia, and praise resembles a stream of consciousness. In fact, its picture of strengths and weaknesses, fears and resolves, is reasonably accurate.

## Psalm 65:(1-8), 9-13 (RCL alt.)
## Psalm 65:10, 11, 12-13, 14 (LFM)

This psalm of praise provides suitable reflection upon and transition between Isaiah and Matthew. The best selection will begin at verse 9. In addition to thematic continuity, this psalmody reminds us that food is a necessity given by God and that weather and crops exist to do more than provide colorful images.

# Second Reading
## Romans 8:1-11 (RCL)

The apostle is working out his view of life in the Spirit given not just the law's shortcomings, but, more importantly, grace's possibilities. The opening two verses state the thesis: since Christ has liberated believers from the power of death, the faithful have been acquitted. Rather than immediately contrast life-giving spirit to death-bringing law, Paul postulates two models of law, as it were. The apostle envisions a dualism of realms, for which different terms may be used. Christians do not elude condemnation because they are without sin, but because Christ has freed them.

Despite his diplomatic goals, Paul clearly states his belief that Torah cannot give life. He associates law with the sphere of "flesh." Verse 3 seems to verge upon docetism (the theory that Christ was not fully and truly human). The term *likeness* results from "sinful flesh." By it Paul avoids labeling Christ as a sinner. Intimations of incarnation are present, but the consequences of particular terms and frameworks have not been worked through. Similarly, it is not desirable to look for a distinction between the

"Spirit of God" and the "Spirit of Christ." Because of Christ, God's Spirit can get to work, as it were.

English does not distinguish between singular and plural in the second person. We tend to prefer the singular: my possession of the Spirit. The text is, however, distressingly corporate. The apostle is talking to the community about the community. This means that moralizing does not give interpreters the best set of lenses for examining this passage. With judgment out of the way, people are free; justification means that we can work together.

The closing two verses come as a reminder that possession of the Spirit and new life is not the result of a choice. It is a divine action. Finally, Paul suggests the possibility that even these mortal bodies may, through God's power, get in better shape. The apostle exhibits a number of tools that have different histories and achieve specific functions. He likes to use dialectical pairs, such as slavery versus freedom. The result, to oversimplify a bit more than is prudent for some purposes, is that we can pick the model that is most relevant or appealing in our particular situations. Paul is not offering a list of the only options. He is showing ways of getting at problems and exposing possibilities. The model is more important than his terminology. Some will simplify this to "anything goes." Others will use it to establish a complete set of rules. For Paul the question is never "What are we allowed to do?" but "What can we, under grace, do?"

## Romans 8:18-23 (LFM)

For comments on this text, please see the second reading under Proper 11, below.

# Gospel
## Matthew 13:1-9, 18-23 (RCL)
## Matthew 13:1-23 or 13:1-9 (LFM)

In the Matthean scheme, Jesus teaches in cryptic, figurative utterances because of his rejection. By withholding revelation, the parables punish those who will not believe. Scholars view this construction as, at best, half true—and mostly the wrong half. This highlights one problem of preaching upon parables on a lectionary basis. One approach is to utilize as the "text" the results of historical-critical reconstruction. One criticism of this approach is that it overlooks the contribution of each evangelist, exposure of which was a major goal of the three-year lectionary. On the other hand, the reconstructions are often illuminating and exciting. It is arguably legitimate to use both. Either may be elected; neither merits consistent neglect. The preacher who does not recognize that Isaiah 55 is the close of a book detracts from its meaning and value. A major function of parables is to get people to think. Reconstruction is a part of that thinking.

The basis of Matthew 13 is Mark 4, where parables constitute the initial detailed teaching of which the Parable of the Sower is central. The Sermon on the Mount serves those functions in Matthew. Matthew has substantially expanded and even more substantially revised his source. The structure is difficult. The simplest model sees two parallel sections in verses 1-35 and 36-52, each with four parables and different settings. Matthew is a bit cagey (or careless) with dramatic audiences. Here he evidently mixes up crowds and disciples. A good working division sees parallel units in verses 3b-23 and verses 24-52, each containing parabolic material and interpretation.

Parable is more easily defined by effect than by form. Ideally, parables are narratives. Modes of interpretation can, and should, vary. Although parables are not allegories, they are readily transformed into allegory. The fundamental principle is that we do not interpret parables so much as parables interpret us. More simply, parables force us to see things in different ways. Multiple interpretations, including conflicting interpretations, are signs of success. Parables get us to think. The primary—but not exclusive—referent is the reign/rule/dominion of God, the kingdom.

This inaugural parable is pretty boring. The traditional title should not mislead. The focus is upon the types of soil. This wasteful method of sowing is called broadcast (which provided a metaphor for wireless transmission). Triplets dominate the picture: three failures and three successes, each act of sowing summarized in three parts. The literary effect of this monotonous and repetitious structure is a bit soporific. Life has its cycles and patterns. One season or year is quite like its respective predecessors. The challenge is whether we can ever see more than we want to see, if we have let our eyes become dulled. Is this all there is? Results may vary, as we learn from the small print in television commercials. In Mark they run thirty, sixty, one hundred. This is a bit unusual—whatever the reference, about which scholars argue. Thirty, sixty, one hundred twenty would be logical, or, thirty, sixty, ninety. Failure is much easier to describe than is success.

Does one wish lessons? Growth is unpredictable and almost indefinable. A modest harvest is a divine epiphany. A fine harvest is an epiphany. A huge harvest is . . . an epiphany. No one needs to be told about the hundreds. The thirties require well-tuned ears. God's rule is not restricted to the hundreds. Word and sacraments enable us to see the marvelous in the mundane, advents in bread, oil, water, and wine.

If we apply this story to the kingdom of God, the ending suggests that growth is not guaranteed. Some use apocalyptic thought to lock God into perfection glowing with clarity and cemented in certainty. The parable says both that the rhythm of normality is deceptive and that God's presence is easily missed by those lacking ears to hear. The advent of God's rule, this parable suggests, is neither an explosion that moves from zero to one hundred in the flash of an eye, nor a clearly rising curve in which things are gradually but indisputably getting better and better every day. The parable paints a picture of failure and success, both enduring in diverse kinds. In this context Matthew makes his most noteworthy contribution.

He replaces Mark's fine crescendo, thirty . . . sixty . . . one hundred, with its antithesis: one hundred, sixty, thirty. It won't take much to get people to praise God when yields double one year and increase by two-thirds the next. Downward trends are a bit harder to handle. This is not to suggest that downward trends are positive benefactions; it does mean that our standards of success, growth, improvement may be at variance with those of the Most High. Some evident thirties turn out to be great successes. An example, should one be desired, is the career of the roughly thirty-year-old Jesus, whose apparent end in a hideous execution was not, in fact, the last word.

The parable is anything but an enticing narrative. Advocates of the slogan "Cut to the chase" miss the centrality of the routine and mundane in life. We sow without knowing what will sprout up, but sow we must. Learning to appreciate the thirties and sixties takes work. Everyone can brag about the hundreds. "Learning" is an apt word, for, although the early interpretation relates the parable to mission, in antiquity the image was commonly applied to education. The word *seminary* shows that the metaphor enjoyed a long life. *Mission* and *education* are terms with a good deal of overlap; the mission of the church does not end with planting. It requires constant nurture.

The parable provides some consolation. You can't grow wheat in rocks. The teacher/preacher/pastor/missionary may thus say: "God, how can you expect me to soar like an eagle when I've got all these turkeys to work with?" Say it, but don't ever completely mean it. Our mission—and here this inept model of agriculture helps—is not restricted to the finest soil. In the end we know that weeds and soil will often win, but we must act as if everything depended upon us.

The structure of Matthew 13 also exhibits ancient notions of instruction, with general teaching in simple forms like parable followed and complemented by private instruction to the select few. An antepenultimate observation is that this is no warrant for understanding mission as protection of the seed. The penultimate comment is that the dominion of God and the proclamation of it are inextricably linked. Its sequel is that sowers sow; they do not create the seed.

Verses 10-17 are an alternate in the LFM. If read, this material requires comment, logically in sequence to Matthew 11:25-27 (from the previous week). The plural "mysteries" (v. 11, vs. Mark) points in that direction, as does the macarism in verses 16-17, which in Luke 10:23-24 follows the parallel to Matthew 11:25-27. The mystery is God's unlikely choice of the unlikely. The presumption of this unit, based upon Mark 4:10-12, is that "parables" cannot be understood without a key. Matthew's disciples do not ask what the parables mean but why Jesus speaks in riddles. How do the activities of (inspired?) seeing and hearing relate to knowledge of divine secrets? Those who don't wish to act as Jesus acted will not understand his deeds. Those who don't like his words will misunderstand the parables. The contrast between hidden and revealed, promise and fulfillment, runs throughout the Gospel and is prominent in this chapter.

Verse 11 establishes an antithesis, supported by the general, aphoristic content of verse 12. Verse 13 establishes this lack of communication as intentional. Passages like this arise in a situation of intense conflict. They may justify disagreement, but they are not useful tools for conflict resolution. Verses 14-15 intensify the condemnation. They represent a late (probably Byzantine) addition to Matthew. The closing announcement intends to reassure and thus uplift the community. The key word is "understand" (vv. 13, 19, 23, and 51).

The interpretation provides a window into (and a mirror of) the divine mysteries. This explanation does not appear to unlock cosmic mysteries. It would disappoint any new-age aficionado. That is not entirely accidental. Many of the parables argue that secrets lie about in plain sight, and the early tradition, to which this unit belongs, did not entirely forget that. The technique reflects allegorism, understanding each item in the parable to correspond to a religious fact. The method can be restrictive, but it shows appreciation for the limits of literalism. The soils are the focus. The failures present a diagnostic manual for church leaders. Rocky soil (vv. 20-21) receives the most substantial elaboration and exhibits the most alteration. The major problem is those who are initially energetic and attractive, but turn out to be inadequate. Some things don't change. . . .

This method of interpretation is not the only method; for more than a century it has been officially old-fashioned. It shows that from very early times (c. 70 C.E.) the parables were seen not just as stories *from* Jesus but as stories *about* Jesus, that is, stories with christological significance. More than that, this primary and paradigmatic parable was viewed from an ecclesiological perspective, as an attempt to perceive the nature of the body created by God's seed.

# July 17, 2011
## Fifth Sunday after Pentecost
### Sixteenth Sunday in Ordinary Time / Proper 11

**Revised Common Lectionary (RCL)**

Genesis 28:10-19a or Isaiah 44:6-8 or
  Wisdom of Solomon 12:13, 16-19
Psalm 139:1-12, 23-24 or 86:11-17
Romans 8:12-25
Matthew 13:24-30, 36-43

**Lectionary for Mass (LFM)**

Wisdom of Solomon 12:13, 16-19

Psalm 86:5-6, 9-10, 15-16
Romans 8:26-27
Matthew 13:24-43 or 13:24-30

## First Reading
### Genesis 28:10-19a (RCL)

Those who intend to utilize this passage as a preaching resource should read through verse 22, the formal, if not entirely edifying, end of the unit. Jacob is on the run, a banished exile because he entered into a cabal with his mother to abscond with his brother's blessing (which conveys prosperity and is, like all magical things of this nature, irrevocable). This deceiving creature stops in just any old place because it is time for rest and makes what is for us an uncomfortable pillow of a convenient stone. An unperson in an unplace. Readers suspect that the narrator has reasons for these details. Jacob is certainly not an item from the top drawer. He is an immoral and irreligious rogue. No religious seeker, he will have to be run to ground by God, who is not without experience in handling hard cases.

A convenient means for getting through to such types is via dreams, when they are asleep and their defenses are down. There may be others who could more readily and often discern God's will if their defenses were not set so high. The revelation combines two notions, the entrance ramp to heaven and a direct theophany. In the background are Babylonian temples, with a penthouse apartment for the god and a ground-level chamber for formal receptions. Movement from one to another takes place via a ramp (rather than a ladder in our sense). Associated with this was the notion of a window in the sky (or ground), a narrow aperture providing direct access to the divine. Such gates of heaven were nearly unique. No one would be surprised to learn that this site became a great religious center. For the very early auditors of the story, part of the excitement was hearing about Bethel when it was devoid of buildings. The erstwhile pillow became a pillar—such stones were quite tall, duly consecrated with oil.

The passage reeks of primitivism, even without a stone pillar to represent a male god. By juxtaposing the picturesque vision of heaven's gate with the simple—and cruder—notion of the Almighty popping by for a chat, the editor was combining two sources but also more than hinting that neither picture is adequate to portray an encounter with the divine. Each is but a vague and vulgar shadow of an ineffable reality. So much for the framework, splendid as it is.

God quite explicitly reiterates the promise to Abraham. Jacob cannot claim ignorance of his family's history and responsibility. Indeed, the promise is expanded: God is stuck with Jacob, and vice versa. The Lord promises to be with him until the promise is accomplished. The claim of continuing presence in verse 15 resonates with Matthew's theme of Emmanuel (1:23; 28:20). Then Jacob comes to his senses and realizes his own insensitivity. This will often happen to all of us, and we pray that we shall react so boldly and generously.

### Isaiah 44:6-8 (RCL alt.)

This is a trial speech like others in Deutero-Isaiah (cf. Isa. 41:1-5; 41:21-28; 43:8-15), but blended with an oracle reassuring the hearers of salvation ("Do not fear," v. 8). The condemnation is interesting and the effect apparently ironic at first impression. By ordinary standards the God of Israel, despite the fine titles of King, Redeemer, Lord of hosts, would not start on a weak junior varsity in the league of minor deities. The people of Israel and Judah had been hammered, conquered, crushed, exiled, all but pulverized. By the criteria of common sense: as goes a people, so goes its god. For this puny godlet to diss the mighty members of triumphant pantheons who have dispensed their benefactions upon the ruling powers is risible. Unless . . .

Judgment supplies an overt link with the Gospel text. Among the questions raised are: Who gets to judge God, and by what criteria is God to be evaluated? These are not idle questions. The Bible does not, to be sure, lack examples of vanquished idols and displaced deities. They are good and fun. Faith (and theology) really comes into play when things are tough. Dramatically, claims like this assert that the generously endowed soprano has not offered her final aria. Theologically, this passage affirms that God makes the rules. That is one of the hardest of all points to grasp—particularly when we don't like the rules.

### Wisdom of Solomon 12:13, 16-19 (RCL alt., LFM)

This passage connects with the selected Gospel through its focus on judgment, with emphasis upon mercy and forbearance. Wisdom 11:15—12:27 reflects on the subject of divine mercy. The generating issue is the difficulty of the nationalist tradition in an age when many Israelites lived in Egypt. The question is not devoid of contemporary relevance.

Power and mercy go together. God's universal dominion places some limits upon playing favorites. Justice, fairness, and equity are concomitants of strength. Hellenistic ideas have contributed to this picture. God not only exercises restraint, forbearance, and mercy, but also serves as a model for human beings. Verse 19 further implies that God is more than an example to inspire the faithful; God empowers believers through repentance. Forgiveness, the fruit of repentance, is itself power and it empowers the forgiven to show kindness and mercy. Some of the loudest voices for godliness in political and civic life do not talk about these godly qualities. Without mercy and kindness hope cannot take root, and justice will wither.

# Psalmody
## Psalm 139:1-12, 23-24 (RCL)

This is a long, complicated, and beloved psalm. The selection is rather long for an interlude. The omitted verses contain a personal lament over apostasy. Verses 1-3 and 23-24 form an inclusio. The selection reacts, somewhat ironically, to the story of Jacob, which is testimony to its truth, but more from God's perspective, as it were. Verses 7-12 celebrate, in stirring words, the omnipresence of the Most High. Although the original Hebrew text of verse 12 is unfortunately uncertain, it remains one of the simplest yet most powerful of images.

## Psalm 86:11-17 (RCL alt.)
## Psalm 86:5-6, 9-10, 15-16 (LFM)

This is an individual lament that constitutes a kind of library of classic Bible verses. Both selections underline elements found in the reading from Wisdom, notably God's rule over all the nations, related in an individual key. The Ruler of the universe hears the prayers of mere individuals.

# Second Reading
## Romans 8:12-25 (RCL)

Paul is moving toward the close of his reflections on grace (Romans 5–8). Verses 1-11 continue his thought on life in the Spirit; verses 12-17 reflect on the meaning of being children of God. The subsequent sections in verses 18-30 and 31-39 treat the eschatological dimension. Although the outline seems clear and each statement is intelligible, following his argument requires some work on the part of the reader. Verses 12-13 reiterate the opposition between flesh and spirit and modes of existence. The "deeds of the body" in verse 13 refer to, sinful actions. The Spirit is a death-killing force. Verse 14 says, in effect: because you are children of God, you are led by the Spirit. Examining Mark 1:9-11 and Galatians 3:26-28 will illuminate the background.

As a story about Jesus, the baptism creates difficulties, readily observable in the varied stratagems of Matthew, Luke, and John. A major function of that story is to explain the link between baptism, the Spirit, and believers' standing as offspring of the Most High.

The term used in verse 14 is, literally, "sons," just as the noun "adoption" (v. 15) is, hyperliterally, "adoption as sons." Paul was more egalitarian than some males in his day, less so than others. His language includes females (Gal. 3:26-27). The forms represent the privilege accorded to male heirs. "Children" and "adoption" are good renditions. In verse 16 he can take up a more general Greek term for children. The proof of this status is the cry "Father," an Aramaic term of endearment evidently used as a postbaptismal acclamation by initiates. That is the Spirit's work (cf. 1 Cor. 12:3).

From this status follows our position as heirs and, logically, co-heirs with the Son of God. Paul can now spring a little trap. If we are going to get what Jesus got, that will include suffering. At this points he expands the notion to include all creation, the notion of suffering that is, not the idea of present glory. The entire universe is traveling the same road, awaiting the irruption—birth—of the ultimate. The background owes much to elements upon which various Gnostics will erect religious systems, but the concept, like the apocalyptic vision of renewed creation, is magnificent.

The subject is that of the parable in Matthew 13:24-30, the end, but judgment is not in view, nor does this flatter our individualized eschatologies that equip every soul with a cloud and a harp. At times, and Romans 8 is one of them, Paul's view of the end more closely approximates that of the nonreligious Arthur C. Clarke's *Childhood's End* than it does the harp-for-every-cloud model. This should give one food for thought, the conclusion to which should not simply be that Scripture offers many images, among which we may have preferences so long as we realize that no single picture can capture all that God has to offer.

The Pauline "eschatological reservation" makes a surprise appearance in verse 23: our adoption is not / will not be complete prior to the redemption of our body. "Body" is singular in Greek. It does not mean the church, the body of Christ. Paul declines to view ultimate victory as shuffling off the mortal coil. All that is subject to sin and decay, corruption and error will be transformed. In short, redemption is not the amputation of the body from the soul. Verse 24 is not as much of a leap as it may seem. Because salvation is unfinished, hope is our mode of existence. This hope is not a fine wish, like the "wait 'til next year" of Chicago Cubs fans. It is grounded in a promise. Because it is true hope rather than a goal clearly glimpsed, patience is the other course that drives the chariot. Paul says patience is good. He also knows that suffering permeates our existence. The two do not add up to the sum: pie in the sky by and by. This epistle will do its best work if it can shake up the preacher, and thus the hearers, shake up to challenge, but also to reassure.

### Romans 8:26-27 (LFM)

For comments on this text, please see the second reading under Proper 12, below.

## Gospel
### Matthew 13:24-30, 36-43 (RCL)
### Matthew 13:24-43 or 13:24-30 (LFM)

The LFM offers the broadest choice: either the Parable of the Weeds in the Wheat without the included interpretation, or three parables with a rationale for their use and an interpretation. I recommend that the focus be upon one parable, whichever option is selected. The introductory formula, "The kingdom of God is like . . . ," is not in standard simile format, in which God's reign is being compared to a person or something else, but means, in effect: God's rule may be compared to a situation in which . . .

Matthew has revised Mark 4 in characteristic ways. The contrast between insiders and outsiders is intensified and ecclesiological interest is prominent. The first parable dealt with bad and good *soils*. This story of wheat amid weeds takes up the question of the *seed*, the nature of what is sown. In evident place of the Markan parable about secret growth (4:26-29) stands the allegory about weeds and wheat. This may be a (probably Matthean) revision of the Markan text or based upon a different parable. For the task of preaching, the difference is not important.

The allegorical nature of the text is clear because of the ease with which each referent is assigned a meaning in verses 36-43 and because of details that do not work well. Why do the slaves start shrieking when they do? Anyone who has ever grown anything outdoors has had experience of weeds. Their origin is not relevant. In short, the dialogue of verses 27-30 was generated to serve the interpretation of verses 36-43.

The images are those of the sower (last week): planting, which often refers to education and mission, and harvest. This story attends more to growth, with its obvious references, and treats harvest in a different manner. Harvest is a favorite biblical image for judgment, fully developed here. The images thus relate to community origins, growth, life, and fate. On "sleep" note Matthew 25:5; 26:40-45 (and cf. 1 Thess. 5:6); for "both" see 9:17. The weed in question is possibly a wolf in sheep's clothing, that is, a weed camouflaged as grain, and/or a plant with pernicious roots that intertwine with the grain, making extrication almost impossible.

The story is a mystery for the slaves. Readers and master know who committed the crime. There are three characters, two collective: the householder, who is, of course, the boss, his slaves, and some reapers. The boss plants the seed and the reapers gather the harvest. Now the slaves, whom we should expect to do all the work—at least all the hard and unpleasant work—do none at all. They only talk. Their talk consists of a question, which turns out to be a proposal, a plan for dealing with that perennial problem of weeds. Surveying the field which they have not planted and which they will not harvest, they cast their eyes upon a mess of weeds, to which they appropriately direct their master's attention. The master replies: "No! That isn't your job. By killing the weeds you may ruin the wheat as well." Evidently maturity will enhance discernment.

After the crowds have been dismissed, the disciples eagerly seek clarification about the weeds, ignoring the intervening material. The interpretation (vv. 36-43) and the story have cross-fertilized, although the interpretation focused on verses 24-25, 30. The details are treated as ciphers: X stands for Y. The Son of Man and the devil are both active in sowing. The field is the world, rather than the church. The owner and his slaves disappear. The thrust is upon the contrasting fates of righteous and wicked at the last judgment, spelled out in the fullness of apocalyptic detail (and dualism). The wicked will be used as fuel, while the righteous shine like the sun (cf. Dan. 12:3 and Matt. 17:2). This may be compared with Paul's poetic flight in Romans 8.

The varied parousias of the parables of the historical Jesus and the notion of temporal imminence are discarded. The moral thrust is apparent. The implication for the wicked is not that "the devil made me do it," but that "the devil made me." Opportunity for growth is absent. In short, dualistic pictures have their limitations. The evangelist does not, fortunately, consistently stick to this deterministic formula. Better edification will emerge from the parable itself, which views growth as revelation and reminds believers that judgment is not a part of our job description.

One approach, perhaps the simplest and often the most appealing, is that taken by the slaves. They see the coexistence of weeds and wheat as a summons to get rid of those weeds. In church terms they speak for those in every generation who long for a community of the elect, a band restricted to the perfect and the pure. In brief: they want to clean house and sweep out the trash, perhaps those with whom they disagree or whom they identify as troublemakers. We all have such lists of weeds. We are also aware of the weed catalogs cherished by others. One hears that "everything is a weed somewhere in the world." Let us then assume that each of us is on some group's list of items to be uprooted and trashed. In the jargon of today, weeds are "the other." Everyone is "the other" to some group. The master in the story politely suggests to the servants that such purification is not their job. Slaves are to do as they are told and not make plans for the owner. Judgment is, after all, the province and responsibility of God. It is also one of those jobs humans would most love to usurp. Fortunately, God does not intend to give it away.

Today's parable about weeds and wheat addresses us about the church, about the kind of community God calls us to be and to become. God has not, to the occasional disappointment of all of us and the constant frustration of some, summoned us to the creation of a community of the perfect and the unstained. Whenever a church body decides that this is their vocation, the whole group must focus on the possible presence of a bad apple, and all must worry whether the person next to them is good enough, and ultimately whether we are good enough ourselves.

That is difficult. More difficult still is to be a church, for a church will always contain a number of types about whom we worry, and we shall have to struggle painfully with moral and social questions. Churches are to be hospitals for sinners rather than assemblies of the saints. They are hard to bear. The only thing that can be said in their favor is that this is how God wants it to be. We can, however, gather each week and pray every day for growth. *Growth* is the key word. Hospitals are places in which to get better, not clubs in which we can all be sick together, comforting one another in our misery. God has invited us to gather rather than to judge, to get together and learn to live with one another, weeds and wheat alike. There is wheat within each of us as well as those all-too-visible weeds. From this patchy crop God can fashion a miraculous bread, transforming each of us by the pure wheat of this holy offering, making us into beings shaped by hope.

# July 24, 2011
## Sixth Sunday after Pentecost
### Seventeenth Sunday in Ordinary Time / Proper 12

| **Revised Common Lectionary (RCL)** | **Lectionary for Mass (LFM)** |
|---|---|
| Genesis 29:15-28 or 1 Kings 3:5-12 | 1 Kings 3:5, 7-12 |
| Psalm 105:1-11, 45b or Psalm 128 or | Psalm 119:57 + 72, 76-77, 127-128, |
| Psalm 119:129-136 | 129-130 |
| Romans 8:26-39 | Romans 8:28-30 |
| Matthew 13:31-33, 44-52 | Matthew 13:44-52 or 13:44-46 |

## First Reading
### Genesis 29:15-28 (RCL)

The homilist who has already drawn from the well of the mysterious ways in which God works may wish that that card had not been played. Equal redundancy applies to the melody "How checkered our family history is." Speaking of wells, the interval (29:1-14) has provided another encounter at the well, in which Jacob falls for one whom he might address as "my cousin Rachel."

Genesis 29:1—31:55 constitutes a well-crafted narrative, with marked boundaries. The focus continues to be on the difficulty of producing heirs to fulfill the promise. Jacob remains the sort of fellow who has no difficulty finding conflict. The story is quite humorous, often broadly so, creating difficulties for a family program.

The story opens with bargaining. Jacob can negotiate (e.g., to get a birthright), but here he quickly offers to work seven years for the hand of Laban's younger daughter. That is a long term of service, suggesting that she is quite a beauty and Jacob irrationally smitten. This is reinforced by the fine sentiment of verse 20. Daughters were unmitigated commodities, to be sold for the best price. Still, he did the work. What is seven years in the course of true love? One almost begins to feel sorry for Jacob.

That feeling gains force when the deceiver is cruelly deceived. Weddings lasted a full week, a custom still sometimes observed. The heavily veiled bride was escorted to a dark wedding chamber. Readers are to believe that only with the light of day is the bride's identity revealed. The same device—sometimes including the "bride's" sex—is found in Roman comedy. The range of opportunities this scenario offered for jokes of varied quality can be imagined. Jacob takes umbrage. This was not the deal.

Laban's excuse is lame: daughters must be married in chronological order. He quickly recovers and promises Rachel, on credit. They will marry after he has completed the seven days needed for proper consummation of the nuptials with Leah. In the end Jacob is married to two sisters, both his cousins, and is embedded in the household of his father-in-law. If you like this, you'll love the plot of Wagner's *Ring*.

Nearly all of this is morally reprehensible to us, and some of it would have been questionable, albeit amusing, to its early audience. Morals do change, like it or not. Some arguments against this or that change may be effective and convincing. The claim that this is how it has always been done is not such an argument. Just as Christians believe that Jesus Christ came to save sinners, so our Israelite forebears demonstrated time and again that God did not always choose the virtuous. Two homiletic charges are (1) to reinforce through repetition the cliché that God writes straight in crooked lines and (2) to do so in ways that make this an always fresh and often unpleasant discovery.

## I Kings 3:5-12 (RCL alt.)
## I Kings 3:5, 7-12 (LFM)

A male reading of this passage out of context is likely to elicit the response: "I would have hated this kid when I was a boy!" Context is not unimportant. Up to this point Solomon has been much closer to a model scumbag than to the perfect boy. He has been the kind of person our parents warn us against. Moreover, he is no boy. Verse 7 uses a typical statement of those summoned to a substantial task (cf. Jer. 1:6). The context further notes that Solomon has contracted a diplomatic marriage with an Egyptian princess. "Furrin women" will eventually lead him into difficulty. Nonchalantly, the text also notes that Solomon routinely offered a thousand sacrificial victims at Gibeon, one of those notorious high places.

To this unpromising monarch in these far from salubrious circumstances God appears in the customary mode of a nocturnal dream to announce: "Ask what I should give you." From what we know of this fellow, his wish will be for the status-and culture-appropriate equivalent to faster horses, looser women, and cheaper whiskey. In short, the slogan "Be careful what you ask for" could have been crafted for this creature. One may begin to question the Almighty's judgment. Wrongly.

Solomon surprises us. Responsibility can change people. Responsibility or not, people can change. It helps if we let them do so and acknowledge their progress. After a suitable introduction that combines praise of God's greatness, thanks for the divine role in David's accomplishments, and an acknowledgment of his own weaknesses, Solomon asks for the ability to govern well, so that God's elect might prosper.

Solomon is shaping up! God is pleased and grants the request. (Indeed, in verses 13-15 God grants most of those things for which Solomon had *not* asked.) These gifts will benefit the entire people. The subsequent episode will relate Solomon's famous judgment.

In contrast to the series of readings from Genesis selected for the RCL, which set forth God's determination to fulfill the promise without fussing about the résumés of its agents, this passage belongs to the sphere of covenants, that is, contracts, agreements, and deals. The promise, which is unconditional, shows God's unconditional love. Covenants do not alter that love. They summon people to act as if God loves them.

The scene utilizes a dialogue to help paint the portrait of an ideal ruler, a model to which other rulers may be compared. It is thus important in the history of messianic thought. As a ruler who more or less defined wisdom—most of the time— Solomon offers a precedent for a Messiah who would be Wisdom personified.

## Psalmody
### Psalm 105:1-11, 45b (RCL)

For comments on this text, please see the Psalmody (RCL) under Proper 14, below.

### Psalm 128 (RCL alt.)

This is a wisdom psalm, based upon the principle that the fear of the Lord is the beginning of wisdom. Temporal reward for the wise and God-fearing is promised. The psalm has an androcentric orientation. The psalms, like all Scripture, are written for us, not to us. This one requires many to put themselves in the place of another. The movement is outward: self, spouse, children, Jerusalem, grandchildren, and all Israel. Wisdom begins with the self and moves out to embrace all of God's children.

### Psalm 119:129-136 (RCL alt.)
### Psalm 119:57 + 72, 76-77, 127-128, 129-130 (LFM)

Psalm 119 is a lengthy meditation upon the Torah, written in acrostics, in which each word of the eight lines of each stanza begins with a successive letter of the alphabet. The psalm wonderfully blends petitions of various sorts with fulsome praise of God's word, a varied and swelling prayer for direction to follow in the path set out by the Lord.

## Second Reading
### Romans 8:26-39 (RCL)
### Romans 8:28-30 (LFM)

This is the justly famous conclusion to Paul's discussion of God's plan for overcoming the forces of wickedness, that is, justification. Verses 26-30 are the close of the unit in verses 18-30. Patient endurance (v. 25) is not easy, leading Paul to turn to the Spirit's aid. Prayer is not magic, nor does it work through magical words. Is our problem due to failure to formulate the proper prayers for the situation? Certainly not! The Spirit will fill in the blanks, but we must supply those blanks. The limits imposed by human thought and speech do not apply to God's Spirit. The presence of the Spirit is one sign of the irruption of eternity into time. One meaning of "pray without ceasing" is to pray without stopping to monitor and censor our prayers.

One ground for confidence is God's goal, universal good for believers. The translation of verse 28 is disputable. The tradition represented by the NRSV is preferable. Paul did not see things through spectacles tinted pink. He was, however, confident that the powers of evil had been defeated and were losing ground. Although the apostle generally speaks of faith as human response and love as God's mode of relating to us, he writes here of human love toward God, although immediately glossing this as vocation. To acknowledge God's call is love of God.

Paul takes up his famous *climax*, the figure based upon A yields B, B yields C. . . . The object of this rhetoric is parenetic; he wishes to build his readers' confidence. The ground for that confidence is the divine drive to vindicate the human race. This is sculpted by rhetoric, but it is not verbiage. Rhetoric can be a means for shaping passion and channeling ardor. The sequential themes are vigorously religious, but they do not derive from a system nor do they provide the foundations for a system. Verse 29 indicates that, in the course of religious debate and conversation, the image of God's Son will be a future Christian possession (cf. 1 Cor. 15:49). From the anthropological perspective, Paul is somewhat pessimistic, but pessimism does not lie at the heart of his hope and thought, as this passage indicates.

From a pessimistic viewpoint predestination leads to apathy or paralysis. For Paul predestination equips believers with the confidence to confront the personal and corporate challenges of existence. Justification, God's power, is far superior to covenantal and related models. That has been the point of these four chapters, since life without a system for pleasing God and a clear framework can be more than a bit difficult. Nothing remains but a peroration. Preachers are more likely to learn from Romans 8:31-39 than to improve upon it. The passage is framed as a series of questions with answers. This is the style of the diatribe, a popular technique for producing vividness. Verses 35-39 are marked by an inclusio: Who can separate us from God's love? This addresses the covenant theme tangentially. Broken covenants produce separation.

Verse 31 states the thesis in the form of a rhetorical question. Since God is on our side, it makes no difference what the opposing team can field: an all-time dream team of baseball all-stars? Napoleon, Alexander the Great, Julius Caesar, U. S. Grant, and the Duke of Wellington? Claudette Colbert, Hedy Lamarr, and Susan Sarandon? A symphony comprised of the outstanding instrumentalists of the world? and so on. Paul assumes that he has made his point. He does not say, "If I should happen to be right, it follows that . . ." Nor, most emphatically, does he say, "If we are on God's side . . ." The thesis is that God is on our side.

Verse 32 is a supporting argument: Since God gave us the Son, will God say no to a request for a safety pin? The next verse (33) returns to the forensic framework used in Romans 1-4. One may construe verses 33-34 as two questions with answers or as four rhetorical questions. The former is somewhat preferable. "Elect" in verse 33 is unusual for Paul, selected to emphasize confidence. Verse 34 looks like a creedal formula. The one seated at the right is well placed to intercede, a link with verses 26-27. The next question presents a catalog of earthly hardships, which do not lack eschatological significance. (Love of Christ refers to Christ's love for us.) These things, verse 36 asserts, with Scripture to support it, are part of the deal. We shall win, but it will not be a walkover.

The final verses present the climactic catalog: a list of spiritual forces. Life and death can be demonic forces when they rule existence: life as something to cling to at all costs and death as a manifestation of our fallen state. The other terms are cosmic forces, the powers noted by astrology, culminating in the almost anticlimactic final word, "or any created entity," including and subsequently drubbing the varsity of every evil empire in every galaxy. Point, game, set, and match.

## Gospel
### Matthew 13:31-33, 44-52 (RCL)
### Matthew 13:44-52 or 13:44-46 (LFM)

Even the shortest of the options offers two parables. The longest is a rich harvest indeed, if you will pardon the metaphor. In addition to a staccato series of parables, the chapter provides a unique close (vv. 51-52) that sharply contrasts with Mark. Whereas in Mark the disciples never grasp the teaching of Jesus and understand less the more he teaches, Matthew's disciples *do* understand. The community's leaders, at least, are reliable. Matthew assigns high status to the "scribe," a role generally reserved for vituperation, but honored by this evangelist, whose Gospel reflects the attention to details one might expect of a learned person. The scribe in mind has been trained for the kingdom of heaven, rather than in traditional contracts and rulings. Good scribes attend to both new and old. The general ancient view was that the old is always best. Matthew knows that the new (e.g., Gentile converts) is the wave of the future and wishes to bring about the transition without driving out the old (cf. Matt. 9:17). The language is succinct, but the idea deserves lengthy reflection. The conclusion is somewhat jolting in that basically the entire chapter has worked with the categories of good and bad. Newness is implicit. One possibility is the encouragement to see the newness and presence of God's rule in mundane events.

In the context the two parables of the Mustard Seed and the Leaven (vv. 31-33) follow the narrative about the wheat intermingled with weeds. Both parables appeared in Q, but only the Mustard Seed parable in both Mark and Q. The obvious contrast is between small beginnings and grand endings, with emphasis upon the beginning (Mark), as well as growth (Q). Matthew conforms this to the unit through repetition of the introductory formula and by speaking of a man sowing seed in his field. "Field" is a leitmotif in this chapter. God's rule is manifested in both seed and bush, in being and becoming. Christologically, it would be viewed as a contrast between the humble Jesus and the glorified, all-powerful Christ. The parable evokes two miracles: the manifestation of God's rule in the infinitesimally small and its inclusiveness. Birds of all sorts find shelter.

In this parable's early form, the object was to urge people to see puny parousias, God's presence in utterly ordinary and amusingly minuscule phenomena. Big miracles are readily recognized. When Jesus told this piece, it must have shocked. Mustard is, after all, a bush, however effervescent in a season, a bush not a true tree, and an annual rather than an enduring part of the landscape. The comparison people expect is to the tree of life, a mighty growth with roots in the underworld and branches touching heaven (cf. Ezek. 17:22-24; 31:2-9; Dan. 4:10-17). The tug toward this understanding has affected the parable, but a mustard bush remains a mustard bush. The kingdom may not look like much. If God's reign is comparable to something this ephemeral, it could result in a Messiah who got killed. It also embraces a God enmeshed amid ephemera, a God who delights in popping up during nonmajestic events.

Jesus did not restrict himself to sports metaphors, metaphorically speaking. The second member of the parable pair turns to the woman's world, as the male sphere comprised the out of doors while women managed the home. Leaven is a somewhat surprising choice for an image, as it usually plays a negative role. The contrast is like the preceding, but the emphasis rests upon the hidden character of the agent. (The verb rendered "mixed" usually means "hide.") Leaven is a mysterious substance that makes dough rise. Both parables relate to growth that is both ordinary and yet mysterious. All people have experienced the touch of leavening hands. The challenge is to see in them the hand of God. Parables would seek to lead us to perceive once again with the freshness of discovery the graciousness and surprise of the ordinary, the myriads of miracles erupting in our daily lives; would lead us to see these wonders and then urge us to find the presence of God's reign in just such apparently prosaic routines. Look, our Lord says, for the advent of God in the ordinary, for appearances of the kingdom in people and deeds that seem no more important than mustard seeds and pieces of yeast.

Following a theological rationale for the use of cryptic speech and the private interpretation of the wheat and weeds (vv. 34-43), the next pair (vv. 44-46), evidently delivered to the disciples alone, propels us away from the painfully mundane to the domain of the unique and exciting. The preceding parables have been rather humdrum. These vault into the world of the folk tale.

The two little vignettes are drawn from contrasting lives: one the world of a (possibly struggling) day laborer, hired help working someone else's land, the other the arena of a wealthy and industrious merchant. The laborer was engaged in no quest. Plowing along and occupied with whatever thoughts plowers may have, perhaps dreams of wealth that would relieve him of the need to earn his bread by the sweat of his brow, the farmhand was rudely returned to reality when his plow struck a jar. Ancients often hid their money in buried jars, especially in time of war and disaster, and sometimes no one returned to claim it. Our discoverer in this case is no Boy Scout. He does not dash off to find the owner and share news of his find, in hope of some reward. Instead, he carefully conceals the evidence and, by liquidating all he can lay claim to and mortgaging his life to the eyebrows, he secures enough to purchase the field. Then the treasure is his. Out of the blue he discovered potential wealth, and he spared no energy and strained no morals to obtain it. This farmhand was not about to let a unique opportunity slip away.

The merchant, for his part, was *always* on the lookout, the quest for fine pearls. When this shrewd entrepreneur came upon a stunning example, an item that would blow the roof off of a well-advertised auction, he knew that the moment had arrived. Likewise liquidating his assets, he was able to acquire this treasure, from the sale of which he could probably buy an estate, hire laborers, and retire in luxury.

The treasure story is linked with the reference to field and the word *hidden*. This is not the story of a quest for a buried treasure, but of what to do when it has been found. The previous parables presented the kingdom as something so obvious that one might overlook it. This is the opposite. Interpreters can and should conjure up all of the sayings about seeking first the kingdom of God, seeking and finding, and the like. Something like this evokes an immediate and total response. If you would take such action for a treasure found in a field, what would you do to participate in God's dominion? "Selling all" brings to mind the calls to discipleship. Among the things one is to give up may be ideas about what is right (cf. the weeds), possibly even images of the divine (mustard bush vs. tree of life). Advent is both discovery and opportunity. As stories each begins in the wrong place—with finding, rather than (having) finding) losing, and seeking. [AQ: This still doesn't make sense; can you please rewrite?] Although they end on nearly the last page, when the boy has finally found the girl again, after he has met her and lost her, they close much too quickly. One needs a "happily ever after" in some form or another. The kingdom involves stories of a different sort.

The presence of at least two engaging parables will probably lead most preachers to set the Net (vv. 47-50) aside as a reinforcement of the Wheat and the Weeds. That it is so indicates that for Matthew the point of the community as a *corpus mixtum*, an entity inclusive of both good and bad people, was important. Fishing evokes mission (e.g., John 21:1-14). Just as the two previous parables evoked various call stories, so this recalls the vocation of the disciples.

In contrast to the weeds, this narrative does not discuss the origin of "bad" fish. They are just there. Whereas the association of harvest with judgment aided allegorical interpretation of the Wheat and the Weeds, here judgment (sorting) follows immediately upon the catch. This final parable, like the close of the Sermon on the Mount, summons one toward a decision, albeit awkwardly, in that one will hope to be a good little fish deserving a place at the table. Such lines are best left to commercials about Charlie the Tuna—in other words, know when to quit.

Some of the images will reward users of a concordance and dictionary. Among these are the sea, the fish, and, of course, the net. The last indicates that the distinction between kingdom and church is fading, but the general thrust is toward comprehensiveness and inclusion. Verse 48 makes a nice inclusio with verse 1, in that it is inartistic and obtrusive. While listeners have sat and listened, judgment has occurred.

# July 31, 2011
## Seventh Sunday after Pentecost
### Eighteenth Sunday in Ordinary Time / Proper 13

| **Revised Common Lectionary (RCL)** | **Lectionary for Mass (LFM)** |
|---|---|
| Genesis 32:22-31 or Isaiah 55:1-5 | Isaiah 55:1-3 |
| Psalm 17:1-7, 15 or 145:8-9, 14-21 | Psalm 145:8-9, 15-16, 17-18 |
| Romans 9:1-5 | Romans 8:35, 37-39 |
| Matthew 14:13-21 | Matthew 14:13-21 |

## First Reading
### Genesis 32:22-31 (RCL)

This completes the lectionary survey of Jacob/Israel's story. This section provides retardation, delaying the climactic resolution of the Jacob-Esau confrontation, but it makes that encounter all but anticlimactic. Genesis 25–36 is carefully arranged in five segments, in each of which Jacob is paired with another character. Every scene is set in a particular location. The clear counterpart to chapter 32 is chapter 28. In both cases Jacob is alone and encounters God at night. Nothing else about the passage is particularly clear. This is one reason for its attraction. Passages like this should not be read without some comment, however it is supplied.

These verses are so primitive that they are too sophisticated for most of us. The narrative outline is uncomplicated: Jacob, justifiably anxious about an encounter with the brother from whom he fled after fleecing him of birthright and blessing, is returning as a rich and generous sibling. He passes the night wrestling with a strange "man," leaving early the next day with a new name, a fresh blessing, and a limp. He had a similar experience on his first wedding night, consummating a marriage to an invisible woman (Gen. 29:23-25). Questions arise. The match is described as if such things happened regularly. "What did you do last night?" "Nothing. Oh yeah, some guy wrestled with me the whole time."

The antagonist is a male of undefined status. Brevity is added to opacity. Much of the force of this text lies in what we do not learn. It appears that the match was about even. Jacob may have won on points. The other got out of it as well as he did with a possibly magical dislocation of Jacob's hip. Questions arise, not well answered by the three two-line exchanges in verses 26-29.

The history of religions informs us that nocturnal encounters with demons were not unfamiliar. When invisible beings become visible, one needs to learn their name, which is to say their nature and purpose. If their attacks fail, humans can grasp some of their nature and power. We could have put up with such a story, but the narrative has been altered to make the rival none other than God. There is demythologizing and there is hypermythologizing. Questions arise. The match lacks a clear ending. Jacob is strong, but he does not prevail. The opponent also fails to prevail, although he can injure, supply a new name, and grant a blessing. Possession of a new name makes Jacob a new being. The new name comes equipped with an appropriate, albeit inaccurate, etymology. Israel was brought to life by a divine assault. With name and blessing the hero has acquired a bit of divine power. Ironically, the birth of Israel was accompanied by an injury to his reproductive organs, if one takes "thigh" as a euphemism. Still, it may have been worth the limp. His questionable blessing (32:11-12) has been superseded by one of unquestionable validity.

The most fundamental of all the questions is: What kind of god will get into a nighttime brawl with a mortal and come out no better than even? From the perspective of spirituality, the answer is: the kind of God we need. This passage represents the longing for contact with the divine as the highest human spiritual need. However knocked around, God does not supply a name. Mystery remains even after this most intimate of encounters. The spiritual image evoked, wrestling with God, is valid and precious. A sermon, an essay, a book could be written on the subject without exhausting more than a fraction of its surface. Anger with God is a legitimate form of spirituality. Doubters are urged to leaf through the psalter.

For the gallery of feminist theology, this unabashedly masculine tableau of two (presumably) naked guys rolling around on the ground all night is so undisputedly symbolic that even the most staunchly patriarchal of readers must concede as much and, willy-nilly, watch other pictures begin to dissolve. (Another feminist question, the use of [sexual?] assault imagery for divine encounter may be quite appropriate, but conducive to few homiletical situations, particularly because unresolved questions evade pat answers to this approach.)

For the male and female Marks and Johns and Pauls among us, this is one of the most profound representations of theological irony. For Christians it intimates the one who wrestled long into the night with God in Gethsemane and then went to an ignominious death. And more, for it is not possible to sort out victor from victim, weak from strong, profit from loss here. Power appears in weakness, but the definition of each is debatable. Not all will long for a postmodern wrestling match, but all can benefit from two lessons: less in story, sermon, and account may not be more, but it can be superior, for it leaves us room to wrestle with the material. Second, spirituality includes rolling up our sleeves (for starters) and getting our hands dirty.

### Isaiah 55:1-5 (RCL alt.)
### Isaiah 55:1-3 (LFM)

For a general discussion of the close of Deutero-Isaiah, see the first reading (RCL alt., LFM) under Proper 10. Despite the appeal of the Genesis passage for users of the RCL, this option is recommended, for it explicates the Gospel selection, not by way of background and comparison, but through emphasis upon the meaning of the feeding stories.

The selection, which effectively evokes the noises of merchants hawking food and beverages in the streets, is marked by thrice-repeated imperatives: "come" and "listen." The invitation is like that of personified Wisdom, both in form and in function, since the nourishment is metaphorical—but not exclusively so. The poet warns hearers about the dangers of spiritual junk food—a perennial problem in various forms—while evoking the utopian promises of the "messianic banquet." Those without some loaves and fishes are not in optimum condition to hear the word. The invitation climaxes in verse 3 with the promise of life. Verses 4-5 (RCL) make of David a universal model. Those fed with word and sacrament are strengthened for "witness." This is witness not only to the Christian creed, but to lives that show its power and display its fruit through kindness and charity, quests for justice and efforts for peace through serving others and, a sometimes greater challenge, accepting service from others as valuable missionaries. That meal, that message, that life are available now. Grace is free; it is not cheap.

## Psalmody
### Psalm 17:1-7, 15 (RCL)

This is an excellent psalm for those planning to wrestle with God. Verse 15 perfectly echoes the reading from Genesis. The declaration of innocence in verses 3-5 tends to offend our notions of propriety and is much the better for the offense. Victims of injustice are not rare; many believers have treated other members of the community unjustly. In these words we remember not only our own grievances, but the occasions when we have been agents of injustice, and all who have suffered unjustly.

### Psalm 145:8-9, 14-21 (RCL alt.)
### Psalm 145:8-9, 15-16, 17-18 (LFM)

For comments on this text, please see the Psalmody for Proper 9, above. This is a fine "gradual," a bridge between the reading from Isaiah and the Gospel.

## Second Reading
### Romans 9:1-5 (RCL)

This is the first of three samples from Romans 9–11, in which Paul takes up God's faithfulness. After his essays on God's righteousness and grace, the outstanding question is, If God has fulfilled the promises through Jesus, why have most Israelites not accepted this solution? Have the Jews missed the boat and doomed themselves?

No Christians can approach these questions without accepting the terrible consequences of Christendom's mistreatment of the Jewish people, climaxed by an anti-Christian horror (the Holocaust) built upon foundations Christians erected. Paul approached the theme with anguish, as do we, but with anguish generated by different circumstances. For the apostle the problem was not the inhumanity of mortals but the consistency of God.

The Gentile "yes" and the Jewish "no" are not made explicit, but they inform and motivate every element of the discussion. Paul does not view himself as an apostate. He is a loyal Jew. The running qualification to his comments is "the human (vs. the divine) perspective," in verses 3 and 5. This not very subtle qualifier exposes Paul's critique of his people: they have tended to view their privileges "humanly," rather than asking God's purposes in bestowing them. These privileges are real, but like all privileges, they can be viewed as entitlements rather than opportunities for the furtherance of God's purposes. One need not look very deeply or unusually far to discover ways in which other bodies, including the Christian church in general and our own religious bodies in particular, have not used our privileges to the best advantage.

The opening strong statements attempt to convince his audience that Paul's remorse is genuine. "Conscience" is similar in meaning to our use of the term, although Paul writes as if it possessed independent judicial status. We evaluate conscience from behavior, as when acts betray a "bad conscience." The list of privileges marks the exodus as constitutive of Israel. The items in verse 4 need not be ranked; all are of more or less equal importance, for all point to God and derive from God; that is, one cannot delete the liturgy and refine a moral code of enduring validity from Torah and end up with enduring moral and discarded ritual law. Others will make cases of that nature and Paul uses the unity of the system against them (e.g., Galatians). Ancestry comes only at the end and may indicate a lesser standing. Paul is not about to make "race" (the term is anachronistic) a requirement. Paul does imply that the Israelites have missed the boat, but—and this is important—he does not suggest that they are condemned eternally. God will use the Gentile response to prod the people.

*Notes*: The singular "covenant" is well attested in verse 4, the singular "promise" somewhat less so. Since it is difficult to argue why the singular nouns would be pluralized, the plural is more probable, although not certain. The punctuation of verse 5 is a famous crux. The syntax supports a reading that would identify Christ as "God." Paul never makes this claim elsewhere in his uncontested letters. Since calling Christ God in this context would be provocative, it is probably preferable to separate the doxology. Reflection upon what the text might mean with each of these variants will promote understanding.

## Romans 8:35, 37-39 (LFM)

For comments on this text, please see the second reading for Proper 12, above.

## Gospel
### Matthew 14:13-21 (RCL, LFM)

The context demands attention. The preceding verses (3-12) narrate the death of John the Baptizer. This places the feeding under the shadow of the Passion. The two stories share a number of parallels. These generate ironic contrasts. Examples include the two banquets, the audience, a head on a sumptuous platter versus food overflowing humble baskets, and the contrasting gifts. Herod's celebration of life leads to a death. Association with the Passion establishes a contrast between that birthday party and Jesus' Last Supper.

The feeding stories used to be classified as "nature miracles." All miracles deal with nature. Gerd Theissen's term "gift miracles" identifies their function. They show that God cares whether people have nourishment. All miracle stories have a broader application: this story means more than that, on one particular night, five thousand families of average size did not go hungry. Such applications may be called symbolic.

Parallels come from two ends of the spectrum: the exodus (cf. Rom. 9:1-5 and "wilderness" in Matt. 14:13) and the "messianic banquet" (cf. Isaiah 55). They link the story to salvation history and to eschatology. In this context one function of the feeding stories would be portrayal of Jesus as a "new Moses." Examination of the stories in Mark 4–8 allows the inference of cycles of wonders, each of which includes a water miracle (e.g., Mark 4:35-41) and a feeding story. Such cycles portrayed the Christian journey as a glorious triumph, initiated in baptism and sustained in the Eucharist. The sacramental and social elements of the feeding stories are mutually reinforcing.

The eucharistic connection is apparent in the fourfold (take, break, bless, and share) formulae (Matt. 14:19). This establishes a link to the Last Supper, strengthened by the evangelists through the context. In their earlier setting the feedings were not associated with the death of Jesus. A vital question is whether the feeding stories symbolize the Eucharist or does the Eucharist symbolize the miraculous meals? Early and enduring controversies (1 Cor. 11:20-32; 14) note discrepancies among those with more and fewer resources and leisure. The position of the poor would have been "Let's pool all our resources and give all an equal share." That solution is represented in the feeding of the five thousand. Those lacking food would have little difficulty interpreting this story. The body of the faithful is assembled around Jesus in worship. His disciples (i.e., subsequent leaders) propose that Jesus get rid of these creatures so that they might enjoy a fine and undisturbed meal (cf. 1 Cor. 11:34). Jesus does not disagree. He directs them to feed the people. The point is that this is part of their pastoral role.

Jesus does not say, "Don't worry; I'll take care of it," or "My repertoire of powers includes the miraculous multiplication of loaves. Healings are not the only thing I do, you know." Rather than promise to feed the people and ease their need, he tells the *disciples* to take care of it. This astonishes those worthies, who quickly retaliate with the inventory they have quite properly made before undertaking their mission. Like many of us, they think initially only of difficulties. The cupboard is nearly bare:

"We have nothing *here* but five loaves and two fish."

"Bring them *here* to me," replies Jesus.

Those two "heres" constitute the pivot and hinge of this story. For the disciples "here" is merely the unpromising place in which they find themselves, the empty wilderness. To Jesus "here" is the possibility of grace. Matthew simply ignores their objections and the circumstantial details. The focus is upon the dialogue. The resources total seven items, a number overflowing with symbolic value. After the appropriate acts Jesus gives the disciples the loaves. They in turn distribute them to the crowd. (Matthew drops the fish.) Jesus has shown his disciples how to feed the people.

One characteristic feature of these stories is that the miracle is neither narrated nor even recognized (cf. John 2:1-12). From these five loaves five thousand families were fed, and really fed. The verb in verse 20 means to eat to one's heart's content. Note its metaphorical use in the beatitude of Matthew 5:6. The utopian, messianic element is manifest in the pigging out of the multitude that still left a dozen baskets brimming with leftovers. The final number is a good trick of miracle stories. Only at the climax do readers learn that more than thirty, more than sixty, more than one hundred families, in fact *five thousand* families were nourished. A thriving urban house church of Matthew's era might include fifty families. Five thousand would fill an amphitheater, overflowing many. This was the messianic banquet for sure. That banquet was not just something to dream about on hungry days. It was a model for the present and a challenge to community leaders.

Food supply was a major problem for ancient cities, not to mention countrysides that might be stripped to feed urban mobs. One obligation of cities was to provide, through the generosity of the wealthy, grain at more or less affordable prices. The largest city was Rome and the chief benefactor the emperor. Eligibility criteria for donations and subsidized grain existed and were contested. In short, the people who told stories like the feeding of the five thousand knew something about food fights and looked to their leaders for relief.

One of Matthew's contributions is to place this story within the context of healing (v. 14). Hunger is a disease that generates compassion and motivates healing (cf. Rev. 22:2). Hunger is a social illness that Jesus shows his disciples how to cure. All are to be healed; all fed. All of this can be summed up in familiar words that follow the Great Thanksgiving: "Give us today our daily bread." Bread for me is a personal matter, perhaps also a spiritual matter. Bread for others is a social and economic issue.

When confronted with the needs of our world, we often react like those disciples in Matthew, seeing only problems, not potential. Needy creatures that we are, we can be overwhelmed by the needs of others and long for someone to send them away, so that they will not bother us, so that we can meditate in tranquility and pray in peace. The history of social problems in our land and personal issues in our own families and within our own souls strongly and urgently refutes this solution. Problems do not disappear just because we try to banish them from our sight.

Our power comes from that capacity, inspired by word and sacrament, to stand outside of ourselves and our surroundings, to see from a supernatural perspective, to be free of the bonds of social custom and the prison of political wisdom, free to be able to see more than problems and obstacles, the hungry mobs and ailing masses of humanity. The presence of Christ makes here the place for grace and for action, now the time to feed others because we have been fed.

Here is also the "wilderness." Ancients, like moderns, often envisioned the wilderness as close to God, a region uncluttered by the effects of civilization and its problems. In the Bible the forty years of wilderness wandering by the liberated Israelites is viewed as a kind of ideal and magic time. It was also a time of infestation of plagues and sin, nor should one forget that out there in the country God set up and ran a soup kitchen that served 100 percent of the population for an entire generation. To get close to God is also to get close to suffering and hunger—and solutions to them. Whenever we eat the bread of heaven and drink the cup of salvation, we return in some mysterious and inexpressible way to the wilderness there to find ourselves briefly swept beyond the bonds that limit us, joining with angels and archangels and with all the company of heaven in an endless celebration. Therein lies the power of the church to influence society. Our strength does not reside in particular platforms or programs, for Christians endorse and support many conflicting philosophies. Our power resides in our ability to reject the notion that we should get rid of these people, these problems, these concerns. Jesus does not ask what we have. He says of what we have, "Bring them here to me." And the rest is more than history, more than fantasy.

# August 7, 2011
## Eighth Sunday after Pentecost
### Nineteenth Sunday in Ordinary Time / Proper 14

**Revised Common Lectionary (RCL)**

Genesis 37:1-4, 12-28 or 1 Kings 19:9-18
Psalm 105:1-6, 16-22, 45b or 85:8-13
Romans 10:5-15
Matthew 14:22-33

**Lectionary for Mass (LFM)**

1 Kings 19:9a, 11-13a
Psalm 85:9a + 10, 11-12, 13-14
Romans 9:1-5
Matthew 14:22-33

## First Reading
### Genesis 37:1-4, 12-28 (RCL)

The story of Joseph (Genesis 37–50) provides the bridge over which the ancestral narrative crosses into the collective story of Israel in Egypt. Joseph's own story foreshadows the bondage of Israel in Egypt. The story has been that of a family, an extended, perhaps hyperextended, can-of-worms family. Problems have come from within the family. External oppression will replace internal oppression in Exodus. The former is far preferable. Although we prefer our problems to come from others, history indicates that their origin is often closer to home, frequently as close as ourselves. All of those insights, easy to affirm and difficult to accept, are in this story.

Although inconsistencies indicate the existence of different sources, this material is not an assembly of originally independent episodes, nor does it resemble a collection of short stories. The Joseph material is rather too complex to be called a novella. Formally it resembles a short novel and shows affinities to works like Tobit. If earlier portions of the ancestral narrative portrayed God writing straight with crooked lines, here the divine hand becomes so fine that it seems invisible. The touch of providence emerges only in retrospect and through interpretation. Dreams are prophetic, to be sure, but they need show no more than the immutability of fate. This view of providence is not uncongenial to modern sensibilities. The Gospel text presents, by way of contrast, a full-fledged theophany.

This opening episode deals with the fall of a favored son. Jacob, the old rogue, has grown sentimental in his advanced maturity. He has picked a favorite, not the eldest. It worked for him, why not for Joseph? The lad does not initially win our hearts. He is a little snitch. Furthermore, he has a dream of power and shares it with his family. Omission of this dream (vv. 5-11) alters the story. A literary function of dreams like this is to foreshadow, in indirect and elusive ways, the subsequent plot. The second dream reinforces the first. The dreams were of divine origin and indicated preeminence for Joseph. Because dreams of this nature were tools for understanding the future, failure to report them—an omission that we should regard as prudent—is unthinkable. The entire family is revolted, although Jacob takes note of the matter.

Motivation for sibling enmity is building. To these blows Jacob adds the insult of endowing Joseph with a gorgeous outfit. Clothes like these marked their wearer as a person of leisure and high status. He is a petit prince, a little Lord Fauntleroy ahead of his time. Jealousy bursts into flames.

Possibly in an evidently unwise effort to patch things up among the siblings, Jacob sends this spoiled brat on an errand for which he is neither well equipped nor appropriately dressed. Verses 12-17 provide retardation, but eventually his brothers catch sight of Joseph and their rage explodes. Reuben and Judah suggest means to avoid the stigma of fratricide, keeping the plot at a boil. (The doublets probably represent different sources.) In the end Joseph has been sold, for two-thirds of the price that Jesus would elicit, and shipped off for servitude in Egypt. The lectionary selection ends before the brothers concoct proof of Joseph's demise and reduce his father to abject mourning.

The story of Joseph exhibits elements of the pattern of the righteous sufferer that will influence the shape of the Passion narrative and invite many to find christological parallels. Thus far it has told of one exalted and then thrust down into the pit of degradation. Vindication will come. These stories make good reading and teach that God is the amply endowed soprano who will not end the story before the final aria. Providence means that hope remains, even at the direst moments.

The particular manifestation of hope in this story is the dream. Joseph is not just a dreamer. He is inspired with power to forecast the future. On the surface his brothers wish to kill him. In fact, they want to kill the dream. Readers ought to be ambivalent about Joseph's dreams at the beginning. By the conclusion of this material, however, they will be on his side. He has been stripped of all—the robe is a fine symbol—but the dream. For the oppressed, to which category our hero now belongs, dreams are power, for they point to change. What counts most is not status or favor but possession of that dream, not an opiate but a weapon, not an escape but a key to the prison door.

I Kings 19:9-18 (RCL alt.)
I Kings 19:9a, 11-13a (LFM)

This selection, if less brilliant than the reading from Jonah 2 in the Book of Common Prayer lectionary, complements the Gospel as a story of a struggling believer. Elijah and Peter are both on the biblical A-list, but even they have their moments of despair. For Elijah this story plays against his rather vigorous stand against the hundreds of rival prophets on Mt. Carmel (1 Kings 18), where he also claimed to be the only one left (v. 22).

Another obvious parallel is to the experience of Moses, who utilized "the cave" to protect himself from divine glory (Exod. 33:22-23). Elijah, however, is on the lam from an angry monarch. As in the earlier account, the repertory of theophanic symbols is produced. (In the background are the characteristics of the theophany of a storm god on a mountain, long demythologized.) Wind, earthquake, and fire appear, but God does not put in an appearance after any of them. Then comes something less. The NRSV's captivating "sound of sheer silence" is a guess that may improve upon the venerable "still small voice." Elijah responds to this "sound" and goes to the mouth of the cave, face reverently wrapped.

Cecil B. DeMille could teach God nothing about getting an audience's attention. Before all of the *son et lumière,* "the word of the LORD" had arrived, not to issue a charge, but to ask a question, "What are you doing here, Elijah?" (v. 9). After the full range of special effects, a voice asks, "What are you doing here, Elijah?" (v. 13). The thundering prelude has apparently accomplished nothing. The question stands; Elijah quivers. Even great prophets can burn out. God may agree, for Elijah is commissioned, charged to send in a new team, two new kings and a prophet in his own place. The use of triplets in this passage is quite effective, climaxing in verse 17.

Oh, there is one other matter. Elijah is not quite so isolated as he imagined. Seven thousand faithful people remain. Any number beginning with seven is propitious; seven thousand is large *and* propitious. Elijah is not the only person who has ever imagined that he was isolated and alone against the world. God does not mind our complaints, but we are never so alone as we imagine, and having God on one's side is not a little something, although, and this is the main point: those almost imperceptible somethings—shall we call them "mustard seeds"?—may be just where the Most High is to be found.

## Psalmody
### Psalm 105:1-6, 16-22, 45b (RCL)

For general comments on Psalm 105, please see the Psalmody for Proper 12, above. This selection will be chosen if the reading from Genesis is followed, as verses 16-22 summarize the story of Joseph.

Psalm 85:8-13 (RCL alt.)
Psalm 85:9a + 10, 11-12, 13-14 (LFM)

> Psalm 85 begins as a lament for the nation followed by an oracle. The selections derive from the latter. The leitmotifs of land, peace, steadfastness, righteousness, and salvation permeate this psalm, which climaxes with a series of bold and beloved images.

## Second Reading
### Romans 10:5-15 (RCL)

> The general framework is Paul's reflections on why Israel has generally said no to the proffer of salvation through Jesus Christ (Romans 9–11). His general answer is that they will ultimately say yes, but that their initial negative means the possibility of a Gentile "yes." The selection omits the first four verses, which should be perused as an aid to interpretation. The final two verses belong to a subsequent section, but follow well upon the preceding declaration.
>
> Paul's reflections utilize, in rabbinic fashion, a series of quotations from Scripture, centered upon Deuteronomy 30:11-14. The apostle seeks to push the meaning of the Torah in a fresh direction, since the Deuteronomist argued that the Torah was not too difficult to fulfill, while Paul applies these verses to Christ. The language of ascent and descent reverberates with much ancient thought, for descending and ascending gods conveyed salvation, while some mortals made the journey to the other world. For Paul such striving transforms salvation into a human enterprise. We cannot get God's attention, compel God to love us, through our behavior. Paul stresses the accessibility of the message, which can be discovered without an epic quest.
>
> After glossing "the word" as the message of salvation by faith, Paul invokes an apparent early baptismal creed (cf. 1 Cor. 12:3) in support of his case. Verse 10 seeks to correct the notion that repetition of a verbal formula suffices. Belief comes from the heart; what begins in the heart will result in action. The theme of belief generates another scriptural affirmation, issuing in the declaration that one God rules and thus is open to all people. Good rhetoric can help inspire good preaching.
>
> Verse 13 initiates the famous climax, the charter of and warrant for evangelism. The closing quote from Isaiah 52:7 in verse 15 employs a surprising (to us) synecdoche: feet. The passage that opened with disparagement of using one's feet for excursions to heaven or hell ends with a macarism upon . . . evangelistic feet. Many readers would expect a blessing upon mouths, in keeping with the verbal orientation of this passage. Beautiful words are one thing, beautiful feet another. It is not likely that Paul's focus is aesthetic, that he is waxing eloquent over shapely feet. The most recurrent image in these verses is not the mouth, but the heart (vv. 6. 8, 9, 10). "Heart and hands" is a common phrase, something of a hendiadys: compassionate, committed hands. "Heart and feet" generates a fresh perspective. Hands indicate action, feet motion, the journey of the people of faith, a journey made by redeemed

people with beautiful feet, people who not only talk the talk but also walk the walk. This image of feet will walk us right into the Gospel.

### Romans 9:1-5 (LFM)

For comment on this text, please see the second reading (RCL) for Proper 13, above.

## Gospel
### Matthew 14:22-33 (RCL, LFM)

This is a story no less charming and vivid than it is primitive and complex. Here there is room for a child to wade and an elephant to swim. We shall make the most of it by embracing both the trusting child and the wise elephant. One way to grasp its mystery and its majesty is to envision a cinematic depiction of the scene. The result would make most honest adults titter. This is an epiphany and shares with the reading from 1 Kings the response of a frightened disciple to divine revelation.

Matthew has transformed the source in Mark 6:45-52 through the insertion of verses 28-31 (and by replacing Mark 6:52 with a new, positive ending). Mark quite probably took the passage from a collection of wonders that presented Christ as the leader of a new exodus. Two editions of this cycle were evidently in circulation, each of which included a miracle at sea and a miraculous feeding. This story was, however, different from that of Mark 4:35-41. It was an appearance—probably the first—of the risen Lord, who appeared to his disciples on the water (cf. Luke 5:1-11; John 21:1-14). Stories in which the risen one could be mistaken for a ghost or other person (cf. John 21:1-14; Luke 24:13-35; Ignatius, *Smyrn.* 3.1-3) tended to be relocated or altered. Background coloration comes in part from depictions of God or Wisdom walking upon or moving through the water (cf. Isa. 43:16; Job 9:8; 38:16; Sir. 24:5; Wis. 10:15-21). A Wisdom Christology lies in the background.

Comparisons to the exodus spring rightly to mind. In early Christianity baptismal applications were common, as can be found in some of the early Christian hymns called the *Odes of Solomon*, notably *Ode* 39. Other important images include the sea as a symbol of chaos, of hostility to God, as well as the storm at sea as both the epiphany of a god and a symbol of danger and attack, and, last but not least, the image of the church as a boat, which, if not hinted in Mark 4:35-41, is patent in Matthew's adaptation of that story (8:23-27). Much of the background can be placed in the file labeled "Easter power." The storm motif gives the added fillip of a rescue miracle. Even without the demons, water continues to possess the capacity to remind us, through its rapid changes, that much of life and nature is uncanny.

Following the feeding (last week) Jesus sends the disciples across the lake and ascends "the mountain" to pray. "The mountain," unnamed, evokes both Moses and Elijah. With darkness comes wind (cf. 2 Kings 19), against which the boat can make little progress. (The verb rendered "battered" in v. 24 is used of demonic activity: Matt. 8:6, 29; Rev. 9:5; et al.) The fourth watch covers the time from 3:00 to 6:00 a.m., adding the kind of detail that lends veracity, indicating how long the poor disciples had been struggling, and setting the encounter in the early light of Easter discovery. The sight of this apparition ambling across the stormy water terrified the storm-tossed disciples, who concluded that a malevolent ghost was about to add to their miseries, if not put them out of the same. (On such ghosts see Matt. 14:1-2.) Jesus' encouragement is typical. The "I am" is as powerful as epiphanic announcements get. The corresponding response of believers is "you are" (as in the hymn *Te Deum*), a formula found in verses 28 and 31. Under pressure the church may believe that the Lord is absent. In Matthew Christ is with us always (28:20).

Verses 28-31 are typically Matthean, a didactic story with a message comprehensible to all. It is also amusing. Peter's demand is less a test than a recognition that the appearance of Christ empowers, that Christ's epiphany sets us free to practice our faith without fear. "Walk" is an ethical term referring to a manner of living. Believers walk amid the billows of chaos and the winds of wickedness. The doubt in view is not creedal, but that lack of trust and confidence that allows us to be overwhelmed. Still there is the gentle healing hand for those who pray, a hand that leads Peter back into the boat. The episode closes with an unabashed christological confession and obeisance of all. Whereas Mark emphasized the lack of understanding (Mark 6:52), Matthew stresses their positive reaction.

Peter left the boat to get closer to Jesus, a fine sentiment, if not a terribly bright idea, not least for a fisherman. God, however, rescued this now better-educated worthy and leaves him to us as a useful example and pattern for faith: stay on the boat, or, should you find yourself overboard, start praying. Or so it seems. One infelicity of this position is that God is not the kind of perfect lifeguard we should like to be on constant duty.

The very presumption that one ought to stay on the boat is open to question. The presence of Christ gave Peter the chance to take a risk. His little promenade, hesitant and stumbling as it is, presents us with a marvelously vivid and *honest* picture of the life of faith. The presence of Christ in our lives *does* give us the courage to move in some improbable directions and to take some significant chances, even to look more than a little stupid and utterly foolish. There is probably no day in our lives when we do not have the opportunity to walk on water, to venture away from the familiar and secure toward the unknown, to walk in faith, to walk by the Spirit.

We should like to believe that the God who invites us to take risks also promises us that we shall never find ourselves over our heads. That is not faith. Faith emerges when we are in over our heads. The position of "little faith" is that to be in over our heads is failure. It is not. Jumping in without looking is not faith; it is idiocy. Never taking a risk, never going beyond our depth leaves us without knowledge of what we may accomplish. The only real failure would be to give in to that fear which holds us back in the boat, the fear which keeps us from seeing that Christ appears in the midst of darkness to set us free. The call of our Lord does not lead us first to the safety of a boat or to the warmth of the shore, but into the depth and midst of that mysterious and ambiguous sea, the realm in which we live.

# Time after Pentecost / Ordinary Time
## Propers 15 through 22

### S. D. Giere

These next eight weeks bring us from the doldrums of Ordinary Time (aka the dog days of summer) into what is for many the beginning of the program year in the parish. For many parishes in both Canada and the United States, the passing of Labor Day (the first Monday in September; in 2011 following Proper 18, on September 5) means a shift from a summer to a fall schedule. Among other things, this shift often means that worship attendance swells. It often means that many activities, groups, and programs within the parish ramp up after the more relaxed summer schedule. It means that Sunday school rooms begin to buzz with students and teachers telling, learning, and engaging our collective Christian story.

It is a strange convergence of the ecclesial, solar, and civic calendars.

In some places the Sunday after Labor Day is called Rally Sunday. This is interesting, given the primary sense of the word *rally*, which, according to the *Oxford English Dictionary*, is "a rapid reunion for concentrated effort, *esp.* of an army after repulse or disorganization."[1] With a faint bugle call playing somewhere over the horizon, this convergence of calendars marks a rallying point. In what is in many places a de facto beginning of a second church year—the program year—clergy, parish workers, and committees call people back to church, to participation in the life together that we share as Christians. As people return from vacations and students return to school, the "forces" are recalled to the assembly. Anyone for a rousing rendition of "Onward, Christian Soldiers"?

This particular Rally Sunday marks the ten-year anniversary of the Al Qaeda attacks on the World Trade Center and the Pentagon on September 11, 2001. It would be inappropriate, it seems, to sing such a song as our rallying cry on this somber anniversary. In point of fact, the lessons for that Sunday coalesce around threads of release, forgiveness, and community *in Christ*. The Gospel lesson for that Sunday, in particular, speaks of a divine forgiveness that is lavishly imprudent *and* that we Christians are called to emulate, if only imperfectly. While the first and second readings provide the preacher rich and interesting texts when juxtaposed with this anniversary, the parable of the unforgiving slave on this rallying Sunday provides an interesting mirror for us Christians (and preachers!) to look into.

And so, what should we sing on such a rallying day? Perhaps Harry Emerson Fosdick's twentieth-century hymn "God of Grace and God of Glory" should be our collective songful prayer for this day. Emerson captures well our impulse to run contrary to the divine will, contrary to God's kingdom, as we hear in verses 2 and 3:

> Lo! The hosts of evil round us
> Scorn the Christ, assail his ways!
> From the fears that long have bound us
> Free our hearts to faith and praise.
> Grant us wisdom, grant us courage
> For the living of these days,
> For the living of these days.
>
> Cure your children's warring madness;
> Bend our pride to your control;
> Shame our wanton, selfish gladness,
> Rich in things and poor in soul.
> Grant us wisdom, grant us courage,
> Lest we miss your kingdom's goal,
> Lest we miss your kingdom's goal.[2]

With all the divisions and strife in the world—between nations and people, in cities and towns, in parishes and families—on this day of rallying with its particular anniversary, what else can we pray but "Grant us wisdom, grant us courage"? And for what? That we might forgive as we have been forgiven, for such is the kingdom of heaven (Matt. 18:23).

So amid this convergence of calendars, the strange annual phenomenon of a rallying Sunday and this particular remembrance of a hurt- and sorrow-filled day ten years past, the proclamation of the Word goes on. For uninterrupted through the movement of all calendars and through all the upheavals in the church's history in the world the church's mission remains—to proclaim the gospel and administer the sacraments—the identifiable marks of Christ's church and its mission.

## Notes

1. James A. H. Murray, ed., *The New English Dictionary on Historical Principles* (10 vols.; Oxford: Clarendon, 1888–1926), 8:126.
2. Harry Emerson Fosdick, "God of Grace and God of Glory," in *Evangelical Lutheran Worship* (Minneapolis: Augsburg Fortress, 2006), #705.

# August 14, 2011
## Ninth Sunday after Pentecost
### Twentieth Sunday in Ordinary Time / Proper 15

**Revised Common Lectionary (RCL)**

Genesis 45:1-15 or Isaiah 56:1, 6-8

Psalm 133 or 67

Romans 11:1-2a, 29-32

Matthew 15:(10-20), 21-28

**Lectionary for Mass (LFM)**

Isaiah 56:1, 6-7

Psalm 67:2-3, 5, 6 + 8

Romans 11:13-15, 29-32

Matthew 15:21-28

## First Reading
### Genesis 45:1-15 (RCL)

The story of Joseph begins with jealousy and betrayal and comes to a climax[1] in this theologically packed moment of reconciliation and preservation. To think through this pericope, I suggest reviewing chapters 37–44 to see the longer narrative arc. Suspense has been building since the beginning of Genesis 42. Famine reaches the land of Canaan, the land of Joseph's family. With one of the most amusing lines in Scripture, Jacob, the father of the twelve tribes of Israel, aware that he needs to provide, looks around at his sons and asks, "Why do you keep looking at one another?" (42:1). The implication is simply, "Do something!" And to Egypt he sends them. They go looking for sustenance, not knowing that the brother they hated and betrayed into slavery, the brother they assume died so many years before, would be their savior.

Through trials and testing and Joseph's seeming desire for revenge,[2] Joseph's anonymous encounters with his brothers prove to him that there has been a change. Judah's willingness to give himself into slavery to spare their father the absence of his dear Benjamin is Joseph's evidence.

Joseph's story erupts with uncontrollable emotion, the shouting so loud that the Egyptians could hear and the news of the incident reached Pharaoh's palace. Yet, after all these years, his words to his brothers are simple. "I am Joseph. Is my father still alive?" (45:3). The brothers' response is terser still. So flummoxed are they by this revelation that they are dumbstruck. Against all odds, what transpires is a tear-drenched reconciliation and embrace of brothers long separated.

Interesting in the midst of this is Joseph's theologizing. Not underplaying his brother's actions, Joseph sees this moment as a culmination of God's activity. "I am your brother, Joseph, whom you sold into Egypt. And now do not be distressed, or angry with yourselves, because you sold me here; for God sent me before you to preserve life" (45:4b-5; cf. 50:20 [Proper 19, below]). This statement frames what comes before it and (perhaps less intentionally so) what follows.

Jacob's favoritism, along with the brothers' ensuing jealousy and hatred and Joseph's movement by way of his gift of dreams from the rank of slave to that of governor of Egypt, culminates in Joseph's ability and willingness to bring them all to Egypt to avoid starvation in Canaan. What follows are good times for the Israelites in the land of Egypt. But it is also written, "Now a new king arose over Egypt, who did not know Joseph" (Exod. 1:8). Thus, Joseph's story sets the story of the Israelites on its trajectory toward the exodus.

From within this narrative, but also as if sitting back looking at the larger scope, Joseph witnesses to God's activity woven together with human actions, traditionally understood as concurrnce.[3] While it is his brothers' despicable actions that land him in Egypt, at the same time God's action and its purpose are to "preserve life."

## Isaiah 56:1, 6-8 (RCL alt.)
## Isaiah 56:1, 6-7 (LFM)

The Lord God, "who gathers the outcasts of Israel," has expansive designs for the gathering of God's people—designs that culminate in the grand proclamation, "For my house shall be called a house of prayer *for all peoples*" (56:7b)—designs that open God's favor to those beyond even the outcasts of Israel.

That said, the way that the pericope is partitioned partially blunts its full impact. Isaiah 56:1-8 is clearly a whole that addresses those excluded from the Lord's house. More specifically, the text takes up, and the pericope excludes, the enigmatic case of eunuchs and foreigners, outsiders by cultic definition, who keep the Sabbath and observe the Lord's covenant with Israel (vv. 3b-5). Also left out is the deliberate connection between maintaining justice, doing what is right, and the Lord's deliverance and keeping the Sabbath (v. 2). This proportioning can and should be reconsidered by those preaching on this text.

This text represents a dynamic and radical inner-biblical reinterpretation of who is in and who is out of the Lord's chosen. While the worldview of Deutero-Isaiah frequently challenges other texts in the Old Testament, the worldview in this pericope meets these texts head-on.

The text is framed with the Lord's imperatives and promises: "Maintain justice, and do what is right, for soon my salvation will come, and my deliverance be revealed" (v. 1). In a real way what follows indicates this salvation and reveals the deliverance.

"Happy is the mortal" who keeps the Sabbath and does not do evil. The Hebrew word for "mortal," 'enosh, has no cultic or religious connotation. It is not connected to the chosen people. This declaration is for all.[4] The Sabbath is not Israel's to own and to control. It is the Lord's,[5] and it is open to all.

What follows are two specific examples of this: eunuchs and foreigners. While there is some ambiguity about eunuchs—some were "proper" eunuchs with their boy bits crushed and/or missing, and others were "functional" eunuchs sworn to sexual abstinence—Isaiah 56 is certainly speaking about proper eunuchs, who would be excluded from the assembly of the Lord and therefore the temple (cf. Deut. 23:1; see also Jer. 38:7-13; 39:15-18; Acts 8:26-40). Verses 3b-5, however, stand in tension with the exclusion that is elsewhere proscribed. For eunuchs who keep the Lord's Sabbath and who hold fast to the covenant, much is promised: inclusion in the Lord's house and a name better than son or daughter—a name that is everlasting and unable to be cut off (pun intended!). In short, in spite of the fact that Scripture and the community exclude, the Lord here privileges faithfulness and therefore restoration and inclusion.

Likewise, foreigners who are faithful and keep the Sabbath are no longer outsiders but lavishly included. Excluded from celebration of the Passover (Exod. 12:43), from participation in the eschatological temple (Ezek. 44:6b-9), and later literally of foreign wives and children (Ezra 10:3; cf. Neh. 9:2), foreigners had only the most limited access to the temple by way of the Court of Gentiles, the outermost court, more a marketplace than worship space. The picture in Deutero-Isaiah, however, is quite different.

The foreigners who join themselves to the Lord, love the Lord's name, are the Lord's servants, and keep the Sabbath will be gathered by the Lord to the holy mountain to participate joyfully and fully in prayer and sacrifice. In a real sense, this proclamation of God's people fulfills the Lord's designs for the world. For, presumably without their prayer and sacrifice, humanity's (recall 'enosh) veneration of the Lord would be incomplete.

As Christian Scripture, it is important to note that in the Synoptic Gospels, when Jesus cleanses the temple, he teaches on Isaiah 56:7b, though it is only Mark who includes the clarifying "for all peoples" (Matt. 21:13; Mark 11:17; Luke 19:46; all coupled with Jer. 7:11, "But you have made it a den of robbers"). And just as important is the alignment of the expansive nature of Isaiah 56:1-8 with Jesus' own practice of expanding the vision of the kingdom of God.

# Psalmody
## Psalm 133 (RCL)

In a world and a church rife with division and disunity, the singing[6] of and preaching from Psalm 133 may be most needed. "Behold how sweet and pleasant it is that brothers and sisters live together in unity!" (my trans.). As an abstract concept this statement is amorphous and has had many different incarnations in the course of both human and ecclesial history. Throughout the last five hundred plus years of Western church history, Christians have found many, many reasons to break unity with one another. Yet, when we are so eager to split over our "righteous" differences, how do we wrestle with this bold claim by the psalmist about sweet and pleasant unity?

The psalmist provides us two similes with which to compare this living together in unity. The first is a priestly (but messy!) image of precious oil cascading from the head of Aaron down over his beard and robes that recalls the holy oil used for anointing (Exod. 30:22-33; see also Exod. 29:1-9) and imparts the notion of consecration, of being made holy (cf. Lev. 19:2).

Second, the sweetness and pleasantness of living together in unity "is like the dew of Hermon, which falls on the mountains of Zion" (v. 3a). If we understand this in a purely locative sense, Mt. Hermon is the collection of snowcapped peaks marking the boundary between Israel/Palestine and Syria. Assuming this is a geographical reference to the area of Jerusalem, perhaps the simile suggests that as the snowcapped mountains to the north share their moisture with the arid mountains around/of Jerusalem, so is the blessing of this brotherly unity.[7]

The poem concludes with a grand theological proclamation. The reference of the "for there" (*ki' sham*) that begins verse 3b can be either (1) the mountains of Zion or, more likely, (2) living together in unity, given the two similes. The grand theological proclamation, then, is that in this sweet and pleasant living together in unity the Lord has ordained the blessing of life forevermore. But one might ask a speculatively dangerous question rooted in this psalm: "What does the Lord God think of Christianity's penchant for disunity?"

## Psalm 67 (RCL alt.)
## Psalm 67:2-3, 5, 6 + 8 (LFM)

Psalm 67 begins and ends with invocations of God's grace and blessing[8] with a clearly expected outcome—that the Lord's way and saving power may be known throughout the world (v. 2). Akin to the call to God's people to be a light to the nations in Deutero-Isaiah (chaps. 40–55), Psalm 67 proclaims the ubiquitous nature of God's grace. The hortatory call to the whole world is a call to worship. With the staccato of the *hiphil* in verses 3 and 5, the psalm calls all peoples to praise God together. This praise is not empty, gum-flapping praise. The gladness and joyful singing of the world are rooted in God's equitable judging and guidance of all the nations of the earth.

A question comes out of this, however. Where do we see such guidance? For all the chaos, trouble, and violence in the world, God's involvement is not clear. The psalm, rather, projects a world that is as yet still coming into being. What consolation is there for us who do not yet fully see? "The earth has yielded its increase; God, our God, has blessed us" (v. 6). As the seeds sprout and grow and yield the produce of the land, so our vision of this blessing, this knowing, this praise of God is sustained, and we are nourished as we move forward into God's future.

## Second Reading
### Romans 11:1-2a, 29-32 (RCL)
### Romans 11:13-15, 29-32 (LFM)

Central to this section of Paul's letter to the Romans (chaps. 9–11) is his understanding of God's mercy in relation to the people of Israel, the descendants of Abraham and God's chosen people, and to the Gentiles, those outside God's covenant with Abraham. God's mercy is at the heart of this chapter. *But . . .* There is a big "but" here because it is not a namby-pamby mercy like the fake whipped cream that comes out of an aerosol can. God's mercy, especially regarding the relationship of Israel and the Gentiles to God, is, as Paul says, a mystery (11:25).

The lectionary leaves out what, especially since the Shoah/Holocaust, is between uncomfortable and repulsive. While Paul says clearly that "all Israel will be saved" (v. 26), the verse immediately prior to the second half of these pericopes and the proper beginning of the sentence (!) is as follows: "As regards the gospel they are enemies of God for your sake; but as regards election they are beloved, for the sake of their ancestors. . . ." Then to verse 29, ". . . for the gifts and the calling of God are irrevocable."

Recall Paul's question at the outset of the chapter, "I ask, then, has God rejected his people? By no means!" (v. 1). And again from earlier in Romans, "What if some [Jews] were unfaithful? Will their faithlessness nullify the faithfulness of God? By no means!" (3:3-4a). What is clear here is that we humans, Jews and Gentiles, are all unfaithful. What is clearer here is that it is God alone who is faithful.

Paul, himself a Jew, is not being anti-Jewish and/or anti Semitic (which certainly does not mean that the church has not been so over the centuries). Paul's iteration of the mystery reaches a climax in verse 32, "For God has imprisoned *all* in disobedience so that he may be merciful to all." In the end it is not about Jew or Gentile; it is about God. It is about God and God's mercy, rooted in the seriousness of our collective and individual human disobedience. At this point, Karl Barth is right in pointing to Luther's words: "Take to heart this great text. By it the whole righteousness of the world and of men is damned: by it the righteousness of God is alone exalted, the righteousness of God which is by faith."[9]

## Gospel
### Matthew 15:(10-20), 21-28 (RCL)
### Matthew 15:21-28 (LFM)

The focus of the following comments is on the story of Jesus' encounter with the Canaanite woman (vv. 21-28). While there may be some real connections between this story and the conclusion of Jesus' interchange with the Pharisees and scribes about the "traditions of the fathers" (vv. 1-9), as well as with the broader crowd regarding issues of defilement (vv. 10-20), the knock-your-socks-off story of the Canaanite woman[10] has plenty of homiletical fodder for a collection of sermons.

The setting of the story is in the district of Tyre and Sidon. From Gennesaret and the northwestern shores of the Sea of Galilee (14:34), Jesus and the disciples have pushed deeper into Gentile lands, in particular the lands known then as Phoenicia. While earlier in Matthew's Gospel Jesus suggests that the lands of Tyre and Sidon are better off than some other Gentile cities (11:21-22), the setting of the story and the fact that the unnamed woman at the center of the story is identified as a Canaanite provide the narrative and theological backbone of this encounter.[11] For the questions that encircle this story remain germane today: For whom did Jesus come? Or for whom is God's mercy and love?

With a liturgical and confessional force unmatched by "the faithful" around Jesus, the Canaanite woman approaches Jesus in desperation. While the word order in Greek is different, the punch is roughly the same as the global Christian community's weekly cry: *kyrie eleison*—Lord, have mercy! The Canaanite woman, however, is even more precise: "Have mercy on me, Lord, Son of David!" Worshiping (?) at the top of her lungs, she reveals her desperation: ". . . my daughter is tormented by a demon!" Her raucous prayer is rooted in the concrete reality that her daughter, her flesh and blood, is not well. From Jesus she seeks help.

And what does Jesus do? He apparently ignores her. In spite of her faithful cry, Jesus' first response is silence (though the disciples' response is even worse insofar as they seek to remove her like an annoying fly). And then, when it appears the disregard shown for this poor, hurting parent has hit a low point, she and Jesus have an interchange wherein we hear the reason for Jesus' silence. At this point, Jesus understands himself as having been sent only to the house of Israel—the children of Israel, of which this woman and her ailing daughter are not a part. Clearly, Jesus himself is *not* keen on dealing with this foreigner. In spite of the fact that she approaches Jesus from within the tradition (or at least the tradition's language: "Have mercy on me, Lord, Son of David!"), she is a Canaanite, cursed from the time of Noah (cf. Gen. 9:25). According to Jesus, they are dogs.

The desperate mother, however, does not retreat at this insult, this disregard for her desperation. Metaphorically at least, she stands toe to toe with Jesus. "Yes, Lord, yet even the dogs eat the crumbs that fall from their master's table" (v. 27). Steadfast in her commitment to the fact that this Jesus can in some way help her child, she is unwavering and clever.

And what does Jesus do with this? Whatever it is that this Gentile woman brings to the encounter, Jesus declares it to be faith. In the very least what she brings is desperation, but it could also be a swirl of desperation, superstition, hearsay, love, and/or terror. Jesus calls it faith—great faith!—and it is so. Her daughter is healed *from that very hour*. She persuades Jesus that there is enough mercy to go around. Could it be that this unnamed Canaanite woman stirs something in the Son of God? Is such a notion any more outlandish than our own asking for healing or mercy or forgiveness?

In our rational world, we preachers too often pooh-pooh what appears out of the ordinary, unusual, strange in the realm of faith, dismissing people's actions and thoughts as unorthodox. Perhaps rather than worrying about people's motivations or grasping at straws, we should consider meeting people where they are and with the faith of Jesus, which takes what we bring and declares it faithful.

## Notes

1. Gerhard von Rad, *Genesis,* trans. John H. Marks, Old Testament Library (London: SCM, 1961), 392.
2. Joseph's plot to accuse his brothers of espionage in order to coerce them to bring their father's new favored son, Benjamin, to Egypt (Gen. 42:14ff.).
3. An example of concurrence, defined within Lutheran orthodoxy, specifically by Hollazius (1646–1713): "Concurrence, or the co-operation of God, is the act of Divine Providence whereby God, by a general and immediate influence, proportioned to the need and capacity of every creature, graciously takes part with second causes in their actions and effects." Quoted in Heinrich Schmid, *The Doctrinal Theology of the Evangelical Lutheran Church,* trans. C. A. Hay and H. E. Jacobs, 3rd rev. ed. (1899; repr., Minneapolis: Augsburg), 172.
4. Cf. Ps. 8:5. Also, it must be said that while *'enosh* is masculine, it is safe to say that it functions as close to an inclusive as any word in Hebrew.
5. The Lord later refers to the Sabbath as "my holy day"; cf. Isa. 58:13.
6. Consider *"Miren qué bueno* / Behold, How Pleasant," a hymn by Pablo Sosa, based on Psalm 133, *Evangelical Lutheran Worship* (Minneapolis: Augsburg Fortress, 2006), #649.
7. Augustine, who reads Psalm 133 as an explanation of monasticism, understands Christ to be the source of the dew; see St. Augustine, *Exposition on the Book of Psalms,* in P. Schaff, ed., *Nicene and Post-Nicene Fathers,* series 1 (14 vols.; Edinburgh: T&T Clark, 1886–1889), 8:623; http://www.ccel.org/ccel/schaff/npnf108.ii.CXXXIII.html, accessed August 13, 2010.
8. Perhaps an echo of the Aaronic blessing in Num. 6:24-26.
9. Karl Barth, *The Epistle to the Romans,* trans. Edwin Hoskyn, 6th ed. (London: Oxford University Press, 1933), 421.
10. The parallel story is found in Mark 7:24-30.
11. Mark locates her as a Syrophoenician, but adds for emphasis that she is a Gentile (Mark 7:26), an unnecessary moniker with the punch of "Canaanite" here in Matthew.

# August 21, 2011
## Tenth Sunday after Pentecost
### Twenty-first Sunday in Ordinary Time / Proper 16

| **Revised Common Lectionary (RCL)** | **Lectionary for Mass (LFM)** |
|---|---|
| Exodus 1:8—2:10 or Isaiah 51:1-6 | Isaiah 22:19-23 |
| Psalm 124 or 138 | Psalm 138:1-2a, 2b-3, 6 + 8 |
| Romans 12:1-8 | Romans 11:33-36 |
| Matthew 16:13-20 | Matthew 16:13-20 |

## First Reading
### Exodus 1:8—2:10 (RCL)

"Now a new king arose over Egypt, who did not know Joseph." The times, they are a-changin'! From the time when Joseph, a Hebrew and the son of Jacob, saved Egypt from drought, to the time when the Egyptians wept for seventy days in mourning for Joseph's father, Jacob, to the "now" of this text seems a gulf of time . . . to the present, perhaps.

The new pharaoh incites fear of the Israelites. Why? "Look, the Israelite people are more numerous and more powerful than we. Come, let us deal shrewdly with them, or they will increase and, in the event of war, join our enemies and fight against us and escape from the land" (vv. 9-10). The Israelites are a risk to the Egyptians' homeland security. Such enslavements have been threatened and accomplished on similar grounds for centuries right into the present. In the United States alone, one need only consider the African slave trade together with the likes of Jim Crow in the time after emancipation, the Trail of Tears, the incarceration of Japanese-Americans during World War II, let alone contemporary sentiments against Muslims and people of Hispanic descent. So it became for the Israelites in Egypt under the pharaoh who did not know Joseph.

There are a number of heroes in this story. Shiphrah and Puah, the Hebrew midwives, are the first (vv. 15-22). In the midst of the Egyptian king's systematic attempt to weaken and oppress the Hebrews, we find these two faithful, strong, and clever women. They boldly defy the royal edict to kill all boys born to the Hebrews, letting only the girl babies live. Their actions safeguard all the newborns, girls *and* boys. Their allegiance to God is stronger than their allegiance to their master, Pharaoh.

Pharaoh, however, expands the edict given that the Hebrew midwives have been "ineffective" to him. He now instructs "all his people" to throw every boy born to a Hebrew into the Nile. By this time in the narrative, we, the readers, know that he is wicked and bent on oppressing the Hebrews and presumably assimilating them. If only the girls live, they must marry Egyptian men.

Such is the dramatic background for the beginning of Moses' story, which is the remainder of the pericope. Again this is a time for heroes, and again they are women. To seemingly ordinary parents, a child is born. The unnamed mother and her sister[1] bravely secure this child's future and with him the future of the Hebrew people. Placing him in a waterproof basket, Moses' mother let him float away downriver toward the daughter of the one who would have him killed. It is likely no coincidence that the Hebrew word used here is the same used in the flood story (Gen. 6:5—9:17). The infant Moses is placed in an ark (*tēbhā*; NRSV: "basket"). For his mother, securing Moses' future (and Israel's) meant a complicated confluence of retaining and relinquishing: as the child's wet nurse, she retained the ability to feed and nurture her son, and at the same time she relinquished some of her role as mother to the point of not being able to name her son.

It could be a real gift to a parish to preach on this foundational story. The dynamics of Moses' birth, the strong female heroes, and the difficult beginnings of this chapter in the biblical story provide a rich array of images and a powerful narrative. It is also an important piece for the biblical consciousness of Christians in that Matthew's birth narrative is so informed by the beginning of Moses' story. As with Moses, there is a threat to the life of the Christ child, refuge is found in Egypt, and, by way of his escape of the sword of Herod, he lives to die and thereby to save, not a specific people but the whole world.

## Isaiah 51:1-6 (RCL alt.)

From the richness of Deutero-Isaiah come these verses that demand the attention of both ears and eyes and that draw both to the Lord's promise of salvation. The prophet employs the imperatives "Listen!" (vv. 1a, 4a), "Look!" (vv. 1b, 2a), and "Lift up your eyes!" (v. 6a) to alert us to the convergence of past and future in the present. "Look to Abraham your father and to Sarah who bore you. . . ." The promise of the future for the present was born in the past. Such is the Lord's faithfulness.

The promise, which is the Lord's comfort, renewal, justice, deliverance, and salvation, will break into the present in such a way that will transform barren wilderness into Eden. In the first person, the Lord promises that a teaching (*tōrah*) will come forth from the Lord and that the Lord's justice will be a light for the peoples.[2]

This is not, however, a namby-pamby promise that does not take into consideration the lived reality of death. "Lift up your eyes," says the Lord. And to what? To see that "those who live on [the earth] will die like gnats" (v. 6a). So it is as well with the heavens and the earth. The Lord's promise is *not* some flimsy thing disconnected from the messiness of life. Rather, it acknowledges the messiness and announces loudly that our hope is not in some earthly happiness but in the Lord's salvation, which is forever, and the Lord's deliverance, which will never end (v. 6b).

### Isaiah 22:19-23 (LFM)

The text comes from one of the narrative bits in First Isaiah wherein the prophet in the name of the Lord addresses corruption within the administration of King Hezekiah (c. 739–c. 687 B.C.E.). In particular, Isaiah is addressing the misuse of power by Shebna, the steward/treasurer of Hezekiah's palace,[3] which seems to have to do with his having a tomb hewn for himself, an action by which he improperly elevated his status (v. 16). The Lord's judgment upon Shebna, at the end of which today's pericope begins, is fulsomely violent like a fight scene in a spaghetti western (22:17-19). The remainder of the pericope speaks of Eliakim son of Hilkiah,[4] who is Shebna's replacement. The transfer of Shebna's power to Eliakim is more than complete insofar as what is promised to Eliakim includes the status[5] that Shebna attempted to grab improperly.

While fundamentally every text in Scripture is preachable, this text pushes the envelope. One avenue the preacher might take regards how the role of the Lord God of hosts in this story is central, which may first appear strange. What is the Lord doing involved in administrative workings of the king's palace? It seems too menial for the Creator of the universe. Yet it is not. The Lord is not disinterested in what might to us appear too small.

## Psalmody
### Psalm 124 (RCL)

This song of "communal thanksgiving"[6] extols the Lord's protection and salvation from the enemy. One can imagine the historical use of the psalm, with verse 1 sung by the cantor and the congregation responding in unison with this great witness of God's deliverance that may poetically echo the exodus from Egypt (vv. 4-7). This pattern of performance internal to the psalm—"let Israel / *the congregation* now say"—itself should be considered for use in the assembly today.

The final verse is of particular confessional and liturgical importance as it locates the community's help in the name of the one true God. "Our help is in the name of the LORD, who made heaven and earth." Calvin's liturgy, originally published in 1542 and used in Geneva and Strasbourg,[7] began with this verse as "he understood that this declaration said the truth about the congregation gathered for worship as well as any one sentence could."[8]

Psalm 138 (RCL alt.)
Psalm 138:1-2a, 2b-3, 6 + 8 (LFM)

This psalm is a song of individual thanksgiving as is evident in the opening line, "*I give you thanks, O LORD, with my whole heart.*" The psalmist sings of personal devotion (vv. 1-3), of hope for the whole earth rooted in the LORD's positive disposition toward the lowly (vv. 4-6), and of confidence in the LORD's help and deliverance (vv. 7-8).

The power of the last half of the final verse, "Your steadfast love, O LORD, endures forever. Do not forsake the work of your hands," was used in what may be the oldest known full liturgy, *The Liturgy of the Blessed Apostles, Composed by Sts. Adaeus and Maris.* Dating from c. 200 C.E., verse 8b is recited by the priest at the altar on behalf of the faithful gathered around the table preparing to receive the Risen Lord. Perhaps this prayer, as contemporary as it is ancient, should be our prayer as well, for it introduces a prayer for peace that begins: "O Christ, peace of those in heaven and great rest of those below, grant that Thy rest and peace may dwell in the four parts of the world, but especially in Thy Holy Catholic Church. . . ."[9]

## Second Reading
Romans 12:1-8 (RCL)

There is a shift in Paul's argument from the theological (chaps. 1–11) to the lived reality of the community of believers (12:1—15:13). The content of Paul's message remains consistent, as he shifts to speak specifically about what this all means for Christian life.

The vision of Christian community that Paul urges the church in Rome to consider is rooted in the radical mercy of God and nowhere else. This section of Romans is not about moralizing the gospel so that a certain checklist of behaviors can be ticked off with the goal of achieving some state of *self*-righteousness. Rather, says Karl Barth, Christian living flows from and is enlivened by the mercies of God, which are none other than the mercies "of grace and resurrection, of forgiveness and Spirit, of election and faith, of the varied refractions of the uncreated light," which he sharpens even further: "We have found the world one great, unsolved enigma; an enigma to which Christ, the mercy of God, provides the answer."[10]

In short, we the church (especially its preachers!) cannot confuse what God has done in Christ with what we do as sisters and brothers in Christ and as the church. Embarking on these next weeks' readings from this last major section of Romans, we need to keep Paul's clarity about this before ourselves and before our parishioners.

While there are many elements in this particular text that deserve further attention, two in particular stand out. The first is verse 2, "Do not be conformed to this world, but be transformed by the renewing of your minds, so that you may discern what is the will of God—what is good and acceptable and perfect." Preaching on this text at a baccalaureate service at Wartburg Theological Seminary in 1993, Ralph F. Smith asked this graduating class if they really knew for what they were asking regarding this transformation of which Paul wrote. Such a transformation, said Smith, is a radical thing "rooted in [Paul's] conviction that the good news of Jesus Christ, crucified and risen, will do the renewing and the transforming."[11] The ministry of the good news of Jesus Christ, with all its challenges and burdens, is a beautiful gift, for at once it both proclaims and participates in this transformation.

Finally, then, we learn again that the church is an instrument of God, not of uniformity, but of unity in diversity. This image of the body of Christ (vv. 4-8), consistently and continually evocative and itself calling the church and her members toward this transformation, declares that so much of what we account as important for oneness is not. The church's strength and our unity with one another are not located in sameness or uniformity but in Christ alone.

### Romans 11:33-36 (LFM)

Paul is wrapping up the section in which he lays out Israel's role in God's providence. What we have in Romans 11:33-36 is a doxological conclusion to his earlier words: "So that you may not claim to be wiser than you are, . . . I want you to understand this mystery" (11:25)—a doxological conclusion that draws an absolute line of distinction between God and humanity, between Creator and creation.

Paul's argument is informed and framed by Isaiah and Job. First from Isaiah, "For who has known the mind of the LORD? Or who has been his counselor?" (Isa. 40:13a LXX). And then from Job, "Or who has given a gift to him, to receive a gift in return?"[12] From the verse in Job, Paul does not quote the second half, which reads, "Whatever is under the whole of the heaven is mine" (Job 41:11b RSV). It seems, however, that Romans 11:36 is an expansive rendering of Job 41:11b: "For from him and through him and to him are all things." What clearer statement is there of this absolute distinction between who God is and who we are?

How do we reconcile with this mystery of which Paul speaks? How do we deal with the drastic distinction between us creatures and the one Creator who is all in all? If we stand back, experience tells us that life is more like that which poet Robert Burns described: "The best-laid schemes of mice and men / Often go awry" (my trans.). The problem is that these schemes that we mount against God's divinity are our attempts to usurp God's divinity. And, lest we claim to be wiser than we are, this perpetual problem is only addressed by our faithful participation in and reception of this mystery with Paul's doxology: "To God be the glory forever. Amen!" (v. 36b).

## Gospel
### Matthew 16:13-20 (RCL, LFM)

Within Jesus' question to his disciples is the reality that his cosmic identity was not altogether apparent *and* that there were others claiming to have cosmic identities—claiming to be messiahs. In the midst of this pericope, Simon Peter, who quite frequently ends up with a throbbing thumb, actually hits the nail on the head: "You are the Christ, the Son of the living God," he declares (v. 16). Amid the wide and varied opinions floating around about Jesus' identity, Peter's confession is bang on. Jesus himself confirms Peter's confession by blessing him and affirming that this cosmic knowledge of Jesus' identity comes *not* from a this-worldly reality but from the heavenly Father. This said, it is important to recall that soon after Simon Peter's confession, he gets a reality check when Jesus rebukes him with the razor-sharp "Get behind me, Satan!" (16:23). Peter's blessing does not assure inerrancy.

Echoing from a fifth-century sermon on the passion of Christ, Leo the Great (c. 400–461 C.E.) points to Peter's confession in Matthew 16:15 as the very root of the rule of faith, as the first acknowledgment that Christ, fully God and fully human, *is* the center of faith, which, in Leo's words

> fears not the gates of death, acknowledges the one LORD Jesus Christ to be both true GOD and true Man, believing Him likewise to be the Virgin's Son, Who is His Mother's Creator: born also at the end of the ages, though He is the Creator of time: LORD of all power, and yet one of mortal stock: ignorant of sin, and yet sacrificed for sinners after the likeness of sinful flesh.[13]

At the heart of this Gospel text as well as Leo's ancient reading of it is the confession of Christ! Like mariners on the sea, we the church continually need to gain our bearings. It is no accident that in our weekly gathering, when we hear the Word and receive the Supper, we also confess together our faith. The very faith itself that, in Leo's day and also in ours, doesn't fear death . . . that knows one Lord, Jesus Christ, as both truly God and truly human, born of a virgin and also his mother's Creator . . . born at the end of the ages and also the Creator of time . . . Lord of all power, yet human like us . . . not knowing sin himself, yet sacrificed for sinners!

In our continual search for that which saves us and with such a smorgasbord of possibilities before us, Peter's confession centers our faith. It provides us a bearing—a bearing to which we might all be able to say *credimus!*—we believe!

## Notes

1. It is not until later in the narrative that the parents of Moses, Aaron, and Miriam are named; cf. Exod. 6:20. Moses' aunt, Jochebed's sister, remains unnamed.
2. More so than the Hebrew, the Greek of Isa. 51:4 makes clear that this light is justice for the nations (*ethnōn*).
3. It is possible (even probable) that this Shebna is the same person identified as a scribe in the service of Hezekiah; cf. 2 Kings 18:37: 19:2; Isa. 36:3, 11.
4. Like Shebna, Eliakim is mentioned elsewhere as the steward/treasurer of Hezekiah's palace; cf. 2 Kings 18:18; Isa. 36:3.
5. "He will become a throne of honor to his ancestral house" (Isa. 22:23b).
6. Erhard Gerstenberger, *Psalms, Part 2, and Lamentations,* Forms of Old Testament Literature (Grand Rapids: Eerdmans, 2001), 335.
7. Bard Thompson, *Liturgies of the Western Church* (Philadelphia: Fortress Press, 1961), 197.

8. James L. Mays, *Psalms,* Interpretation: A Bible Commentary for Teaching and Preaching (Louisville: John Knox, 1994), 397.

9. Cf. Alexander Roberts and James Donaldson, eds., *Ante-Nicene Fathers* (9 vols., Buffalo: Christian Literature Publishing, 1885–1896), 7:565.

10. Karl Barth, *The Epistle to the Romans,* trans. Edwin Hoskyns, 6th ed. (London: Oxford University Press, 1933), 427.

11. Ralph F. Smith, "Transformed by Renewal" (May 16, 1993), in *Gentle Strength: Homilies and Hymns of Ralph F. Smith*, ed. Norma Cook Everist (Dubuque: Wartburg Theological Seminary, 1995), 92.

12. Job 41:11 (41:3 in Hebrew and LXX). The NRSV translation of this verse is inadequate and obfuscates the point, which Paul understands. While Paul leaves off the last half of the verse (in Hebrew or Greek), what he gets to in Rom. 11:36 may well be his summary.

13. Leo the Great, "Sermon LXII," in P. Schaff and H. Wace, eds., *Nicene and Post-Nicene Fathers*, series 2 (14 vols.; Edinburgh: T&T Clark, 1890–1900), 12:174; http://www.ccel.org/ccel/schaff/npnf212.ii.v.xxxi.html, accessed August 13, 2010.

# August 28, 2011
## Eleventh Sunday after Pentecost
### Twenty-second Sunday in Ordinary Time / Proper 17

| **Revised Common Lectionary (RCL)** | **Lectionary for Mass (LFM)** |
| --- | --- |
| Exodus 3:1-15 or Jeremiah 15:15-21 | Jeremiah 20:7-9 |
| Psalm 105:1-6, 23-26, 45c or 26:1-8 | Psalm 63:2, 3-4, 5-6, 8-9 |
| Romans 12:9-21 | Romans 12:1-2 |
| Matthew 16:21-28 | Matthew 16:21-27 |

## First Reading
### Exodus 3:1-15 (RCL)

This story is no less than a theophany[1]—an encounter of the Lord with Moses on Mt. Horeb, the holy mountain of God, where Moses and by extension the whole people of Israel would be encountered by the Lord and the Lord's Torah.

Moses' story, of course, begins in the reeds under the threat of death (1:22), is wrapped with the question of true identity (2:10-11),[2] and reaches a crisis with his ineffectual attempt to use violence to free his people (2:11-15). And now he is again a foreigner in a foreign land (2:22) and married to Zipporah, the daughter of this foreign priest for whom Moses tends sheep.

Lest we think that this story is about Moses, it is important to note that the pharaoh whose daughter had adopted Moses has died (2:23). There is a new pharaoh and the burden of the Hebrews has increased and so has their groaning. The Lord has heard them and remembered the covenant. It is by way of Moses that God will deliver God's people from their bondage in Egypt.

The theophany in today's text is Moses' calling, in which we learn more about God than about Moses, whom the Lord uses for the Lord's purpose of deliverance and redemption. (1) *The Lord intervenes in history.* While it is difficult to wrap our modern, scientifically conditioned minds around the idea of a bush burning but not being consumed, so it is with the Lord who is both knowable and unknowable. Perhaps it is our curiosity (aka faith?), like that of Moses, that leads us to approach and dare to know the unknowable. (2) *The Lord is holy and therefore wholly other.* Not the bush itself, but the presence of God in the flames addresses Moses and tells him to take off his shoes in honor of the Lord's holy presence. So also the holiness of the Lord comes to Moses when the Lord reveals to him that the Lord is the God of Abraham, Isaac, and Jacob. Not only is this land made holy by the Lord's presence, but also the story of the Lord's relationship with the Lord's/Moses' people is sacred, so much so that Moses hides his face. (3) *The Lord hears and has compassion for the Lord's people.* While it is no surprise at this point in the narrative, as the reader/hearer has already heard (2:23-25), here the Lord reveals this directly to Moses. The people's groaning under the oppression of Pharaoh reaches the heavenly temple and arouses the Lord's compassion and memory to the point that the Lord comes down to deliver the people into a new land. To do this the Lord will use Moses. The Lord exercises the Lord's compassion by means of this imperfect one, who at this point is already a murderer on the run. (4) *The Lord is the Lord.* The name of the God of Abraham, Isaac, and Jacob is here revealed, and it is a linking verb, in a simple verb of being, of existence: "I am who I am!" The name of God is revealed as the naming of the living God—the God who is, who was, and who will be. Again, as much as the Lord is knowable, the Lord is also unknowable.

### Jeremiah 15:15-21 (RCL alt.)

Within the wild ride that the "gallimaufry of writings"[3] Jeremiah is, we come upon today's text, a prophet's lament of being a prophet and the Lord's response. Jeremiah's second lament (15:15-18, which echoes 15:10) comes in response to this announcement of Jerusalem's impending doom, but the prophet's lament is met, as with an antiphon, by the Lord's reply (15:19-21, which echoes and rectifies 15:11).

Why is the prophet lamenting? For all of Jeremiah's work, Jerusalem has doomed herself. For all of Jeremiah's prophecy, there has been no listening and no repentance. Just prior to today's lesson, the Lord speaks to the city: "You have rejected me, says the LORD, you are going backward; so I have stretched my hand against you and destroyed you—I am weary of relenting" (15:6; cf. also 2:1-27). It is not difficult to imagine the prophet's distress at this. For all his work and speech and suffering, nothing is happening.

The Lord's relationship with the prophet is intimate. "Your words," says Jeremiah, "were found, and I ate them, and your words became to me a joy and the delight of my heart; for I am called by your name, O LORD, God of hosts" (15:16; cf. also Ezek. 2:8—3:3). The words of the Lord have become part of Jeremiah from his guts right on down to his mitochondria. Theologically, one might consider this a sacramental image. And for Jeremiah this supping causes heartburn untouchable by any antacid. "Unable to suppress the divine wrath within him,"[4] as Abraham Heschel writes, Jeremiah continues to belch the judgment of the Lord. And thoroughly irritated by this,[5] he screams out to the Lord, "Why must my pain be endless?" Also, contra

Isaiah 58:11, the Lord *is* to him a spring that fails. It is difficult to imagine images more existentially conflicting than those in verses 15-18—from joy and delight to suffering, pain, and failure.

Yet the Lord responds. If verses 19-20a were the Lord's only response, I can imagine Jeremiah responding, "This still sucks," for the Lord speaks of the Lord's relationship with Jeremiah like a sci-fi tractor beam from which the prophet has no hope of escaping. And God promises him no relief from his persecutors (v. 15), only that he will be fortified, like a walled city.

This second portion of the lesson is like a renewal of Jeremiah's call. First and in relation to Jeremiah's call to speak, the Lord says, "If you utter what is precious, and not what is worthless, you shall serve as my mouth. It is they who will turn to you, not you who will turn to them" (v. 19b). So it is with the call of the preacher as well—to speak God's Word and not worry so much about the people's response, for that is the work of the Spirit. The second moment of promise for Jeremiah is that his foes will not prevail, "for I am with you to save you and deliver you, says the LORD. I will deliver you out of the hand of the wicked, and redeem you from the grasp of the ruthless" (vv. 20b-21). While Jeremiah's discouragement continues (see the comments on Jer. 20:7-9 below), as can happen to us preachers as well, there remains this promise of deliverance and redemption—a promise that is not something beyond the horizon but is present in the crucified Christ.

### Jeremiah 20:7-9 (LFM)

Like Jeremiah 15:15-18 (see above), Jeremiah is again lamenting his role as prophet, perceiving that he has been deceived (*pth*; NRSV: "enticed") into the role by the Lord.[6] He is the object of mocking and derision, compelled to cry out on the Lord's behalf the unwelcome message of divine judgment, which has become to him "a reproach and derision all day long."

Abraham Heschel is correct, I think, when he says that Jeremiah "hated his prophetic mission." Yet "in spite of public rejection, in spite of inner misery, he felt unable to discard the divine burden, unable to disengage himself from the divine pathos. He knew why he had to yield; he knew how to explain his inability to resist the terrible errand."[7] Able to articulate his own misery and malevolence toward the Lord and the Lord's calling, Jeremiah continued to proclaim. He knew and professed that, while those around him were wanting him to shut up, the Lord was with him "like a dread warrior" (20:11),[8] compelling him to speak. How might such a text provide an honest entry point for preaching on and/or discussing vocation?

## Psalmody
### Psalm 105:1-6, 23-26, 45c (RCL)

"O give thanks to the LORD, call on his name, make known his deeds among the peoples." This psalm rehearses God's faithfulness to God's people, and by its singing so does the assembly. This week's portion of the psalm's recollection of Israel's history echoes the beginning of the exodus story, poetically recapping the last two weeks' RCL Old Testament lessons.

God's rule over the whole of history, as partially known as it is this side of the eschaton, is reflected in this psalm. In a sense, we are called to give thanks for the Lord's deeds, even though we do not and cannot know the full extent thereof. We do so confidently, however, because "we believe in one God, the Father Almighty, maker of heaven and earth, of things visible and invisible," who has decisively made himself known in history by way of Jesus Christ and him crucified.

### Psalm 26:1-8 (RCL alt.)

The psalm begins with the singer asking to be judged (*shpht*; NRSV: "vindicate"; cf. also Pss. 7:8; 35:42; 43:1) by the Lord. A positive outcome is expected, as there is little if any humility evident in the words of the singer: "I have trusted in the Lord without wavering." The cultic elements of the psalm (e.g., the altar and the reference to the place where the glory of the Lord abides, which is the Holy of Holies) suggest that this is a priestly psalm.

Whether sung by priests or more generally by the assembly, as it will be in Christian assemblies, how does one deal with the juxtaposition of this psalm and Paul's assertion that all people sin and fall short of the glory of God (Rom. 3:21-26). Perhaps it is with just such juxtaposition. It is not the preacher's job to redeem Scripture; however, holding such a tension in place can serve as a creative tension whereby we can pray and sing this psalm in light of Christ's saving incarnation, death, and resurrection, which judges the sinner and declares her/him righteous in faith.[9]

### Psalm 63:2, 3-4, 5-6, 8-9 (LFM)

Like Psalm 105 commented on above, Psalm 63 has strong cultic elements that may suggest it is reserved for singing by the high priest. In particular, the language "I have looked upon you in the sanctuary, beholding your power and glory" could only have been said by the high priest, the only one allowed and able to enter the Holy of Holies (Heb. 9:1-7).

## Second Reading
### Romans 12:9-21 (RCL)

What might appear to be a laundry list of exhortations for Christian living is a firm foundation for Christian ethics. This is not just inner-Christian business here. It is a foundation for the Christian life *in the world*. What does belief in Jesus have to do with how Christians live? What comes from Paul in this pericope is the exercise of the transformation of the Christian by discerning the will of God (12:2).

"Let love be genuine," Paul writes. What are three little words in Greek are of utmost importance. The love of which Paul writes is *agape*. In Romans (and elsewhere!) *agape* is God's love and not to be mistaken for any other. It is the love of God "poured into our hearts by the Holy Spirit" (5:5) and demonstrated by Christ's death *for us* "while we were still sinners" (5:8). It is the *agape* of Christ, who intercedes *for us*, from which nothing, not even death, can separate us (8:31-39). This *agape* is God's self-giving promise for the creation, as well as the love expected by God of God.[10]

What the NRSV translates "genuine" is the Greek word *anupokritos*, that is, unhypocritical. Our human love is imperfect—expecting, using, manipulating, and so forth. Human love is imperfect insofar as it will never reach the nature of God's love in Christ. Such is the unhypocritical *agape* that Paul urges Christians to observe . . . to live! Such is a love that sees the neighbor and sees what God in Christ has already done for her or him.[11] And nowhere does Paul restrict this unhypocritical *agape* living to the Christian's relationships with fellow Christians. This is an ethic to govern the whole of a Christian's life in relation to sisters and brothers in Christ, to the other, to the earth, to the cosmos.

What follows in the pericope spells out just how wild and crazy this unhypocritical *agape* is[12]—a love that "hates what is evil" and holds "fast to what is good." With all the possible preaching avenues to pursue, three stand out.

1. *Share with the saints / people of God who are in need* (12:13a). While it would be a far clunkier translation, the full gist of this might be better conveyed by "*koinonia*-ize sisters and brothers in need." So often our Christian practice these days is to have little to do with one another even in the space of worship. Many Christians like to blend into an anonymous participation. Exercising this unhypocritical *agape* means active caring for, respect of, and involvement with the needs of the Christian community and not that which resembles drive-up church.

2. *Extend hospitality to strangers* (12:13b). In an age of rampant xenophobia, there is no clearer call to something very different. The word that Paul uses here is *philoxenia*, a word that defies attaching adjectives like "illegal" to those from outside. *Philoxenia*, then, is yet another exercise of this unhypocritical *agape*.

3. *It is true that evil only begets evil* (12:14). And evil can only be overcome with good. How difficult this unhypocritical *agape* is! It is as difficult to envision as it is to live. What Paul is saying is not that evil will not be judged. What he does say clearly is that the judgment is God's and *not ours*. Quoting Proverbs 25:21-22a, Paul comes close to Jesus' crazy language about loving the enemy (cf. Matt. 5:43-48).

This business of living the Christian life is a bugger. It is incredibly easy to be conformed to this world—to live as if Jesus is still in the grave. Yet let us continue to pray that we Christians and the church may be transformed toward this unhypocritical *agape*, thereby discerning the will of God (12:2).

## Romans 12:1-2 (LFM)

For comments on this text, please see the second reading (RCL) for Proper 16, above.

## Gospel
### Matthew 16:21-28 (RCL)
### Matthew 16:21-27 (LFM)

Immediately on the heels of Peter's insight into Jesus' identity, we encounter Jesus' passion prediction (vv. 21-23) and its implications for his followers (vv. 24-28). It is important to back up just a bit. The whole of this week's Gospel flows from Jesus' identity: "You are the Christ, the Son of the living God" (16:16). Peter's faith-filled confession in last week's Gospel pericope is met in this week's by Jesus adding precision and Peter's resulting miscalculation. From the love fest of Matthew 16:13-20, the dire reality of the trajectory of Jesus' ministry and the life of discipleship comes into full view. There is no outcome for Jesus or his disciples other than the suffering of the cross.

In the immediate wake of Peter's confession, Jesus' blessing of Peter, and his gag order to his disciples, Matthew indicates that Jesus began to show his disciples how it was necessary that he must suffer and be killed and on the third day be raised from the dead. This marks a turning in Jesus' ministry where the cross increasingly comes into full view.

The language that Matthew uses here is of interest, particularly the word *dei*, a form of the verb *deō*, translated "it is necessary." It occurs in this particular form perhaps in large part to maintain its force as a word that offers no wiggle room, no exit clause, no loophole, no plan B. Rather, *dei* indicates a singularity of trajectory. Thus, when Matthew writes that "from this time on, Jesus began to show his disciples that he must [*dei*] go to Jerusalem and undergo great sufferings at the hands of the elders and chief priests and scribes, and be killed, and on the third day be raised," he is saying that the trajectory is set. Suffering, death, and resurrection are inevitable for Jesus of Nazareth.

How often in our contemporary Christian practices and especially the North American pop-Christian incarnations thereof do we want to downplay the centrality of the crucifixion? Peter does. The one whom Jesus just lauded and to whom were entrusted the keys of the kingdom, when faced with the ugly reality that the ministry of the Christ, the Son of the living God, necessarily culminates in suffering and death (it's not the resurrection piece that upsets Peter!), rebukes the very Son of the living God. How stupid and unnecessary for one with such power! How foolish of Jesus to use this *dei*.

"Get behind me, Satan! You are a stumbling block to me; for you are setting your mind not on divine things but on human things" (v. 23). No sooner after Jesus proclaims a blessing upon Peter for his confession does he then refer to Peter as Satan, the deceiving, fallen angel who is the enemy of God (e.g., Matt. 4:10; Luke 10:18; Rom. 16:20; 2 Cor. 11:14; etc.). He says that Peter is "a *skandalon* [scandal] to me!" How do we explain such a shift?

Jesus' identity ("You are the Messiah, the Son of the living God," v. 16) is incomplete without suffering and death . . . without the cross. Jesus' thorough vexation with Peter is that the Son *must* suffer and die. In the pithiness of Gustaf Aulén: "The incarnation is perfected on the cross."[13]

Couldn't Jesus be saying such things to us as well? To his contemporary disciples, we who no less than Peter would rather be rid of the suffering and cross of Christ? We who would sanitize Jesus and thereby make God irrelevant to a messy, suffering world?

Lest we think that Jesus' concern is only for Peter here, he does turn at this point in the pericope to address the whole of his disciples: "If *any* want to become my followers, let them deny themselves and take up their cross and follow me" (v. 24). Not the best recruiting slogan one can image for participation in the church! And it gets worse: "For those who want to save their life will lose it, and those who lose their life for my sake will find it" (v. 25). Funny thing that the contemporary church has not plastered these verses on billboards around the world! But isn't this the point? Advertising Jesus and following Jesus mean something . . . cost something. Though here we want to be careful to avoid the pitfall of Peter insofar as he heard the *dei*—the "it is necessary"—only from a human vantage and not from the divine. For what is true for Jesus' disciples is that Jesus himself has taken our death upon himself that we might not be afraid to take up the cross, to serve the other, to proclaim the love of God in word and deed.

## Notes

1. I agree with Umberto Cassuto, *A Commentary on the Book of Exodus*, trans. I. Abraham (Jerusalem: Magnes, 1967), that the language "an angel of the LORD" in v. 2 means a "manifestation of the LORD" (31). This suggests that Moses' encounter was with the Lord, not a messenger of the Lord.
2. In the space between these two verses, Moses grew up into a man. And, raised as a son by Pharaoh's daughter, he recognizes and empathizes with the plight of his *own* people. It is difficult not to speculate on the question of identity, given that he was reared by both his Hebrew mother (cf. 2:11) and his Egyptian adoptive mother. Note that upon his first encounter with the daughters of Reuel/Jethro, they recognize him as an Egyptian (2:19).
3. Robert P. Carroll, *Jeremiah: A Commentary*, Old Testament Library (Philadelphia: Westminster, 1986), 38.
4. Abraham Heschel, *The Prophets* (New York: Harper Perennial, 1962), 148.
5. Later Jeremiah articulates his distressed irritation poetically: "My heart is crushed within me, all my bones shake; I have become like a drunkard, like one overcome by wine, because of the LORD and because of his holy words" (23:9).
6. Properly, the pericope should be 20:7-12.
7. Heschel, *Prophets*, 151.
8. The Hebrew here (*'arîtz*) used to describe the Lord is ironically used to describe Jeremiah's persecutors in 15:21.
9. Similarily, cf. James L. Mays, *Psalms*, Interpretation: A Bible Commentary for Teaching and Preaching (Louisville: John Knox, 1994), 127–30.
10. The Septuagint translation of the *Shema* commands *agape* love.

11. "Love beholds the concrete neighbor, sees his positive 'Yes', and knows it to be a veritable 'No'; and yet, nevertheless, apprehends him as he has been already apprehended by God." Karl Barth, *The Epistle to the Romans,* trans. Edwin Hoskyns, 6th ed. (London: Oxford University Press, 1933), 454.

12. I am compelled to note the interesting parallels between this section of Romans and Jesus' Sermon on the Mount in Matthew 5, parallels first suggested to me by my colleague Duane A. Priebe.

13. Gustaf Aulén, *The Faith of the Christian Church*, trans. E. H. Wahlstrom and G. E. Arden (Philadelphia: Muhlenberg, 1948), 221.

# September 4, 2011
## Twelfth Sunday after Pentecost
### Twenty-third Sunday in Ordinary Time / Proper 18

**Revised Common Lectionary (RCL)**
Exodus 12:1-14 or Ezekiel 33:7-11
Psalm 149 or 119:33-40
Romans 13:8-14
Matthew 18:15-20

**Lectionary for Mass (LFM)**
Ezekiel 33:7-9
Psalm 95:1-2, 6-7, 8-9
Romans 13:8-10
Matthew 18:15-20

## First Reading
### Exodus 12:1-14 (RCL)

The institution of the Passover is at the heart of this pericope. Lest the impetus for the Passover be forgotten (a danger that should be taken seriously with any pericope), recall these words:

> Moses said, "Thus says the LORD: About midnight I will go out through Egypt. Every firstborn in the land of Egypt shall die, from the firstborn of Pharaoh who sits on his throne to the firstborn of the female slave who is behind the handmill, and all the firstborn of the livestock. Then there will be a loud cry throughout the whole land of Egypt, such as has never been or will ever be again. But not a dog shall growl at any of the Israelites—not at people, not at animals—so that you may know that the LORD makes a distinction between Egypt and Israel." (Exod. 11:4-7)

At the peak of the crescendo of the plagues against Pharaoh and the Egyptians is this wailing at the death of the firstborn. The Passover is something between a promise of deliverance and an antidote against the angel of death.

Today's pericope begins with the time. This event and its remembrance take place at the beginning of the year, the first month of the year.[1] While we could at this point in the narrative get wrapped up with tradition/redaction-historical questions, the observation about this timing by Umberto Cassuto is corrective: "On the first day of the first month of the new year—that is, at the beginning of a new period of time in human life—God communicates with them joyful tidings; the new calendar period marks a new historic epoch in the life of Israel."[2] Against the backdrop of both Israel's suffering in slavery at the hand of Pharaoh *and* the wailing of the Egyptians, creeping in from the future of this narrative is this promise of life and deliverance. It is *not* a fragile promise. It is a promise that comes in the midst of the untidiness and brokenness of life.

The perpetual observance (*huqat 'olam*; 13:14) of the ritual of Passover becomes the backbone of history, as it comes to symbolize the remembrance of Israel's deliverance in the past and the perpetual promise of God's faithfulness into the future, both of which inform and frame the present. For Jews this Passover celebration remains alive and formative as much today as in centuries past. For we Christians, this Passover is understood in light of Christ's own death and resurrection, the lamb who was slain (1 Cor. 5:7; John 1:29, 36). This perpetual ordinance, then, becomes the weekly celebration of the Eucharist. Therein we taste, see, smell, and hear, though still partially and penultimately, the fullest revelation of who God is and what God does.

## Ezekiel 33:7-11 (RCL alt.)
## Ezekiel 33:7-9 (LFM)

These pericopes come within the larger unit of Ezekiel 33:1-20, which deals with Ezekiel's role as a prophet of the Lord and, perhaps more importantly, the possibility of a future for God's people. I recommend that the preacher include the whole of verses 7-11, as ending at verse 9 misses the promise of verse 11.

Clear in Ezekiel is that the Lord cannot be imagined solely in terms that are safe and cuddly. God is righteous and holy and demands that the Lord's people be righteous and holy. Up to this point in the book, the Lord's judgment has been all-inclusive—upon the religious leaders (8:1-18; 14:1-5) and the whole of Israel (9:1-11), extending to the prophet himself (24:16). The Lord has even abandoned the temple (10:1-22; 11:22-25) because of Israel's idolatry and unrighteousness.

In today's text, however, we have a glimpse of a future made possible by repentance. The prophet's call is to call the wicked to turn, to repent (*shuv*) from their wicked ways. If the prophet does not follow through with this preaching, the Lord will require the death of the wicked at his hand. If, however, the prophet does follow through and the people do not respond, the prophet's life will be spared. So it is with proclamation. We preachers cannot control the response of the congregation (and we will be sorely disappointed if we think we can!). We only announce God's Word to the world as it is normed by Scripture and comes in the single Word of law-gospel, naming our idolatries and transgressions and proclaiming forgiveness and life from the foot of the cross. If anything, Ezekiel is brutally honest about the idolatries of Israel, and here he also proclaims God's fundamental disposition: "As I live, says the Lord God, I have no pleasure in the death of the wicked, but that the wicked turn from their ways and live; turn back, turn back from your evil ways; for why will you die, O house of Israel?" (33:11).

Proclamation is a holy, wonderful, and dangerous thing. To proclaim God's judgment without God's promise is cruel, dangerous, and unscriptural. To proclaim God's promise without God's judgment is also cruel, dangerous, and unscriptural. God's judgment and God's promise are together God's Word to us and the world. Ezekiel, for all its elements to question and dislike, is honest about this aspect of the role of the prophet and the preacher.

# Psalmody
## Psalm 149 (RCL)

A "Hallelujah!" psalm, this psalm calls for dancing, which makes this author uncomfortable. With visions of Hasidim ecstatically dancing with whirls and kicks, I can see along the wall people like myself shyly tapping a toe. This psalm bespeaks a response to the Lord not necessarily hardwired into all people. May it not be so for all readers!

Why does the psalmist call the singers of this song to dance? Because the Lord takes pleasure, *not* necessarily in the dancing itself, but in the people. The people's response to the pleasure of their Maker and King in them is to dance.

For all this talk of dancing, we ought not to miss that this psalm is also about war. The dancing and praising appear to be in preparation for battle with "two-edged swords in their hands." Perhaps the call here is to read and sing this text metaphorically, for instance, "The word of God is living and active, sharper than a two-edged sword" (Heb. 4:12). Not to condone the warring imagery, how might it be carefully and faithfully interpreted in light of texts that speak of turning swords into plowshares and spears into pruning hooks (Isa. 2:4; Micah 4:3; contra Joel 3:10) and Christ who says, "Put your sword back into its sheath" (John 18:11; Matt. 26:52)?

## Psalm 119:33-40 (RCL alt.)

In this massive acrostic psalm on the Torah of God, today's portion is the letter *he*. It is a prayer that beseeches the Lord, "Teach me, O LORD, the way of your statutes, and I will observe it to the end." As a student sitting before a teacher, the psalmist sings for help in keeping the Torah. It is a holistic prayer asking for knowledge, an intellectual and heady need, and for a change of heart: "Turn my heart to your decrees, and not to selfish gain" (v. 36).

James L. Mays is correct to say that "the Word of God is given but never possessed. Because it is God's instruction, it is not owned apart from the teaching of God."[3] This portion of Psalm 119 has the psalmist longing for willing participation in this divine teaching, in the ways of the Lord—a gift that can only come from God.

### Psalm 95:1-2, 6-7, 8-9 (LFM)

In praise of the Lord's kingship, this psalm calls the assembly to "sing to the LORD" and "make a joyful noise to the rock of our salvation!" In the portion skipped by the lectionary,[4] the Lord is heralded as Creator, which is to inspire devotion, for in addition to creating the world, the Lord is "our Maker" (v. 6). The psalm then transitions to image the Lord as shepherd, who calls to the sheep/people. The psalmist sings, expecting the people's ears to open, "O that *today* you would listen to [the LORD's] voice!" (v. 7b).

## Second Reading
### Romans 13:8-14 (RCL)
### Romans 13:8-10 (LFM)

Again, love is the central concern of this section of Romans 13. It is *agape*, God's undeserved, cruciform love: "But God proves his love for us in that while we still were sinners Christ died for us" (Rom. 5:8). This love of God in Christ crucified is the same love that fulfills the whole of the Torah, and by way of this fulfillment of the Torah, this *agape* love overflows into the world as we relate one to another.

Paul has in view here the relation of the Mosaic Torah and Christ. In referencing a number of commandments from the second table of the Decalogue (cf. Rom. 13:9), Paul resonates with much of early Judaism in saying that the Torah (*nomos*) is summed up by Leviticus 19:18b, "Love your neighbor as yourself." Together with Jesus (Matt. 5:43; 19:19; 22:39; Mark 12:31; Luke 10:27) and others,[5] Paul here points to the command to love one's neighbor as oneself as the fulfillment of the whole law (cf. Gal. 5:14). Important in Romans 13:8-10 is that Paul explicitly connects *agape* to the fulfillment of the Torah of Moses, and this love is first and foremost the love of God in Christ.

Paul's word choice in verse 8 is of interest: "Owe no one anything, except to love one another; for the one who loves another [*ton heteron*] has fulfilled the law." Given that he is progressing toward the classical formulation of the great commandment of Leviticus 19:18b, it may at first seem jarring that he uses the less specific "another" here. Consider this alongside Romans 12, where Paul makes it clear that this *agape* is not to be lived only for one's neighbors. This word choice seems to deliberately conjure Paul's previous points about caring for the needs of the saints (those within the community of believers), showing hospitality to the outsider, and treating the enemy as a sister or brother (12:13-21). Such it is that this *agape* overflows from the cross through believers to the world. *Agape*, the love that is displayed most clearly in the cross of Christ,[6] fulfills the law and *is* the ethic for Christian relationships and interaction with the world.

The second half of the pericope turns to the importance of the expectation of Christ's imminent return to the Christian life. Paul's call to Christians to live in the nearness of salvation (13:11) should be read against the wider backdrop of Romans. In 6:1-14 Paul writes: "For if we have been united with him in a death like his, we will certainly be reunited with him in a resurrection like his" (v. 5). The salvation of which Paul writes in chapter 13 may well be understood as the Christian's baptismal reality, which lives both in our human, worldly time and in a mysterious way in God's time.

For the Christian, then, Paul speaks of living in the baptismal meantime, during which he urges the Christian to "put on the Lord Jesus Christ" (13:14a) as a baptismal garment that symbolizes the Christian's new reality in Christ. It is difficult here not to see that Paul is speaking of Christians as whole beings. That is, one's Christianity— one's baptismal reality—is not one reality among many. When thinking of one's identity, it is not a laundry list that would read, "daughter, mother, wife, Christian, accountant, Mariners fan, diabetic," and so forth. The claim of baptism upon a person is complete without a remainder. Of course, our lives on this side of Jesus' imminent return remain broken. Yet Paul places before us this call into wholeness, which is only completely true in Christ. Earlier he wrote, "By the mercies of God . . . present your bodies as a living sacrifice, holy and acceptable to God, which is your spiritual worship" (12:1). And here he urges his readers to "put on the Lord Jesus Christ, and make no provisions for the flesh, to gratify its desires" (13:14).

## Gospel
### Matthew 18:15-20 (RCL, LFM)

This week's pericope is the conclusion of Jesus' teachings in response to his disciples' question, "Who is the greatest in the kingdom of heaven?" (18:1). On occasion this Gospel lesson is read as a step-by-step prescription for dealing with unruly congregants—those whom clergy consider as the real pains in their clerical butts— those who cause problems at meetings, who monopolize the time of the parish's dedicated leaders, who have lost the missional focus of the church, and so forth. Also on occasion, this Gospel lesson is used by clergy (and others) to coerce the abused, primarily women, to forgive their abusers and remain in abusive situations.[7] These readings are insufficient and shallow! More appropriately, this text is a vision of the kingdom of heaven breaking into our earthly present, whereby forgiveness is indeed central and not empty. There is also communal accountability.

Forgiveness may in fact be one of the most difficult charges for us Christians to take seriously and accomplish. Thank God it is not so for God. For us, however, it may well be the loftiest and least achieved aspect of living the Christian faith.

About whom is Jesus speaking in this passage? While I am professionally and pastorally a proponent of inclusive language, the NRSV translation ("another member of the church") is rather out of line with the Greek and could be read as referring to some anonymous congregant. The Greek is more intimate as it speaks of an *adelphos*, a brother. I suggest a more intimate and accurate means of making this inclusive is by translating Jesus' words, "If your brother or sister . . ." Jesus here is speaking about the kingdom of heaven breaking into the present in the community of believers, and the vision into which he propels us is not disassociated and anonymous. It is intimate and personal.

149

Jesus' instructions here are fourfold: (1) Go to the person one-on-one to show him or her the wrong done. This is a matter of wisdom (Sir. 20:1-3; cf. Lev. 19:17) that the problem/transgression between people is addressed head-on and not left to fester silently. Notice the language that Jesus uses here as it parallels that of the shepherd seeking the lost sheep, which comes immediately prior to today's pericope (18:12-14). Gustavo Gutiérrez articulates the juxtaposition of these two bits of Matthew well: "It is not enough to say that love of God is inseparable from the love of one's neighbor. It must be added that love for God is unavoidably expressed *through* love of one's neighbor."[8] Yet if the brother or sister does not listen, there is a second step whereby (2) he/she is to be approached by "one or two others." This is so that they might corroborate the accusation and thereby convince the sister or brother to listen. And if the weight of testimony of the "one or two others" does not work, then (3) the matter is to be brought before the whole of the *ekklesia* or assembly. And again, if the brother or sister refuses to listen to the whole of the assembly of believers, then (4) the person is to be "to you as a Gentile and a tax collector." Here is the kicker that is often missed. So often, "a Gentile and a tax collector" is read as if the kingdom of heaven is a band of clerically rigid Pharisees, which would suggest that to be so regarded is to be shunned or excluded. Within the context of the kingdom of heaven, however, to be "a Gentile and a tax collector" is to be included. Recall that Matthew frames Jesus' ministry (12:17-21) in Isaiah's terms ("And in his name the Gentiles will hope"), and that from Jesus' encounter with the Canaanite woman (15:21-28), to be a Gentile is no longer to be an outsider to the kingdom of heaven. Recall as well that the namesake of the Gospel, Matthew, was himself a tax collector and that Jesus ate with tax collectors and sinners (9:9ff.; cf. 21:31). How difficult is this?!

Is this empty forgiveness, forgiveness without repentance or accountability? It does not seem so. While Jesus describes a lavish forgiveness, there is also the serious recognition of the inability (or unwillingness?) to hear on the part of the one sinning. This, together with the power to bind and to loose in Matthew 18:18 (note well that the second-person pronouns there are plural!), acknowledges the penultimate reality of the kingdom of heaven in the present—penultimate in that sin and brokenness are and remain real—even (especially!?) within the church.[9]

Of what importance is this set of instructions? Is it about order within the community? Healthy congregations? Perhaps. I suggest that more than order or health it is about Christ's presence, a presence that constitutes the kingdom of heaven on earth and in the present. Recall Jesus' final words in this passage: "For where two or three are gathered in my name, I am there in the midst of them" (v. 20). It seems that in Jesus' framework this work or vocation of forgiveness within the Christian community is primarily about the assembly, as a fractured and fragmented community jeopardizes Christ's presence and thereby the community's witness to Christ in Christ's name.

This is irregular divine unity. It is irregular insofar as Jesus' instructions culminate in these strange words that the Christian assembly is to treat the wayward as a Gentile and tax collector. It is divine in that it reflects and demonstrates a care for the other that is like the shepherd's care for the one lost sheep. It is unity in that it is gathering in the name of Christ.

## Notes

1. Note that beginning the new year with Passover (Exod. 12:1) is a different tradition than beginning the new year with Rosh Hashanah.
2. Umberto Cassuto, *A Commentary on the Book of Exodus*, trans. I. Abrahams (Jerusalem: Magnes, 1967), 136.
3. James L. Mays, *Psalms*, Interpretation: A Bible Commentary for Teaching and Preaching (Louisville: John Knox, 1994), 385.
4. The LFM omits the juicy, uncomfortable bits, such as the Lord's "loathing" of the people (v. 10a) and the Lord's swearing in anger that the people shall not enter the Lord's resting place (v. 11).
5. See James 2:8. Hillel (first century B.C.E.–first century C.E.) formulates his summation in the negative: "What is hateful to you, do not do to your neighbor. That is the whole Torah, the rest is explanation. Go and learn" (Talmud *Shabbat* 31a). Aqiba ben Joseph (c. 50–c. 132 C.E.), like Hillel, though following the positive formulation, taught that Lev. 19:18b was the greatest commandment.
6. Of course, 1 Corinthians 13 is of importance here, not as a relationship map for marriage, but as a display of this cruciform *agape* that overflows into the world.
7. Cf. Susan E. Hylen, "Forgiveness and Life in Community," *Interpretation* 54 (2000): 147–57.
8. Gustavo Gutiérrez, *A Theology of Liberation: History, Politics, and Salvation*, trans. C. Inda and J. Eagleson, rev. ed. (Maryknoll, N.Y.: Orbis, 1988), 114–15.
9. "Our response to victims of domestic violence has been like our reading of Mt 18.21-35. We are horrified by the situation and counsel *them* to forgive, just as we would counsel the unforgiving servant, but we do not notice ourselves (the fellow-servants) in the story. One of the primary tasks of the Christian community in confronting domestic violence is to understand *our* need to repent of violence. Becoming aware of domestic violence requires that we recognize the many ways that the church has encouraged this violence and the ways we personally have accepted or minimized the many forms of violence against women in our culture." Hylen, "Forgiveness and Life in Community," 155. In addition to Hylen's clarion call for the church to address and repent of its often perpetuating stance toward domestic violence against women, we should also include the abuse of power by clergy often resulting in the violation—physical, spiritual, and emotional—of children *and* the covering up of such abuse by the ecclesial powers in so many corners of the church.

# September 11, 2011
## Thirteenth Sunday after Pentecost
### Twenty-fourth Sunday in Ordinary Time / Proper 19

**Revised Common Lectionary (RCL)**
Exodus 14:19-31 or Genesis 50:15-21
Psalm 114 or Exodus 15:1b-11, 20-21 or
 Psalm 103:(1-7), 8-13
Romans 14:1-12
Matthew 18:21-35

**Lectionary for Mass (LFM)**
Sirach 27:30—28:7
Psalm 103:1-2, 3-4, 9-10, 11-12

Romans 14:7-9
Matthew 18:21-35

## First Reading
### Exodus 14:19-31 (RCL)

Deliverance comes to the Israelites from the living God, but it does not come without pain and death. What may appear to be a fantastical story of the deliverance of the Israelites from the armies of the Egyptians through the parting of the Reed Sea is centrally about God's faithfulness—a faithfulness that is both delivering and frightful.

With the first Passover just marked and the Egyptians' wailing at the death of their firstborn still hanging in the air, the Israelites, released by a grieving Pharaoh and led by Moses, fled Egypt.

Today's pericope picks up the story at dusk with the Egyptian army pursuing the Israelites right up to the Reed Sea. At this point, both the angel (presence?) of the Lord and the pillar of cloud that had been leading the Israelites in their exodus shift from the front to the rear of the Israelites, thereby protecting the Israelites from the Egyptians. Moses, as commanded by God, stretches out his hands and the Lord parts the sea with the east wind so that the Israelites might escape their hostile pursuers. The threat from the Egyptians inspired among the Israelites both fear of death and change as well as their doubting of Moses and presumably the Lord (vv. 11-12). But the Lord acts, and the people are moved.

The thing is, however, that the Lord's actions include (1) hardening Pharaoh's heart, which evidently entails changing Pharaoh's mind about letting the Israelites go, (2) arousing panic among the Egyptians with the pillar of fire and cloud, (3) mucking up the chariots' wheels, thus bogging down the Egyptian army betwixt the walls of water, and (4) causing the sea to swallow the Egyptian army whole.

The result of this exercise of deliverance is, at least from an Egyptian perspective, destruction and death, from the plagues right on through to the floating corpses along the shore of the Reed Sea. At the same time, the Israelites are freed from captivity and slavery. These two results cannot be separated, and one does not cancel the other.

What happens in the wake of this crossing? The Song of the Sea. In the singing of this song with some combination of elation and relief, the Israelites praise the God who delivers, the Divine Warrior who intervenes and protects. With voices raised there is a collective use of the first-person possessive: "The LORD is *my* strength and *my* song, and he has become *my* salvation; this is *my* God, and I will praise him, *my* father's God, and I will exalt him" (15:2). In the words of Brevard Childs, "Israel left Egypt as fleeing slaves, and emerged from the sea as a people who testified to God's miraculous deliverance."[1] In their singing, they testify that the Lord is *my* Lord— the Lord of the people of Israel. At the same time, this beginning is most certainly difficult![2]

If preaching on this text, it makes good sense to use Exodus 15:1b-11, 20-21 as the psalm for the day (rather than Psalm 114), so that the assembly can sing out with the Israelites. While the lectionary does include some of the more horrific bits, such as "Horse and rider he has thrown into the sea" (15:1b), it curiously omits verses 12-18. It would be preferable to include at least verse 12 and to consider all these final verses, as they round out the whole of the exodus story as it moves into the conquest of Canaan.

## Genesis 50:15-21 (RCL alt.)

While this story comes in the immediate wake of Jacob's death, it marks the pinnacle of the role of the Israelites in Egypt. Yet this is a backdrop to the profoundly theological resolution to which Joseph's story comes with this final encounter with his brothers.

The rubber really begins to hit the road in the pericope in 50:15, when Joseph's brothers realize the impact of their father's death. Their question feels real and urgent: "What if Joseph still bears a grudge against us and pays us back for all the wrong that we did to him?" (v. 16). Their mistreatment of Joseph so many years ago remains raw. With this maltreated brother so powerful and their father dead, what will be the future of these motley brothers?

The emotional back-and-forth between brothers is riddled with drama, and Joseph's words to his anxious brothers are like a balm. "Do not be afraid! Am I in the place of God? Even though you intended to do harm to me, God intended it for good, in order to preserve a numerous people, as he is doing today. So have no fear; I myself will provide for you and your little ones" (vv. 19b-21a; see also 45:4b-5).

153

The spoken word, especially the word of absolution, is a powerful thing. Not only does Joseph soothe the anxious hearts of his now orphaned brothers; he also speaks a word of faith in a God whose purposes are often beyond our limited comprehension. He testifies to the fact that, were it not for the harm caused him by his brothers, he would not have been able to sustain Egypt and Israel through the drought.

Such a faithful response as Joseph's, however, is not to be used lightly or, worse, misused. It is not to be imposed as justification or explanation of an evil done to another. That is, if my sister were to have been abused by her spouse, it is not my place to tell her that "God intended it for good," either in hindsight or worse as a twisted justification for her staying in the abusive situation. One could follow a similar line of thought with someone whose spouse or partner or child died on 9/11 or in the January 2010 Haitian earthquake or in a car accident or of cancer or . . . To superimpose Joseph's response upon another is *not* within the bounds of this text.

Joseph comes to this on his own and only after much suffering and separation and reunion and grief and tears and, frankly, hindsight. His speech to them is heartfelt (*'al-libam* [NRSV: "kindly"]; v. 21). Sincere is Joseph's judgment of the many interwoven elements, good and bad, that comprise a life lived. Only he can say that what humans intend for evil, God can use for good (v. 20).

### Sirach 27:30—28:7 (LFM)

A complement to the Gospel lesson for this week, Ben Sira's offering of wisdom on forgiveness is both theological and practical. For Ben Sira, Wisdom is cosmic and local. Created first and before the beginning of time (24:9), in the assembly of the Most High Lady Wisdom speaks of her glory, of her coming from the mouth of the Most High, and of her throne in a pillar of cloud whence she governs over all peoples and nations (24:2-6). It is *this* Wisdom, woven into the fabric of the universe and located in the Torah of Moses, that is also expressed in the likes of today's poems[3] focused primarily on forgiveness.

Of note is that there is roughly the same reasoning in Sirach 28:2-4 as in the parable of the unforgiving slave, who is asked by the king, "Should you not have had mercy on your fellow slave, as I had mercy on you?" (Matt. 18:33). While one could get into the question of influence here, the correlation between the cosmic wisdom in Ben Sira and the storied wisdom in Christ is more important.

## Psalmody
### Psalm 114 (RCL)

*Fantastic* may be a word for this psalm's poetic portrayal of two significant events in Israel's history: (1) the exodus from Egypt and (2) the entry of the people into the promised land. Regarding the first, the psalmist sings that "the sea looked and fled" (Exod. 14:21), and regarding the second that "Jordan turned back" (Josh. 4:23-24). Not only does the psalmist recall these seminal events in Israel's story, but the psalm attests that the mountains and hills skip like rams and lambs respectively. One can imagine a children's production of this psalm with delightfully awkward and playful kids dressed as sea and stream, mountains and hills, skipping about. Lest we frolic too long in such amusements, the psalmist draws us to the true power that inspires such movement by the Reed Sea and the Jordan River, mountain and hill—it is the Lord "who turns the rock into a pool of water, the flint into a spring of water." Tremble (v. 7), indeed!

## Exodus 15:1b-11, 20-21 (RCL alt.)

See the comments on the RCL first reading, Exodus 14:19-31, above.

## Psalm 103:(1-7), 8-13 (RCL alt.)
## Psalm 103:1-2, 3-4, 9-10, 11-12 (LFM)

This psalm of thanksgiving is chockablock with acknowledgment that the Lord alone is the source of life. It is the Lord who forgives and heals (v. 3), redeems and crowns with *chesed* ("steadfast love") and mercy (v. 3), satisfies with good, and renews youth (v. 4). Notice that the psalmist's praise is not only related to the personal; it is also in recognition of the corporate. "The LORD works vindication and justice for all who are oppressed." The Lord is the deliverer, as is so familiar from Israel's history.

Perhaps the crown jewel of the psalm comes in verses 10-12, wherein the psalmist praises the Lord for forgiveness. The Lord "does not deal with us according to our sins, nor repay us according to our iniquities." For us Christians, it is impossible to read this outside of the cross of Christ. We can pray this psalm because of Christ, who in Luther's understanding becomes the greatest sinner of all as he takes on himself the sins of the world.[4]

# Second Reading
## Romans 14:1-12 (RCL)
## Romans 14:7-9 (LFM)

Paul continues his teaching on living together in community. Of course, the community that he is addressing most directly, the burgeoning assembly of believers in Rome, is a hodgepodge of Jews and Gentiles. Presumably, this community came together with a significant difference of opinion and practice. Notice what Paul says about hospitality[5] among believers: "Welcome those who are weak in faith, but not for the purpose of quarreling over opinions." After addressing different dietary practices, he says, "Who are you to pass judgment on the servants of another?" In short, he says, do not let that which is not central to the faith divide you. He goes on to say in a veiled sort of way that even one's observation of the Sabbath is not to be used as a measure of another's faithfulness (14:5-6).

I trust that the analogy to our lives as Christians today is easy to spot. How often do we feel a need to judge the behavior of our fellow Christians, so often finding ourselves in the camp of the righteous and the "others" outside? While Paul speaks specifically about dietary decisions and Sabbath observance, how many more categories has the church—have *we*—added to this list of inner-ecclesial, inhospitable squabbling? We need to recall Paul's language in verse 3, "Those who ___ must not despise those who ___, and those who ___ must not pass judgment on those who ___; for God has welcomed them." The reason for not passing judgment: God *has welcomed* them (see 15:7).

What this comes down to is the basis for our gathering. What makes the church the church? Is it agreement, right thinking, conformity of behavior, similarity of hairstyle, and the like? No.

In the midst of these early verses of Romans 14 come the theological girders upon which Paul's argument for this understanding of community rest. Romans 14:7-9 tells us about the Christian's living in Christ. The Christian life is a radical thing because, from the point of faith/baptism (Rom. 6:1-14; 12:4-5), the Christian's individuality is no longer simply in and for itself. Rather, the whole of the Christian's life and death is in Christ, who is Lord of the living and the dead. We need not fear and therefore judge the other, our neighbor, but love in Christ. We need not fear death, for the love of Christ does not conclude at our own death but goes beyond. Are we accountable? Indeed. But this accountability seems concerned with love and hospitality—a cruciform love.

# Gospel
## Matthew 18:21-35 (RCL, LFM)

Continuing from last week's Gospel text, forgiveness is at the heart this week as well—and it is nuttier and more radical than we can imagine. The pericope begins with Peter's question of Jesus regarding forgiveness, a question that flows well from last week's Gospel (18:15-20): "Lord, if a brother or sister sins against me, how often should I forgive? As many as seven times?" (v. 15, my trans.; see Proper 18, above). It seems relatively safe here to assume that Peter has taken Jesus' teaching seriously. To suggest that he would forgive one who has wronged him seven times is quite gracious. How many of us could do the same? Jesus' response, however, is incredible insofar as he increases Peter's bid elevenfold.

From this shocking number crunching, Jesus' words move seamlessly (*dia touto*) into the parable that puts these numbers into story. More than an illustration, Jesus' parable embodies the seventy-seven times *and* connects our creaturely forgiveness to divine forgiveness. The creaturely and the divine are not two separate spheres of existence. The creaturely, especially understood as the kingdom of heaven, is a mirror of the divine. Our forgiveness, albeit dimmed in comparison (1 Cor. 13:12), is to mirror God's mercy and forgiveness incarnate in Christ. The ones so graciously forgiven are to be no less gracious and forgiving.

So it is that Jesus begins the parable saying, "For this reason the kingdom of heaven may be compared . . ." The verb here, *hōmoiōthei*, may be better translated as "the kingdom of heaven *has become* like."[6] Within the proper bounds of the Greek, the text accentuates that this kingdom has already come to be in Jesus.

The debt that the slave owes the king is so enormous that it has to be theologically humorous hyperbole. If a talent is worth 6,000 denarii, and a denarius is a commoner's daily wage, then a talent is approximately twenty years' worth of wages. Multiplied by 10,000, the debt that the slave owes the king is approximately 200,000 years' wages.[7] There is no possible way that a slave could end up in such a situation. It is highly unlikely that the king himself in this story could owe such a debt. For the sake of more real-time numbers, if this slave's yearly wage were $15,000, the debt that he owed the king would be $3 billion.

Clearly, the slave was not able to pay. And what is the king's judgment? That not only the man, but also his family and possessions, be sold into slavery to pay the debt. Important here is that even this action by the king, which is a harsh and sweeping judgment, would not get close to denting this massive debt.

Upon hearing this judgment, the slave falls upon his knees (*proskuneō*—perhaps more appropriately "worship") before his lord to beg for patience, saying boldly that he will repay the whole thing. Clearly, the slave's promise is ridiculous, and the king's wits should be questioned. It would take him ten thousand lifetimes to settle this debt.

"And out of pity for him, the lord of that slave released him and forgave him the debt" (18:27). The Greek here is more explicitly theological than the English may first appear. The Greek *splagxnizomai* is a word often reserved for Jesus' compassionate disposition toward the crowds that followed him (Matt. 9:46; 14:14; 15:32; Mark 6:34; 8:2) or to those in need of healing (Matt. 20:34; Mark 1:41; 9:22; Luke 7:13). Jesus also uses it in two parables recorded in Luke: of the good Samaritan (10:33) and of the father in the parable of the prodigal son (15:20). One might go so far as to say that this "pity" (NRSV) is God's loving disposition toward God's creation most clearly seen in the ministry and cross of Christ. For it is this "pity" that moves the lord in the parable to release (*apoluō*) and forgive (*aphieimi*) the outrageous, unpayable debt of the slave.

Such is God's forgiveness of the sinner unable to pay his/her outrageous, unpayable debt. The parable continues and in its continuation the lines are drawn between the divine and the human. The forgiven slave, upon his release from his debts, comes upon a fellow slave who owes him a debt. While still a significant debt, the one hundred denarii is equivalent to about four months' wages; thus, the rough ratio of the debts of these two slaves is 600,000 to 1.[8] Immediately after being forgiven his own outrageous, unpayable debt, the slave grabs his fellow slave by the neck in an attempt to choke the money out of him. The forgiven slave's disposition toward his fellow slave is opposite that of the compassion (*splagxnizomai*) of the lord and king as the forgiven slave ignores pleas for mercy and throws his fellow slave into debtors' prison.

The outrage of the community at the actions of the forgiven slave reaches the ears of the king, who is also outraged. "Should you not have had mercy on your fellow slave, as I had mercy on you?" (18:33). Herein is the crux of the parable. The Lord's mercy, compassion, and forgiveness are lavish, not earned, and provide a model for our creaturely imitation. This imitation can never earn or merit forgiveness, for the Lord's forgiveness precedes all. Our forgiveness, however, flows from being forgiven and can imitate, albeit imperfectly, God's forgiveness of God's creatures. To top off the parable, the king's anger and judgment are harshest when this response does not happen. The forgiven slave, because of the frugality of his own forgiveness, is condemned to ten thousand lifetimes of torture.

The role of forgiveness within the Christian community and the larger world, which is God's creation and dominion, is all-important. Unforgiven sins fester and destroy individuals, communities, nations from within. To hold on to debts/sins perpetuates the debt/sin for days, weeks, generations, to the point that individuals and nations want to grab each other by the neck and choke out payment.

While our human forgiveness is always an imperfect imitation of the forgiveness we have first received in Jesus Christ, it is what God expects. Recall the words we pray so often in the prayer that Jesus taught us: "Forgive us our sins, *as* we forgive those who sin against us." We are praying that God forgive us *as* we forgive those who sin against us. This parable of forgiveness in Matthew 18 is this petition of the Lord's Prayer in story form.

It is not an easy thing to forgive, yet so many of us pray this petition of the Lord's Prayer nonchalantly as if it doesn't matter. Yet what we pray—forgive us our sins, *as* we forgive those who sin against us—is that God's forgiveness of our own transgressions, sins, estrangement, idolatries, and so forth be to us like our forgiveness is to those who sin against us.

There is a certain serendipity (a word that I use when I'm not sure if the Holy Spirit is to blame or not) that the Gospel lections from Matthew 18 center our attention perfectly on forgiveness on the 4th and 11th of September 2011, ten years after the Al Qaeda attack on the United States. This anniversary is not a time to focus on aggression or victory by way of violence and war. Violence only begets violence. While there is and needs to be an accountability, accountability does not heal, retribution does not heal, violence does not heal. Forgiveness heals for it is in forgiveness that we meet the other, sister or brother, as one for whom Christ died.

With the images of that day seared into collective and individual memories of people and peoples around the world and as we still and always will live in a world that is not safe from death, we Christians are called to live more fully in the faith of Jesus Christ, where security comes in the waters and promise of baptism and assurance comes in a little hunk of bread and taste of wine with the words "For you!" and forgiveness comes so centrally and lavishly in Jesus the Christ.

Perhaps *serendipity* is not faithful enough.

## Notes

1. Brevard Childs, *The Book of Exodus: A Critical, Theological Commentary,* Old Testament Library (Philadelphia: Westminster, 1974), 237.
2. "All beginnings are difficult" is a fine bit of wisdom in *Mekhilta Yitro, Bachodesh* 2.
3. Actually, this lesson includes a portion of one poem on "anger and vengeance" (27:28—28:1) and the whole of another on "forgiveness" (28:2-7). Cf. Patrick W. Skehan and Alexander A. Di Lella, *The Wisdom of Ben Sira,* Anchor Bible 39 (New York: Doubleday, 1987), 362–64.
4. See Martin Luther, "Lectures on Galatians 1535: Chapters 1–4," in *Luther's Works*, vol. 26, ed. Jaroslav Pelikan (St. Louis: Concordia, 1963), 276–91.
5. Recall that earlier Paul exhorted, "Extend hospitality to strangers" (12:13b).
6. Arland J. Hultgren, *The Parables of Jesus: A Commentary* (Grand Rapids: Eerdmans, 2002), 23.
7. Ibid., 23.
8. Ibid., 27.

# September 18, 2011
## Fourteenth Sunday after Pentecost
### Twenty-fifth Sunday in Ordinary Time / Proper 20

| Revised Common Lectionary (RCL) | Lectionary for Mass (LFM) |
| --- | --- |
| Exodus 16:2-15 or Jonah 3:10—4:11 | Isaiah 55:6-9 |
| Psalm 105:1-6, 37-45 or 145:1-8 | Psalm 145:2-3, 8-9, 17-18 |
| Philippians 1:21-30 | Philippians 1:20c-24, 27a |
| Matthew 20:1-16 | Matthew 20:1-16a |

## First Reading
### Exodus 16:2-15 (RCL)

While it is a rather peculiar problem that we find the Israelites complaining about a lack of food given the flocks and herds that were with them when they left Egypt (Exod. 12:38), here it is. Hunger. And with hunger, murmuring.

It must have been a drag to be Moses and Aaron. The constant querulous whining and complaining like fingernails on an old blackboard, so viscerally annoying that it made their teeth hurt. And likely making things worse, what the Israelites recall about Egypt is less memory and more reminiscence, like a sieve straining out the nasty dregs, leaving a clear wine that never existed.[1] They long for bread and the meat of their fleshpots, and they accuse the Lord's liberating agents, Moses and Aaron, of dragging them into the wilderness only to starve to death.

Yet the Lord hears their complaint and provides: meat (quail) and bread (manna) (16:13; cf. 16:31). Of course, there is the comic play on words, as this *manna* is closely related to the Israelites' question at the first sight of this heavenly bread, paraphrased, "What the heck *is this*?!" (*man hu'*). Complaining aside, the Lord hears and responds.

As for the beleaguered Moses and Aaron, they are able to say to the Israelites, "This just isn't our fault!" When the glory of the Lord appears in the wilderness before the people, it is clear, if even for a fleeting moment, that the Lord delivered them from Egypt, that the Lord heard of their hunger, and that the Lord responded with bread from heaven.[2]

## Jonah 3:10—4:11 (RCL alt.)

The pericope, which is the final scene in this lovely prophetic novella, comes to an embarrassing conclusion for the prophet. Nineveh, the wicked city, has repented. They have "turned from their evil ways," and God has had compassion (*nkhm*) upon the people of Nineveh, relenting from punishment (3:10). In spite of Jonah's lame attempt to announce the Lord's call to repentance—not only does he run the other way at first, but when he gets to Nineveh he does not even go to the middle of the city, walking for one day when Nineveh is a three-days' walk across (3:3-4)—the people of Nineveh have turned.

The embarrassment comes when Jonah, the prophet of the Lord, is outraged at Nineveh's repentance, *and* when he reveals that his resistance to the Lord's call was because he knew that the Lord is "gracious . . . and merciful, slow to anger, and abounding in steadfast love, and ready to relent from punishing" (4:2; cf. Ps. 145:8). Woe upon Jonah, the stingy prophet attempting to hoard the Lord's mercy and lovingkindness! The story, of course, finishes off with yet another measure of absurdity from Jonah, whose concern is greater for the *qiqayon* weed and his own health than for the whole of Nineveh.

The story of Jonah may be one of the most obviously applicable to the church, parish, and Christian today, as it reveals to us the absurdity of any and all of our attempts to be stingy with the message of God's mercy and lovingkindness. For the Lord will trespass any boundaries or borders that we attempt to place upon this love.

## Isaiah 55:6-9 (LFM)

With the reading of this text, a portal is opened for some of the sounds of the Vigil of Easter to waft across the seasons,[3] perhaps breathing a bit of spring air into what can be experienced as the doldrums of Ordinary Time. This portion of Isaiah 55 is a call to repentance. The series of imperatives—seek, call upon, forsake, return—is followed by two equally powerful reasons: that the Lord might have mercy and because the Lord pardons abundantly (Ps. 86:5). In the words of St. Fulgentius (468–533), bishop of Ruspe in North Africa:

> Let the wicked forsake his own way, in which he sins; let the unrighteous abandon his thoughts with which he despairs of the forgiveness of sins and according to the prophet's statement, 'return to the Lord, for he will abundantly pardon.' *In this 'abundantly,' nothing is lacking. Here mercy is omnipotent, and omnipotence is merciful.* For so great is the kindness of God that there is nothing that he is unable to loose for the converted person.[4]

The ways and thoughts of God are beyond us, far from our human reason and imaginings, yet here the evangelist of Isaiah proclaims the abundance of God's pardon. Perhaps we hear this abundance in Jesus' words to us from the cross: "Father, forgive them, for they know not what they do" (Luke 23:24).

## Psalmody
### Psalm 105:1-6, 37-45 (RCL)

"Remember the wonderful works he has done, his miracles, and the judgments he uttered" (105:5). From the Lord's covenant with Abraham to the Lord's providing quail and manna in the wilderness and water from the rock at Massah and Meribah, Psalm 105 recalls and gives thanks for the interweaving of the Lord's story with that of Israel.[5]

Together with the opening thanksgiving (vv. 1-6), the psalm is structured for the assembly to accent the final portion of the exodus story (vv. 37-42)[6] and the conquest of Canaan (vv. 43-45). Within the RCL, what Psalm 105:27-42 touches roughly correlates with the Old Testament lessons for Propers 19–21, in particular with today's first reading about the Lord's sending of the quail and manna.

A homiletical strength of the psalm is its poetic recounting of Israel's story, and for Israel (and the rest of us!) their story is their identity. How might the church's and/or a particular parish's story be sung with such thanksgiving? How might such a song witness to the weaving of God's story with the world's? In baptism, the Christian and her/his story are woven together with the church's story and the church's with Christ, and Christ's with the Trinity and the whole of the cosmos.

### Psalm 145:1-8 (RCL alt.)
### Psalm 145:2-3, 8-9, 17-18 (LFM)

Like the genre of children's books with a different letter of the alphabet on each page—books that are both instructive and entertaining—Psalm 145 is one of the alphabetic acrostic poems in Scripture,[7] meaning that each line begins with the succeeding letter of the Hebrew alphabet. While there may be a number of reasons for such poems, it is quite possible, especially with Psalm 145, that this poetic form symbolizes wholeness.

Psalm 145 has played a prominent role in the liturgy and piety of both Jews and Christians.[8] The singing of the psalm in worship is a beautiful thing given the height and breadth and depth of praise of the Lord. Interestingly, this psalm is found in a version of the psalter from among the Dead Sea Scrolls that includes a refrain between the verses: "Blessed be the LORD, and blessed be his name forever and ever."[9] Of pivotal beauty in the psalm is verse 8, "The LORD is gracious and merciful, slow to anger and abounding in steadfast love," which echoes throughout Scripture.[10]

## Second Reading
### Philippians 1:21-30 (RCL)
### Philippians 1:20c-24, 27a (LFM)

Today begins a month's worth of readings from Paul's letter to the Philippians. As terse as the 109 verses of Philippians are, each word is packed with rich theological and homiletical possibilities. This first portion of the letter comes from a section where Paul is naming both his own personal situation, which in a nutshell has him in prison (1:7, 13, 14, 17), and his relation to the assembly in Philippi.

Let there be no doubt that the physical location of Paul's writing has a great deal to do with what he is writing. Paul's situation is one of hardship, suffering, and perhaps despair. He is between a rock and a hard place,[11] between desiring an escape from this life and welcome into the next and remaining to serve in the mission of the gospel. Whether exaggeration or not, Paul is inclined to say that his situation is such that death is not so bad: "My desire is to depart and be with Christ, for that is far better" (v. 23b).

At the same time, let there be no doubt that Paul's first concern is God's action in Christ, which is effective both in his imprisonment and in the community of believers in Philippi. Regarding his own self, he desires that "whether by life or by death," Christ be exalted (v. 20b). Likewise, in the shift from focusing on his own self to the Philippian community (cf. "for you," v. 24), Paul's encouragement to the Philippian believers is that they live their lives "in a manner worthy of the gospel of Christ" (v. 27a).

Even from his prison cell and the suffering that he is experiencing for the sake of the gospel, Paul exhorts the Philippians with a realistic, cruciform sense of mission. Lest we think that Paul is simply commending the Philippian Christians with a brand of moralism, the living of which he speaks is missional, and living missionally is not a cakewalk. Together with the joy and rejoicing with which Philippians is laced, there is realism about opposition, struggle, and suffering. But it is not suffering for suffering's sake. Rather, the mission is to "proclaim Christ out of love" (v. 16a).

Such is the missional journey that Christian communities are called to—a journey where the proclamation of Christ is the impetus, the content, and the goal—a journey where this proclamation brings both joy and suffering and at times results in the Christian finding him/herself between a rock and a hard place.

A contemporary example of this comes in the story of a small group of Trappist monks in rural Algeria before and during the time of the Algerian Civil War (1991–2002). The steady, dynamic witness of the brothers together is coupled with their hearty and trusting relationships with their Muslim neighbors. The brothers risked real relationship with their neighbors in spite of the genuine threat of death—a threat eventually realized, though *not* at the hand of their neighbors.

At the funeral of the seven monks of Tibhirine on June 2, 1996, the words of Brother Bernardo Olivera are worth recalling as a witness to the complex mix of joy and suffering that is this missional life "worthy of the gospel of Christ":

> What can a monk say about his brother monks? I know that our order was founded on our commitment to silence, work, and praise of God. But we know that there are times to speak as well as times to be quiet. After fifty years of silence, our seven brothers—Christian, Luc, Christophe, Célestin, Bruno, Michel, and Paul—today

have become spokesmen for all the stifled voices and anonymous individuals who have given their lives for a more humane world. Our seven monks lend their voices today to me as well. They, as others like them, were living manifestations of the good news of the Gospels; a life freely given in the spirit of love is never a life lost, but one found again in Him who is Life. . . . They showed that we must enter into the world of others, be that "other" a Christian or a Muslim. If "the other" does not exist, there can be no love of "the other." Let us learn to go beyond ourselves and to be enriched by those who are different.[12]

# Gospel
## Matthew 20:1-16 (RCL)
## Matthew 20:1-16a (LFM)

"For the kingdom of heaven is like . . ." So Jesus begins this parable.

By itself, this little story could be read as a critique of free-market capitalism, sociopolitical theory, or just labor practices in the first century C.E. Yet if we were to take this tack on the story, it quickly becomes clear just how absurd it is. There is no way that any landowner could or would behave in this way and still expect to secure workers for a whole day. Why work for the whole day when you could get hired onto this fellow's grape-picking crew at 3:00 p.m.—or better yet, at 5:00 p.m.—work a couple of hours, and get the same wage as the poor buggers who put in a full day? The outrage of the worker who has toiled all day only to be paid the same as the one who has worked a couple of hours is evident in the parable itself: "You have made them equal to us . . ." (v. 12). In spite of the fact that the workers all agreed to conditions prior to setting out on their service—that is, their daily work—the outrage by the workers who began work earliest in the day and labored under the hot sun throughout is rooted in an understanding of fairness. From the standpoint of the worker, it is simply not fair, and from a business standpoint it is ridiculous. To think that an employer would retain those who work hard all day long if she/he did not compensate them in a fair and proportional relation to the work they provide is just nutty. In short, without the comparative ("the kingdom of heaven is like"), the laborers in Jesus' parable are justifiably outraged and the landowner is both a fool and an irresponsible businessperson.

And just what is the kingdom of heaven likened to? The foolish, irresponsible businessperson. The kingdom of heaven is absurd and out of touch. It is built upon an out-of-whack sense of fairness and with naïve business and economic sensibilities. Thank God for this!

It is true, I think, that texts project a world into which the reader/hearer is invited to participate. A novel, for example, builds a world into which the reader is invited. While the world of the novel can be similar or dissimilar or some combination thereof from the reader's everyday life, much of a novel's "success" comes in the buy-ability of the world that the story projects.

Jesus' parables also project a worldview, and they do so as a metaphor. Paul Ricoeur, who did much work in the area of metaphor and meaning, suggested that metaphors *redefine reality* by way of holding in tension two unrelated things. As such, metaphor has the power to create meaning ("semantic innovation") and project an otherwise inaccessible world.[13]

So what is the world that this parable projects?

Without the comparative, this parable tells the story of a naïve businessman and righteously outraged workers. It could be read as a farce that points fun at a foolish member of the upper class. Yet with the comparative "the kingdom of heaven is like," the ultimate meaning of the parable is found in the theological reality of God who makes God's self known most clearly in the cross of Christ. In this way, the hermeneutic for reading this (and every?) parable might be summarized by Paul: "For the message of the cross is foolishness to those who are perishing, but to us who are being saved it is the power of God. . . . For God's foolishness is wiser than human wisdom, and God's weakness is stronger than human strength" (1 Cor. 1:18, 25).

The worldview that this parable creates and into which it invites us Christians is one that is topsy-turvy. Those of us who presume to be on top, in the lead, making the big bucks, the most faithful, the clearly righteous may well be surprised. The divine landowner *is* foolish and irresponsible with forgiveness and grace. We Christians *are* so often righteously outraged precisely at this foolish and irresponsible forgiveness and grace. And this *is just the worldview* that this parable projects and into which we are invited. A world in which the divine landowner is free to distribute as the landowner chooses.

The landowner is not stingy either. This is not a world of scarcity wherein there is a limited amount of forgiveness and grace thereby lending itself to hoarding by the "faithful." Not at all. This world is one of abundance. If we consider that one does not need more than the "daily wage," then to seek more is misplaced. What can we seek that is more than God's undeserved justification of us sinners? Is not the daily wage more than enough? This worldview into which we're invited is one that understands that all who enter the vineyard receive this abundance. Such is the scandal of the gospel.[14] And we Christians are called to see others, whether cradle Christians or newcomers or those sitting around in the town square, as worthy of the divine landowner's payment. In this way the kingdom of heaven is perfectly out of whack: "So the last will be first, and the first will be last" (v. 16).

## Notes

1. "This exaggeration is well understandable from a psychological viewpoint, for people are inclined to forget past troubles when faced with new ones, and to picture the past to themselves as far better than it was in fact." Umberto Cassuto, *A Commentary on the Book of Exodus*, trans. I. Abrahams (Jerusalem: Magnes, 1967), 189.
2. The story of the Israelites and their manna is reinterpreted in light of Jesus in John 6.
3. Isaiah 55:1-11 is a traditional text for the Vigil, read each year as the fifth text read according to both the LFM and RCL.

4.  From "Letter 6," as quoted in Mark W. Elliott, ed., *Isaiah 40–66*, Ancient Christian Commentary on Scripture (Downers Grove, Ill.: InterVarsity, 2007), 188, emphasis added.

5.  Psalms 78, 106, and 136 are similar.

6.  This covers roughly Exod. 13:17—17:7.

7.  Others include Psalms 34 and 119, as well as the first four chapters of Lamentations and Sirach 51 outside the Old Testament psalter.

8.  James L. Mays, *Psalms,* Interpretation: A Bible Commentary for Teaching and Preaching (Louisville: John Knox, 1994), 437.

9.  Cf. Martin Abegg Jr., Peter Flint, and Eugene Ulrich, *The Dead Sea Scrolls Bible* (New York: Harper, 1999), 570. For an accessible text on the whole of 11QPs[a] by the original editor of the scroll, see James A. Sanders, *The Dead Sea Psalms Scroll* (Ithaca, N.Y.: Cornell University Press, 1967).

10. E.g., Exod. 34:6; Pss. 86:15; 103:8; Joel 2:13; Jonah 4:2 (see the first reading, above).

11. My paraphrase of what the NRSV translates "hard pressed between the two" (1:23a). On the question of Paul contemplating suicide or not, see N. Clayton Croy, "'To Die Is Gain' (Philippians 1:19-26): Does Paul Contemplate Suicide?" *Journal of Biblical Literature* 122 (2003): 517–31.

12. As quoted in John W. Kiser, *The Monks of Tibhirine: Faith, Love, and Terror in Algeria* (New York: St. Martin's, 2002), 4–5.

13. Cf. Paul Ricoeur, "Biblical Hermeneutics," *Semeia* 4 (1975): 29–148, esp. 75–106. See also Paul Ricoeur, *Interpretation Theory: Discourse and the Surplus of Meaning* (Fort Worth: Texas Christian University Press, 1976).

14. In the more overtly political reading of Pablo A. Jiménez, "the parable would depict . . . how God loves, cares for, and saves people who admittedly do not deserve such divine mercy. In brief, the Parable of the Laborers in the Vineyard is a clear expression of the 'scandal of the gospel': God affirms the full humanity of the 'excluded.'" "The Laborers of the Vineyard (Matthew 20:1-16): A Hispanic Homiletical Reading," *Journal for Preachers* 21 (1997): 39.

# September 25, 2011
## Fifteenth Sunday after Pentecost
### Twenty-sixth Sunday in Ordinary Time / Proper 21

| Revised Common Lectionary (RCL) | Lectionary for Mass (LFM) |
|---|---|
| Exodus 17:1-7 or Ezekiel 18:1-4, 25-32 | Ezekiel 18:25-28 |
| Psalm 78:1-4, 12-16 or 25:1-9 | Psalm 25:4-5, 6-7, 8-9 |
| Philippians 2:1-13 | Philippians 2:1-11 or 2:1-5 |
| Matthew 21:23-32 | Matthew 21:28-32 |

## First Reading
### Exodus 17:1-7 (RCL)

Again, there is complaining in the wilderness camp of the Israelites. Last week's pericope (16:2-15) had them complaining of hunger. This week it is thirst. Their thirst is such that Moses has a near-mutiny on his hands. Again, the people's protest blames Moses for their situation (v. 3). Things have deteriorated to the point that they are about to stone good ol' Moses. Out of desperation, the people complain to Moses, Moses cries out to the Lord,[1] and again the Lord provides. Perhaps this is as much the refrain of our lives as it is of Israel's story.

While it may be that there are natural phenomena like that described here of water flowing just below rock surfaces on the Sinai Peninsula,[2] to explain the event in this way misses the full force of the narrative. More significant is the motif that the people's thirst, which ignites their anger and disbelief, is quenched by the Lord.[3] In spite of their perpetual incredulity, the Lord provides (see also Hagar and Ishmael, Gen. 21:19; Samson, Judg. 15:18-19; etc.). And at the same time, their incredulity toward the Lord and anger with Moses are memorialized in the name of this place—Massah ("test") and Meribah ("quarrel")—as a symbol of this tension between the people's unfaithfulness and God's in-spite-of faithfulness.

## Ezekiel 18:1-4, 25-32 (RCL alt.)
## Ezekiel 18:25-28 (LFM)

"The parents have eaten sour grapes, and the children's teeth are set on edge" (18:2). So goes the familiar proverb that fuels the question of life and death running throughout Ezekiel 18 (cf. Jer. 31:29).

The Lord by way of Ezekiel is asserting the fullness of the Lord's reign over the people in exile. It is not for the people to blame their parents for their own misery and hardship and sin, for their exile in Babylon. Such a mode of thinking, as reflected in the proverb, challenges God's sovereignty insofar as sin and misfortune, parents and children are related like dominoes toppling each other—a human Rube Goldberg machine of cause and effect with the action/sin of the parent determining the action/sin of the child. And so the Lord asserts the Lord's absolute governance: "Know that *all* lives are mine; the life of the parent as well as the life of the child is mine: it is only the person who sins that shall die" (v. 4). It is *not* that sin is ineffectual or inconsequential, but it *is* the choice, responsibility, and burden of the individual.

Yet the people say, "It's not fair!" (also Ezek. 33:17-20). And perhaps we can as well. We are all too aware of systemic sin that plagues our world—that heaps the sin of an individual, corporation, municipality, or nation upon the innocent. While it is certainly not helpful to oversimplify the relation of individual and corporate sin, what is a true reflection of reality is the people's response, "It's not fair!" It's someone else's fault. The current muck in which I/we find ourselves *and* the judgment for it are certainly *not my responsibility.*

Ezekiel does not resolve this tension between the individual and the corporate,[4] but he does emphasize the call to "turn" (*shuv*). And remarkably, amid the sweeping judgment portrayed throughout much of Ezekiel, the Lord's disposition toward both the righteous and the wicked is revealed: "For I have no pleasure in the death of *anyone,* says the Lord GOD. Turn, then, and live" (18:32; also 18:23; 33:11). This revelation of the availability of the Lord's forgiveness and the Lord's willingness to forgive is a strong "yes!" to the life-giving, holy nature of God's sovereignty.[5]

# Psalmody
## Psalm 78:1-4, 12-16 (RCL)

Like last week's psalm, Psalm 78 is a psalm that recalls and gives thanks for the interweaving of the Lord's story with that of the people of Israel. More focused this week is the connection with the RCL Old Testament lesson, wherein the Lord provides water to the thirsty Israelites.

As arranged for the worshiping assembly, two portions of the psalm are used. The first is the opening (vv. 1-4), and the second (vv. 12-16) recalls the exodus from Egypt, from the plagues through the flowing of the water from the rock at Massah and Meribah. Psalm 78, however, does not mention these proper names as given in Exodus 17, perhaps as they represent and recall the griping of the people.

Of interest is that the psalm speaks of secret things—hidden elements of the tradition: "I will open my mouth in a parable; I will utter dark sayings from of old, things that we have heard and known, that our ancestors have told us" (v. 2; cf. Ps. 49:3). This verse is quoted in Matthew's Gospel in the midst of Jesus' parables in Matthew 13. Origen understands verse 3 and Matthew 13:35 together as proof of the multiple layers of meaning in Scripture, including meanings revealed only in faith.[6]

## Psalm 25:1-9 (RCL alt.)
## Psalm 25:4-5, 6-7, 8-9 (LFM)

An acrostic psalm, this psalm is a deeply personal prayer asking for deliverance and instruction in the life and way of faithfulness. It begins with a submissive metaphorical gesture, "To you, O Lord, I lift up my soul" (v. 1; cf. Ps. 86:4)—a posture of prayer that, says James L. Mays, "portrays prayer as an act in which individuals hold their conscious identity, their life, in hands stretched out to God as a way of saying that their life depends completely and only on the help of God."[7]

A significant portion of the psalm is dedicated to the extension of this submission to the truth of the Lord. While the psalm does not mention Torah specifically, the psalmist is seeking from the Lord instruction in the Lord's ways and paths (v. 4), with the goal of "the friendship of the Lord" (v. 14). Arthur Weiser summarizes well the significance of this posture of prayer and desire for the Lord's ways and paths: "Just as the body is in daily want of food, thus the soul needs to be lifted up to God day by day in order that it obtain from him as a gift a true insight into his ways and be instructed in them—and at the same time may also be granted strength to be obedient to his will."[8]

# Second Reading
## Philippians 2:1-13 (RCL)
## Philippians 2:1-11 or 2:1-5 (LFM)

At the center of this pericope is one of the most theologically rich and mined texts in all of Scripture: the Christ Hymn in 2:5-11. When faced with an ocean as deep and wide as the two millennia of Christian praying and thinking through this text, identifying any particular drop or current to explore is as overwhelming as trying to choose one particular sweet in a confectionary. So here are two sweets to savor from amid the shelves full of possibilities: (1) the cruciform nature of God, and (2) putting on the mind of Christ as the *missio Dei*.

First, the church has wrestled for centuries with its understanding of who God is by way of God's revelation of God's self in Christ. What do we know about God by way of Christ? While the councils of Nicaea (325 C.E.) and Chalcedon (381 C.E.) addressed the heart of Christology, as the church lives and moves in the world, the question of God's revelation in Christ remains lively and important. Throughout these centuries-long christological conversations, Christians continually return to the Christ Hymn in Philippians 2.

Of the many areas of the Christ Hymn important to Christology and the mission of God in the world, let us focus on verses 7b-8: "And being found in human form, he humbled himself and became obedient to the point of death—even death on a cross." In the middle of the hymn, between cosmic language of Christ being in the form of God but not wanting to exploit this divinity, the incarnational self-emptying (*kenosis*), and his exaltation for the ultimate purpose of worship in the name of Jesus Christ to the glory of God the Father, comes this bit about Christ's self-humbling, obedience, and death. The hymn is specific in that this is a particular death, a cruciform death (*thanatou de staurou*), which is by definition a public and suffering death. What we have, then, is the cosmic Christ emptying himself in the incarnation, completing the incarnation by way of his crucifixion, and being exalted cosmically—that is, everywhere.

The crucifixion is central to the Christ Hymn's singing about who this Jesus is. And lest we check our trinitarian understanding of God at the door, we can say no less than with the crucifixion of Christ the cross is at the heart of the triune God. More fully in line with the whole of the Christ Hymn, emptying (*kenosis*), humbling, crucifixion, and exaltation are all part and parcel of who God reveals God's self to be.

Second, the hymn is for Paul (and his readers!) the scaffolding for his understanding of who God is and what it means to be in mission. Regarding the scaffolding, N. T. Wright points out that Paul has the Christ Hymn running through him and thus through the whole of his letter to the Philippians.[9] Similarly, Michael Gorman refers to the hymn as Paul's "master story."[10] With the climax of the hymn being the exaltation and cosmic worship of the cosmic, crucified Christ, it should be no surprise that there is an element of imitation encouraged of the Philippian (and cosmic!) Christian community in mission to put on the mind of Christ. But it is not solely the exaltation that the Philippians are invited to imitate, but the emptying,[11] humility, and death of Christ as well (cf. Phil. 3:21).

By way of the Christ Hymn, as it begins, "Let the same mind (*froneō*) be in *you* that was in Christ Jesus" (v. 5), Paul invites Christians into cruciform community and mission. Returning to the beginning of the pericope, Paul provides a disposition, an encouragement (*paraklēsis*) to the community that conforms with the hymn that follows (vv. 1-3). The christocentric, kenotic,[12] and cruciform understanding of who God is, as sung boldly in the Christ Hymn, *is* the framework for Christian community and mission—a mission that begins with singing the name of Jesus throughout the cosmos. The rest is God's business (v. 13).

# Gospel
## Matthew 21:23-32 (RCL)
## Matthew 21:28-32 (LFM)

This week's Gospel has two related but distinct bits: (1) the conflicted interaction in the temple between Jesus and his accusers, the chief priests and elders of the people, over the location of Jesus' authority to teach (vv. 23-27); and (2) Jesus' parabolic teaching that exercises his authority, speaks of the kingdom of God, and goes head-on against the wonky miscalculation of the kingdom of God by the religious leaders of the day (vv. 28-32). The two bits work toward redrawing the kingdom of God.

That this scene takes place in the temple is significant. Throughout Matthew's Gospel there is a recurring theme of the relation of Jesus' authority to the Torah and the temple. In the Sermon on the Mount, Jesus clearly states that he did not come to abolish the Law and the Prophets but to fulfill them. Not even the tiniest *yod* will pass away from the Torah (5:17-20). Yet almost in the same breath, we are privy to his teachings on some important aspects of Torah, all with the refrain, "You have heard it said . . . but *I* say . . ." (5:21-48). Jesus here affirms the authority of the Law and the Prophets (of Scripture) and at the same time asserts his own authority that *is* the Torah's fulfillment.

Likewise, in Matthew 12, Jesus' disciples pluck grain on the Sabbath, effectively working and thereby desecrating the Sabbath (Exod. 20:8-10a). What ensues is an argument with the Pharisees about this Sabbath transgression. Jesus confronts the Pharisees with the story of David and his soldiering companions eating the Bread of the Presence (1 Sam. 21:1-6; see also Mark 2:23-28; Luke 6:1-5), a transgression since this bread was only to be eaten by the Levitical priests in the temple (Lev. 24:5-9). Jesus concludes his response to the Pharisees by declaring, "I tell you, something greater than the temple is here. But if you had known what this means, 'I desire mercy and not sacrifice,' you would not have condemned the guiltless. For the Son of Man is lord of the sabbath" (Matt. 12:6-8, quoting Hosea 6:6).

And now, right on the heels of his triumphal entry into Jerusalem and the cleansing of the Temple (vv. 1-17), Jesus is back in the temple, and it should be no surprise that he is approached by the chief priests and elders of the people. He is a rabble-rouser, a challenge to their authority. The authority of the temple, the setting of this vignette, together with that of the temple leaders, is trumped by Jesus. Jesus' authority (*exousia*) fulfills Scripture and regularly trumps the received tradition/ temple.

This may sound like supersessionism if we don't realize that Jesus is encountering the received tradition from within, in this story literally and spatially so! In our contemporary world, this text should not be used as ammunition against Jews or Judaism. Rather, we should turn Jesus' clever question of authority on the church itself and on ourselves, those entrusted with the leadership of the church. It is true that before Christ there are many things to which we can answer, like the leaders whom Jesus addressed, nothing but "We do not know" (v. 27). We, the church, get so wrapped up in the nonessentials, in judging and gatekeeping, that we forget whose authority we stand under.[13]

The second half of the pericope flows from and concludes the first. Jesus meets the (I think) honest "We don't know" of the religious leaders with a brief

171

parable about a father and two sons. The text of this parable may be one of the most unresolved text-critical questions in the New Testament. While the textual problem itself may well not be preachable, the point behind it is illustrative and informative on the question of what Jesus' authority means for the church.

There are three textual variants in the questions and answers in 21:28-31a: (1) the first son agrees to the father's request but does not follow through, the second son does not agree but changes his mind, and Jesus' hearers (chief priests, elders of the people, and presumably those whom Jesus was teaching in the temple) identify the latter as the one who did the father's will; (2) the first son does not agree with the father's request but changes his mind, the second son agrees but does not follow through, the hearers identify the latter as the one who did the father's will; and (3) the first son does not agree to the father's request but later changes his mind, the second son agrees but does not follow through, the hearers identify the first as the one who did the father's will.[14] The first and third variants have the most significant manuscript support, and the third variant is preferred by nearly all contemporary English translations (e.g., NRSV, NIV, RSV, etc.).

So what does this textual variant matter, especially for preaching? Wendell E. Langely proposes an interesting (though complex) possibility that helps contemporary Westerners to see the otherwise cross-cultural background of the story.[15] While the predominant reading is that this is an allegory for Jews and Gentiles, it is also quite possible that Jesus is not concerned about allegory or even the answer that his hearers offer. Based on Palestinian responses to Jesus' question ("Which one of the two did the will of his father?"[16]), Hebrew linguistics, and readings of early rabbinic methods of interpretation, Langely suggests that both sons are partially obedient and partially disobedient. His reading allows that this parable is not primarily an allegory about two sons, the Jews and the Gentiles, where one ends up on top. Rather, Jesus skillfully uses the rhetorical conventions of the day to allow his opponents to hang themselves (sorry for the violent image!) with their own answer to his question. This is a setup of Jesus' hearers, who are fully disobedient, failing on *both* counts,[17] to the point that "the tax collectors and sinners are going into the kingdom of God ahead of *you*" (v. 31b).

So how does this pericope redraw the kingdom of God? It is the tax collectors (see Proper 18 above on Matt. 18:15-20) and sinners who believed John's message, *not* Jesus' hearers—*not* the religious leaders. It is not that Jesus' hearers will be left out, but the unexpected ones will enter before them. In Jesus' picture of the kingdom of God, the identity of the righteous ones is surprising—especially to the religious leaders. Jesus' authority undermines any and all categories of righteousness that the church and its leaders attempt to impose.

## Notes

1. Umberto Cassuto, *A Commentary on the Book of Exodus*, trans. I. Abrahams (Jerusalem: Magnes, 1967), points out that as much as the people are complaining about Moses, Moses reciprocates by complaining to the Lord about the people (202).
2. Ibid., 203.
3. Notable is that within Jewish tradition water takes on the symbolism of Torah; cf. William H. C. Propp, *Exodus 1–18*, Anchor Bible 2 (New York: Doubleday, 1999), 613; and within Christian tradition water takes on the symbolism of Christ (cf. John 4) and baptism (cf. Rom. 6:4; 1 Peter 3:20-22).
4. Robert W. Jenson, *Ezekiel*, Brazos Theological Commentary on the Bible (Grand Rapids: Brazos, 2009), 148.
5. Moshe Greenberg, *Ezekiel 1–20,* Anchor Bible 22 (Garden City, N.Y.: Doubleday, 1983), 341.
6. Origen, *Against Celsus* IV.49, in Alexander Roberts and James Donaldson, eds., *Ante-Nicene Fathers* (9 vols., Buffalo: Christian Literature Publishing, 1885–1896), 4:520.
7. James L. Mays, *Psalms,* Interpretation: A Bible Commentary for Teaching and Preaching (Louisville: John Knox, 1994), 124.
8. Arthur Weiser, *The Psalms*, trans. H. Hartwell, Old Testament Library (Louisville: Westminster John Knox, 1962), 239.
9. N. T. Wright, *The Climax of the Covenant: Christ and the Law in Pauline Theology* (Minneapolis: Fortress Press, 1993), 59.
10. Michael Gorman, *Inhabiting the Cruciform God: Kenosis, Justification, and Theosis in Paul's Narrative Soteriology* (Grand Rapids: Eerdmans, 2009), 9–39.
11. A number of scholars have recently explored the similarity of Paul's understanding of *kenosis* and the Buddhist concept of *sunyata*, e.g., Teresa Kuo-Yu Tsui, "Seeing Christian Kenosis in Light of Buddhist *Sunyata*: An Attempt at Inter-faith Hermeneutics," *Asia Journal of Theology* 21 (2007): 357–70; Paul S. Chung, *Martin Luther and Buddhism: Aesthetics of Suffering*, Princeton Theological Monograph Series (Eugene, Ore.: Pickwick, 2008), chap. 7.
12. For an argument that takes *kenosis* more fully into the realm of interreligious dialogue and Christian mission, cf. Martha Th. Frederiks, "Kenosis as a Model for Interreligious Dialogue," *Missiology* 33 (2005): 211–22.
13. Recall the Reformation principle *ecclesia semper reformanda*.
14. Paraphrasing both Arland J. Hultgren, *The Parables of Jesus: A Commentary* (Grand Rapids: Eerdmans, 2000), 218–19; and Wendell E. Langely, "The Parable of the Two Sons (Matthew 21.28-32) against Its Semitic and Rabbinic Backdrop," *Catholic Biblical Quarterly* 58 (1996): 228–30.
15. Langely, "Parable of the Two Sons," 228–43.
16. Matt. 21:31a. Langely builds upon the observations of J. A. Findlay, *Jesus and His Parables* (London: Epworth, 1950), who in the mid-twentieth century posed these questions to Palestinians, who identified the negative response of the first son, even with the turnaround, as more disrespecting of the father's will (ibid., 232–33).
17. Jesus' hearers received the Torah and Prophets, saying *yes* but not following through, *and* gave a resounding *no!* to the message of John the Baptist.

# October 2, 2011
## Sixteenth Sunday after Pentecost
### Twenty-seventh Sunday in Ordinary Time / Proper 22

| **Revised Common Lectionary (RCL)** | **Lectionary for Mass (LFM)** |
|---|---|
| Exodus 20:1-4, 7-9, 12-20 or Isaiah 5:1-7 | Isaiah 5:1-7 |
| Psalm 19 or 80:7-15 | Psalm 80:9 + 12, 13-14, 15-16, 19-20 |
| Philippians 3:4b-14 | Philippians 4:6-9 |
| Matthew 21:33-46 | Matthew 21:33-43 |

## First Reading
### Exodus 20:1-4, 7-9, 12-20 (RCL)

"The Lᴏʀᴅ God spoke all these words. . . ." So begins the Exodus account of the Ten Commandments—the basic scaffolding of the way of the Lord and the pinnacle of the Israelites' departure from Egypt and journey to the promised land. While we are not wanting for examples of God breaking into history, as the Lord of history does, the giving of the Decalogue is a gift that keeps on giving.

Speaking in the first person, the Lord addresses the people directly, reminding them, "I am the Lᴏʀᴅ *your* God, who brought you up out of the land of Egypt, out of the house of slavery . . ." (v. 2). The Lord in no uncertain terms claims Israel as the Lord's people. It is not that this is new (e.g., Gen. 12:1-3.), but it is important in that the Lord is putting before the people these ten expectations—commands that the Lord expects the people to observe. And as Terry Fretheim observes, "Obedience is relationally conceived."[1] What the Lord puts before the Israelites and, by extension, us Christians in the Decalogue assumes the Lord's saving relationship (remember Egypt!) with the people.

While there is more than enough material for preaching in this text and it is a great opportunity for the preacher that the Decalogue is in the lectionary for this day, it may well suffice to focus on the First Commandment, from which all the others flow: "You shall have no other gods before me" (v. 3). Herein lies the whole of faith and life: the Lord's expectation that the Lord alone will be the object of our creaturely devotion. As Luther points out in his Large Catechism, "Anything on which your heart relies and depends . . . that is really your god."[2]

From the outset of the Decalogue there is no question of God's faithfulness to God's people. With the First Commandment to have no other gods, God expects God's people to look into our own lives and hearts to examine truthfully our gods, our allegiances, our worship, our faithfulness.

## Isaiah 5:1-7 (RCL alt., LFM)

It is likely that this text appears in the lectionaries as the source for the vineyard imagery in the parable in today's Gospel lesson. In this case, the lectionary correlation between the Old Testament and Gospel lessons is warranted. The relationship is not superficial. Rather, Isaiah 5:1-7 provides the images and language for Jesus' retelling in the parable found with some variation in all three Synoptic Gospels (Matt. 21:33-41; Mark 12:1-9; Luke 20:9-16; also *Gos. Thom.* 65).

Yet what about this text within its more immediate context? Can it be more than background or influence for Jesus' parable? If the whole of Scripture witnesses to Christ (Luke 24:27), how might this text be interpreted and preached on its own? With the strength of the influence on Jesus' parable coupled with the fact that people in the pew will be hearing both together, it may well nigh be impossible—and, for that matter, unnecessary. That said, a couple of thoughts on the Isaiah text.

The text, written in poetic verse, is called a "lovesong" (*shirat dodi*) and functions as what Gale Yee calls a "juridical parable."[3] The judgment (i.e., juridical) is a surprise in that the singer is addressing the people of Jerusalem and Judah with this story about the Lord and the Lord's well-planned and -tended vineyard. Early in the text (v. 3), the Lord asks this audience effectively to judge between the righteousness of the Lord, who poured all this effort into the vineyard, and the vineyard, which has yielded unwieldy fruit. For quite contrary to the Lord's plan, the vineyard has come to yield wild grapes, distasteful compared to their domestic counterparts.

Yee suggests that this audience from Jerusalem and Judah would likely have heard the image of the vineyard as symbolic of the rival Northern Kingdom.[4] Assuming this, Isaiah's hearers would have been in agreement with the exercise of judgment against the vineyard (vv. 5-6). The surprise comes in verse 7: "For the vineyard of the LORD of hosts is the house of Israel *and* the people of Judah are his pleasant planting. . . ." The image of the vineyard and the tale of its unrighteousness are *not* about another. They are about them.

On so many levels, the same is true about us as we cast aspersions upon the righteousness of our neighbors, not recognizing that it is a mirror we are looking into. While Jesus pulls a similar trick on his accusers, it is within the realm of homiletical possibilities that this Isaiah text could be *done* to a contemporary congregation or parish, pulling such a surprise on one's hearers.

## Psalmody
### Psalm 19 (RCL)

"The heavens are telling the glory of God, and the firmament proclaims his handiwork!" So is the bang with which this psalm begins. No less than the very elements of the cosmos are proclaiming the truth about their originator. The psalm comes in two distinct and complementary halves: verses 1-6 speak of God's creative work, and verses 7-14 speak of God's gift of the Torah/law.

The first half has the whole cosmos giving voice to praises of the Lord. The sun, the great light, exemplifies the Lord's providence. With humanity's ability to generate electricity and have light 24/7, the power of this solar image may be lost on us. There is nothing like a night in the wilderness far away from the light pollution of the city to help us regain an appreciation for the sun in our imagination.

The second half, like orange juice concentrate of Psalm 119, bespeaks the beauty of the Torah—the way or instruction of the Lord that is itself interwoven throughout the fabric of the cosmos (cf. Sirach 24). But the Torah is not far removed, like an architect's blueprint archived long ago. The Lord's Torah is alive and well and enduring and personal. So valued by the psalmist (and by extension, the believer) is the law that it is more desired "than gold, even much find gold; sweeter also than honey, and drippings of the honeycomb" (v. 10). One can imagine, with Dietrich Bonhoeffer, Jesus, the Eternal Word incarnate, praying this psalm.

### Psalm 80:7-15 (RCL alt.)
### Psalm 80:9 + 12, 13-14, 15-16, 19-20 (LFM)

Accenting the vine language from the lections from Isaiah 5 and Matthew 21, the refrain of Psalm 80 sings well: "Restore us, O God of hosts, let your face shine, that we may be saved" (80:3, 7, 19). As is indicative of the address of the Lord as "God of hosts," this psalm images the Lord mighty and enthroned in the heavenly temple surrounded by the cherubim (cf. 2 Samuel 22; Psalm 18). The God of hosts is called in to help, to deliver, to restore, to save.

Yet beside the images of cosmic power and might, the Lord is also portrayed as a vinedresser. The vine here is Israel, which the Lord brought out of Egypt (v. 8), and it is the position of the psalmist that the vine needs some divine tending. It is overgrown, sprawling into dangerous places, so that its fruit will be plucked by the unintended and even ravaged by a wild pig! The psalmist beseeches the Lord to pay attention from the heavenly temple and tend this, the Lord's vine, that what the Lord has planted may not go untended.[5]

## Second Reading
### Philippians 3:4b-14 (RCL)

At the heart of this text is the contrast between the righteousness of the flesh and the righteousness of Christ. The contrast flows out of Paul's argument against those (dogs!) who are preaching the necessity of circumcision (Phil. 3:2; Paul shows a similar level of vexation in Gal. 5:12).

With the humility that is *so* characteristic of him (note the friendly sarcasm!), Paul moves headlong into his argument about righteousness, and he does so with elements of self-disclosure. Like one of the "priceless" MasterCard commercials, Paul's progression is aimed at the final piece: "as to righteousness under the law, blameless!" (v. 6b). There is no doubt (at least in Paul's mind!) that he has done all things necessary according to the law to be considered blameless.

Yet all of this he calls "rubbish" (NRSV, NIV), or, more indicative of the force of Paul's language, "shit" (*skubala*),[6] which is picked up in our strange old friend, the KJV, as "dung."[7] Watering down Paul's language misses the full force of this contrast.

The righteousness of the flesh, which Paul can claim fully, is nothing—for Paul "loss"—in comparison to righteousness in Christ. Such is the righteousness "that comes through faith in Christ, the righteousness from God based on faith" (v. 9b).

In a world and in our lives wherein we search for, work toward, and attempt to achieve right standing before God, Paul under no uncertain terms (*skubala!*) calls us to task. He holds up a mirror to himself and his own skilled ability to keep the law, and thereby he holds up a mirror for us to see ourselves as those attempting to justify ourselves. It does not take too much imagination or vision on the part of the preacher to look around the parish and see a plethora of examples of this. It may take more courage to do the same for oneself, for we clergy suffer from using the church, theology, clerical leadership, and the like to justify ourselves. All of which is pure and unadulterated *skubala*! It is not until the preacher reconciles her/himself to this reality, to the helplessness of the sinner before God, that he/she is able to preach it with existential passion and clarity.

I recommend reading or rereading Martin Luther's Heidelberg Disputation of 1518 as a refresher in this fundamental contrast between the righteousness we seek and the righteousness we receive from Christ.

## Philippians 4:6-9 (LFM)

It is no secret that there is conflict in the world—between nations, groups, tribes, families, individuals. How often do our corporate and individual prayers include prayers for the peace of God! How often do we pray for personal safety for ourselves, our loved ones, our friends! But what of our enemies?

Twice in this pericope we hear of the peace of God (vv. 7, 9). Paul's concern at the end of this letter is somewhere between exhortation and blessing.[8] It is important to recall that Paul is writing this letter from prison. Recall Paul's account of his imprisonment (1:12-26), and how he wants the Philippian community to know "that what has happened to me has actually helped to spread the gospel, so that it has become known throughout the whole imperial guard and to everyone else that my imprisonment is for Christ; and most of the brothers and sisters, having been made confident in the Lord by my imprisonment, dare to speak the word with greater boldness and without fear" (1:12-14). From the confines of prison and in the midst of his suffering, which has Paul torn between life and death, he focuses on the good of his imprisonment—the good being "the spread of the gospel" (1:12).

Likewise, in today's lesson at the end of the letter, Paul is urging the Philippian community on a similar course. He exhorts them not to worry but to pray, and he blesses them with "the peace of God, which surpasses all understanding," that will "guard" their hearts and minds in Christ Jesus. While there is a certain irony that Paul uses "guard" (*phroureō*), as it is a term that could well have been used by those guarding him in prison (2 Cor. 11:32), his use of this word also undergirds what he is saying here. The peace of God guards *not* bodies, but the heart and mind.

Paul's exhorting and blessing of his fellow Christians does not promise a life and witness without physical suffering. The peace of God is not a bandage for a superficial wound. The peace of God, "which surpasses all understanding," meets and consoles in the depths of human reality, including the deepest of sufferings, taking away even the sting of death.

## Gospel
### Matthew 21:33-46 (RCL)
### Matthew 21:33-43 (LFM)

Immediately following Jesus' clever redrawing of the kingdom of God in last week's Gospel, this week's begins with an imperative from Jesus that his hearers "Listen to another parable!" This suggests that the parables are related, and the structure of this parable resembles Matthew 21:28-32 insofar as Jesus' question at the conclusion of the parable provides the opportunity for his hearers innocently (pun intended!) to incriminate themselves (cf. 21:25, 28, 40).

Lest we undervalue this parable and its location in Matthew's narrative, it appears in all three Synoptic Gospels (Mark 12:1-12; Luke 20:9-19; also *Gos. Thom.* 65-66). As in Matthew, in both Mark and Luke the parable is preceded (with some varied insertions[9]) by the progression of the cleansing of the temple, the discussion in the temple of the source of Jesus' authority, and then this parable together with the quotation of Psalm 118:22-23 with its reference to the "stone that the builders rejected" (cf. Acts 4:11; 1 Peter 2:4-8). The pericope, beginning with the parable, is from beginning to end on a christological trajectory.

Building again on the image of the vineyard, an image with deep scriptural roots,[10] in today's parable the landowner (*oikodespotēs*) does everything necessary to have a successful vineyard, turns it over to tenants who will tend and harvest on his behalf, and heads off on a foreign holiday. As it is his property and he is therefore entitled to the produce/profits of the harvest, he sends his slaves to collect. Here the parable turns violent. The slaves of the landowner, his emissaries, are more than ill received. They are beaten. Stoned. Killed. One delegation after another.

As a last resort, the landowner sends his son, thinking that these wicked tenants will respect him. They do not. Rather than showing respect, they seek to gain the inheritance of the son by throwing him out of the vineyard and killing him.

With this picture painted, Jesus asks his hearers, who again are the chief priests, elders, and presumably others in the temple, "Now when the owner of the vineyard comes, what will he do to those tenants?" (v. 40). With a righteous vigor they respond, "He will put those wretches to a miserable death, and lease the vineyard to other tenants who will give him the produce at harvest time" (v. 41). By way of their own assessment of the situation in the parable, the religious leaders pronounce judgment upon themselves. What do those who reject the Son deserve? No less, no more than a miserable death.

It is most certainly the case that this parable, especially with the vigor that Matthew records it, has been perceived as and provided Christians with ammunition against Jews. As history recounts in so many times and places, the naming of Jews as Christ killers by Christians throughout the centuries of Christendom has been disastrous. I cannot say loudly or clearly enough: If directed at or used against Jews, this parable is thoroughly misunderstood.

Again, this parable is told within Judaism, and it is directed toward the chief priests and the elders—the religious leaders of the day. Are they Jewish? Yes. Is Jesus Jewish? Yes. If there is a correlation to today, which there most certainly is, it is not about Jews or any other non-Christians. The correlation with today is within the church. This parable is directed toward the religious leaders of the day and their— *our*—rejection of the cornerstone, our shouts of "Crucify him!" Who deserves no less than a miserable death? We Christians, and in particular we Christians who are the leaders of Christ's church.

How might we preach this when we realize that Jesus is speaking about us (v. 45). How difficult and necessary it is to be reminded whose church this is!

## Notes

1. Terence E. Fretheim, *Exodus,* Interpretation: A Bible Commentary for Teaching and Preaching (Louisville: John Knox, 1991), 224.
2. *The Book of Concord: The Confessions of the Evangelical Lutheran Church*, ed. R. Kolb and T. J. Wengert, trans. C. Arand et al. (Minneapolis: Fortress Press, 2000), 386.3.
3. Gale A. Yee, "A Form-Critical Study of Isaiah 5:1-7 as a Song and a Juridical Parable," *Catholic Biblical Quarterly* 43 (1981): 30–40.
4. Ibid., 38. E.g., Hosea 10:1.
5. Outside the bounds of the pericope are the brutal laments of vv. 4-6: "How long will you be angry with your people's prayers?"
6. Frederick Wm. Danker, ed., *A Greek-English Lexicon of the New Testament and other Early Christian Literature*, 3rd ed. (Chicago: University of Chicago Press, 2000), 932.
7. Likewise, Jerome renders it *faciam* or "feces" in the Vulgate.
8. An attempt to convey the thrust of the compelling work of Paul A. Holloway, "Notes and Observations—*Bona Cogitare*: An Epicurean Consolation in Phil 4:8-9," *Harvard Theological Review* 91 (1998): 89–96.
9. Matthew and Mark also include the cursing of the fig tree; cf. Matt. 21:18-22; Mark 11:12-14, 20-25. Matthew includes the parable of the two sons, 21:28-32.
10. See comments on Isa. 5:1-7 above. The vineyard image is also integral to the Gospel lesson, Matt. 20:1-16, for Proper 20 above.

# Time after Pentecost / Ordinary Time
## Proper 23 through Christ the King and Thanksgiving

### Shauna K. Hannan

W e need, therefore, to discard most of the theological baggage that has been imposed on this passage and try to hear it afresh."[1] These words by the late Robert McAfee Brown are ones I hope you will take to heart as you approach the lectionary readings for these final weeks of Ordinary Time. That is, I encourage you to begin attending to the texts themselves before reading my comments. Because some of those comments may challenge you to break away from a traditional interpretation, doing some preparation will put you in a better position either to justify your own stance or to be open to an alternative.

Throughout these weeks you are encouraged to (1) get a bigger picture of what is going on in the text and in your situation; (2) reflect on your role as a proclaimer, pastor, and leader, especially given the number of times in these texts that the religious elite are Jesus' opponents; (3) specify for yourself what you hope each sermon will *do* to your hearers; and (4) engage with some new and hopefully lifelong dialogue partners. It is my hope that you will obtain from each story a sense of both the *what* of Jesus' words and the *how* of Jesus' communication. Jesus establishes his identity and authority not only by the content of what he says, but by the way he says it.

The final Sundays of Pentecost provide a clear picture of Jesus' identity, authority, and reign. The new thing God is doing is not to be missed as Jesus recounts parables, responds to opposition, and describes the kingdom of the one true God. Jesus' ability to prevail against all challenges in his unique way is especially celebrated on Christ the King Sunday, which concludes the church year.

The first four weeks provide somewhat of a continuous reading of Matthew 22 and 23. Even before getting to Matthew 22, we know that (1) Jesus' identity and authority are in question; (2) the religious elite are threatened by Jesus and want to arrest him; and (3) Jesus does not answer his opponents' inquiries directly (e.g., 21:27), suggesting that he has his own way of dealing with the situation.

Beginning with Proper 24, we hear the first of four controversy stories that set the stage for Jesus' utterance of the seven "woes" in Matthew 23. The first is a challenge to Jesus regarding paying taxes (22:15-22). While the second controversy about resurrection (22:23-33) is not included here, the third, regarding which law in the commandments is greatest, is (22:34-46; see Proper 25). The fourth controversy (Proper 26) is a bit different in that Jesus is not responding to his opponents' stirrings, but is introducing his own ideas, which are sure to create controversy (23:1-12). Here Jesus indicts corrupt leaders (particularly religious leaders) and calls for solidarity and equality.

The following three weeks provide another series of continuous readings from Matthew 25. This chapter concludes Jesus' fifth and final discourse (24:1—25:46), which is precipitated by the disciples' question, "Tell us, when will this be, and what will be the sign of your coming and of the end of the age?" (24:3). After two weeks of parables describing what the kingdom of false prophets looks like, on Christ the King Sunday we hear a description of what the kingdom of the true God looks like. All the texts heretofore propel us to this final Sunday on which we hear of Jesus' true identity, authority, and reign.

Matthew is interested in announcing God's reign revealed in Jesus. At this conclusion of the church year, you, a new Matthew, have the opportunity to do the same for your particular people in your particular place in this particular time.

Another potential sermon series in this set of lections is from 1 Thessalonians. While I do not suggest that these texts trump the intriguing and poignant Gospel texts, this is a possibility for those who have an additional midweek worship.

In her book, *If You Cannot Preach Like Paul*, Nancy Lammers Gross argues that because Paul was more of a practical theologian than a systematic theologian, we would do well not to systematize Paul's thinking by saying what Paul said.[2] Instead, Gross calls attention to what Paul did as a practitioner, minister, and missionary and encourages preachers to *do* what Paul did. Heeding this advice, the comments below assess what Paul did with and for the community of Thessalonica in order that we might consider doing the same with and for our own communities.

Remember that at the center of all of these texts is God, not us. We discover right from the start that "making God secondary to one's personal agenda is unacceptable to God." A common theme running through many of these stories is that even when we are disobedient, God remains good, gracious, and present. Thanks be to God.

## Notes

1.  Robert McAfee Brown, *Unexpected News: Reading the Bible with Third World Eyes* (Philadelphia: Westminster, 1984), 129.
2.  Nancy Lammers Gross, *If You Cannot Preach Like Paul* (Grand Rapids: Eerdmans, 2002).

# October 9, 2011
## Seventeenth Sunday after Pentecost
### Twenty-eighth Sunday in Ordinary Time / Proper 23

**Revised Common Lectionary (RCL)**
Exodus 32:1-14 or Isaiah 25:1-9
Psalm 106:1-6, 19-23 or Psalm 23
Philippians 4:1-9
Matthew 22:1-14

**Roman Catholic (LFM)**
Isaiah 25:6-10a
Psalm 23:1-3a, 3b-4, 5, 6
Philippians 4:12-14, 19-20
Matthew 22:1-14 or 22:1-10

## First Reading
### Exodus 32:1-14 (RCL)

I suggest we discontinue referring to this text as the "golden calf" incident and begin calling it the "God changes God's mind at the request of Moses" incident. Incident? Yes. Incidental? No. By this point I mean that it is not shocking that the Israelites' impatience while waiting for Moses leads to idolatry. What is shocking is God's anger and, even more, Moses' ability to quell God's anger.

Given God's own admission of jealousy (Exod. 20:5), perhaps we should not be too surprised at God's anger. But this tirade (32:7-11) is not for the meek. It is a good thing the Israelites were not privy to the tirade; otherwise they most certainly would have run to their gods for protection against God. God refers to the Israelites as those whom Moses brought out from the land of Egypt. That is interesting since God had earlier said God brought them out of the land of Egypt (Exod. 20:2). God calls them names: stiff-necked people. And worse, God wants to be left alone to wallow in anger and to "consume" the idolaters. If that is not enough, God seems to bribe Moses to leave him alone (32:10). If Moses does so, God will make of him a great nation. Anger, tirade, blame, name calling, destruction, bribery; this is not God at God's best. Shocking. The bottom line is that idolatry is a serious offense that will not be ignored by God.

This resolute behavior, seemingly unfit for the Divine, makes it even more shocking when Moses is able to change God's mind. He does so by reminding

God that it was God who brought the people out of the land of Egypt. He reminds God of God's power and might. He reminds God of God's promise to Abraham, Isaac, and Israel to multiply their descendants. Killing the Israelites now would not foster offspring and certainly would give the Egyptians the edge. Moses' threefold imperative—"Turn from your fierce wrath," "Change your mind," "Do not bring disaster on your people"—is bold but effective. God does change God's mind.

As in today's Gospel reading, making God secondary to one's personal agenda (e.g., idolatry, attending to one's field or business) is unacceptable. One wonders if the king's behavior in the Gospel text might have been similarly altered had a Moses stepped in. Psalm 106:19-23 (discussed below) recounts this event.

## Isaiah 25:1-9 (RCL alt.)
## Isaiah 25:6-10a (LCM)

Some are apprehensive of people with visions even if the content is appealing. Isaiah's "I Have a Dream" speech is as appealing as any: rich food, well-aged wine, no more death, no more tears, no more disgrace, the presence of the Lord for whom we have waited so long. There is hope for us all, indeed. The word *all* appears five times in verses 6-8. In other words, inclusivity is not to be missed. (Well, *all* apparently does not include the Moabites, who in verse 10 are "trodden down" like straw in a "dung-pit." I'll let you grapple with that.)

Even with the emphasis on *all*, Isaiah focuses especially on the poor, the needy, those who suffer at the hands of the ruthless. Isaiah grounds his eschatological vision in what God has already begun to do for those who have been disregarded. Isaiah proclaims God's power both to create that which is life giving (e.g., v. 6) and to destroy that which is not (e.g., v. 7). This apocalyptic vision becomes our vision not only for the future redemption of God's people, but also now as many struggle to find not only rich food, but *any* food. The feast / messianic banquet imagery is a common thread in this and the Gospel text.

## Psalmody
### Psalm 106:1-6, 19-23 (RCL)

This psalm begins by proclaiming, "Give thanks to the LORD, for he is good! Who can . . . declare all his praise?" and then highlights the result of living and acting justly and righteously: happiness. Verse 4 begins the transition from that glorious praise-filled opening to what the rest of the psalm will address; that is, the people's iniquity (vv. 19-23 provide one such example as the story in Exodus 32 is recounted).

Verse 4 no longer talks *about* God, but rather is a petition calling upon God to help the people see the riches, rejoice in the nation's gladness, and glory in God's heritage. There is an air of tension here, clarified in the threefold penitential sentences (v. 6): we have sinned, we have committed iniquity, we have done wickedly. Sin abounds. The remainder of the psalm goes on to articulate such iniquity and wickedness. Finally, there is a recognition that God has a part in helping to relieve such guilt; thus, the petition. Praise, confession, faith is a solid template for the movement of a sermon.

## Psalm 23 (RCL alt.)
## Psalm 23:1-3a, 3b-4, 5, 6 (LFM)

Psalm 23's *Wirkungsgeschichte* (the history of its effect) affects its present interpretation perhaps even more than the text itself. In other words, it is difficult to look past Psalm 23's association with funerals. If this psalm is sung, many, if not most, hearers likely will imagine such a setting. The preacher will want to be very attentive to this powerful association.

Without dismissing the incredible comfort mourners receive from this psalm, one can highlight the multiple "job descriptions" assigned to the Lord in this short hymn. The Lord is shepherd, comforter, host, and guide. Not unlike Psalm 106, this individual song has communal implications.

# Second Reading
## Philippians 4:1-9 (RCL)
## Philippians 4:12-14, 19-20 (LFM)

The selected verses focus on Paul's ability to rejoice even in the midst of suffering, akin to this week's psalms. Part of Paul's joy comes as a result of the continued support of the Philippians. Even so, Paul is concerned with the church at Philippi. This is evident in the first part of chapter 4 (vv. 1-9) where the major issue seems to be unity within the church. Paul urges two of the leaders to "be of the same mind." Whether it is a fledgling church like the one in Philippi, a new mission start in the midst of twenty-first-century secularism, or a large congregation in the Bible Belt that has been deeply embedded in its community for decades, unity in the Lord is a mark of Christian discipleship and leadership.

Verses 10-20 are likely a later insertion to Paul's letter to the Philippians. The LFM pericope includes various verses from this section, including one of Scripture's best-known verses: "I can do all things through him who strengthens me" (v. 13).

# Gospel
## Matthew 22:1-14 (RCL)
## Matthew 22:1-14 or 22:1-10 (LFM)

Martin Luther called this parable "the terrible gospel which he did not like to preach."[1] I agree that preaching parables of judgment is difficult. However, when preaching from Matthew, they are unavoidable. In fact, we'll encounter more in the coming weeks (Pentecost 21 and 22 and Christ the King Sunday), so we might as will hit them head-on now.[2] The difficulty lies in the apparent absence of grace. For those who understand the task at hand to preach the gospel as primarily a word of grace, these texts seem to undermine that task. A good question to keep in mind as we make our way through this and other judgment parables is provided by Matthew scholar Ulrich Luz: Does the concept of judgment negate the power of the promise of salvation?[3]

In addition to this theological question, it is helpful to attend to the following questions:

1. What did Matthew hope would happen by recounting this parable?
2. What did Jesus hope would happen by telling this parable?
3. What do you hope will happen as you preach on this parable?[4]

Asking these overarching questions will keep preachers from over-allegorizing the parable. (By that I mean trying to correlate each object/character in the story to the objects/characters in our lives.)[5]

## Matthew

Matthew's Gospel aims to announce God's reign revealed in Jesus. This parable, like every parable in the Gospel, is intended to serve this aim. Historians suggest that the pre-Matthean version of this parable ends at verse 10 (this is reflected in the alternative text for the LFM). Matthew's additional four verses (11-14—these verses do not appear in the Lukan version of the parable found in Luke 14:16-24) change the parable entirely. No longer is it primarily about a king who does everything possible to fill the banquet hall for the wedding feast. It now suggests that even those who make it to the banquet may not be able to stay. Because wedding banquet imagery would have been heard as a connection to the coming new age, clearly Matthew is announcing a new thing here.

## Jesus

Why does Jesus respond to the concerns of the chief priests and the Pharisees by telling a parable? For one thing, parables allow hearers space to place themselves within the story. Jesus is aware that the religious leaders are threatened by him and want to arrest him. If Jesus responds to their concerns directly, he will surely give them justification for an arrest. If he tells a parable, there remains some ambiguity, which is just what Jesus needs. Of course, for those of us who know the whole story, this parable is less ambiguous. Jesus is indicting the elite, those who wish to indict him. But there is more to the story than that.

Preaching on a parable such as this necessitates the preacher recognizing how this parable affects him or her. Does this parable indict you? Does it make you feel secure? Without over-allegorizing, one can still identify with certain characters. Whom do you identify with in the story?

Recognizing with whom you identify in the story will help you preach a sermon that gives your hearers freedom to identify. If you are not aware of what you are doing, you may inadvertently force your hearers to identify with a certain group with which they would not otherwise identify. Now come the bigger questions: Should you preach a sermon that intentionally identifies your hearers with a certain perspective in the story? Is there any way to avoid this? With whom do you think Jesus wants his hearers to identify? Even more challenging, does this necessarily mean that your sermon should do the same for your hearers?

Let's examine a few interpretations in order to respond to these questions. First, identify with the original guest list. Note that these invitees were actually invited three times (always a significant number). The first invite is assumed since the slaves (*doulos*) were sent out to those who had already been invited. The *doulos*'s call was the second invite. We do not know why the invitations were not accepted. The story simply says, "They would not come." Since there could be as many reasons as invitees, there is no homiletical payoff in trying to guess why this is so (but it is curious that no one accepted). The king sends another set of *doulos*, perhaps since the first set was unsuccessful. For this third invitation the king tells the slaves to give more detail about the banquet: all is ready, the menu is generous and exquisite (oxen and fatted calves), come! Not only did the invitees not accept, they "made light of it" and ignored the invitation in favor of their own agendas. As if that is not bad enough, others seized the *doulos*, mistreated them, and killed them.

A sermon focusing on the original guest list may hope that hearers see themselves as those on God's original guest list. It is likely that the sermon would encourage hearers to accept the "king's" invitation the first time and avoid ignoring the generosity of the king and, certainly, refrain from killing the messenger. These exhortations would be heeded when the hearers discover the catastrophic conclusion of the ignorant invitees. The enraged king had them killed and their city burned. While this kind of hortatory sermon may suit this segment of the story, there are a couple of problems: (1) Since you will be preaching to those who gathered at worship, the ones who have responded to the invitation to the banquet, you would be preaching past your hearers, who likely do not identify with the first set of invitees. (2) This interpretation assumes this is the whole story. But, of course, it is not.[6]

Chances are better that hearers will connect with the second group of invitees: the ragtag group that was invited (by the way, by yet a third group of *doulos*) because the original invitees were dim-witted enough not to accept. These are people on the streets, the bad and the good (most translations list "good" before "bad" despite the Greek listing "bad" first); in fact, everyone. As New Testament scholar Arland Hultgren notes, "In the present era God's embrace of humanity is universal; there is no 'sorting out' ahead of time of who shall be welcome into the kingdom."[7] Lest the preacher is tempted to preach a sermon patting the backs of those gathered for accepting the invitation, the story does not at all highlight the initiative, drive, willingness, and/or sacrifice of the second invitees. The story jumps immediately from the invitation to the filled wedding hall (v. 10). The parable does not validate this sermon trajectory. In fact, the Matthean tradition addition (vv. 11-14) wants to move the hearers to the next scene where "the expected are absent and the unexpected are present."[8]

Before those gathered in the wedding hall have a chance to feel lucky or blessed or proud of their own good choices to be at the right place at the right time, the parable inserts an exchange between the king and one of the guests. The king questions the guest's presence given his attire. The guest is speechless. When the king sends him off into the "outer darkness," hearers cannot help but think this is such extreme behavior (and for the second time in the story—recall the killing of the first invitees and the destruction of the city). While no one is likely to identify with this man, there will be some connection. "I am glad I wasn't him," or "I hope I am dressed right," or even "I want no part of this inhumane king." A sermon could use this speechless man as a foil in order to exhort hearers to be prepared when the king invites you to the wedding feast. This seems to make sense, given the Gospel writer's interpretive addition, "For many are called but few are chosen" (v. 14). Indeed, this last line suggests that the parable is a threat to some (particularly those who question Jesus' authority). Klyne Snodgrass reminds us, "More than the other Gospels Matthew consistently reminds his readers that the unlimited grace of the kingdom always brings with it unlimited demand."[9]

### The Sermon

The homiletical question is, How is this parable pertinent to your context? That is for you, the preacher, to discern. Is there anything in your setting that poses a threat to Jesus? That threatens Jesus' authority?

The sermon trajectories listed above do not capture the parable as a whole. In fact, they only point to our penchant to focus on ourselves; on what we have done right or what we have done wrong or what we should do. These interpretations miss the bigger point that the parable is primarily about God (note that the king is the only one who speaks in the parable). Jesus tells this parable and Matthew recounts it in order for hearers to know something about who God is and how God operates in the world. This king tells us something about what the kingdom of heaven has become. That is, the invitation to participate in the kingdom has expanded. It is open to all, bad and good. The king generously invites not once, not twice, but three times. Literally three? Probably not; rather, it's a story whose point is that God invites us to the banquet over and over.

According to this parable, the king does have some expectations. (Jesus says this straightforwardly just before telling this parable: "Therefore I tell you, the kingdom of God will be taken away from you and given to a people that produces the fruits of the kingdom" [21:43].) When invited, we come to the banquet. Also, when God communicates with us, we respond (unlike the man who was speechless when the king questioned his attire). Typical of Matthew, there is a point at which there will clearly be insiders and outsiders.

The preacher will have to choose whether to focus on insider language ("You are chosen") or outsider language ("Do this or else you too will experience weeping and gnashing of teeth"). I prefer the former over the latter, which is validated not only by this parable, but by the Gospel as a whole. Recall that Jesus is in Jerusalem, en route to Calvary where God will sacrifice God's Son for all, the bad and the good. Is there judgment in this text? Yes. It would not be a Matthean parable without it. But, in response to the earlier question, this parable does not suggest that the concept of judgment negates the power of the promise of salvation.

The sermon need not (and should not) be a recounting of the possible interpretations of this parable. Save that for the Bible study. Instead of explaining away this parable (which is never an effective homiletical move), open up a world for your hearers (just as parables do); a world where God invites them over and over to feast on God's generosity and extravagance. For this sermon, choose invitation over threat in order to announce God's reign revealed in Jesus.[10]

## Notes

1. Martin Luther, Sermon from 1531, cited in Ulrich Luz, *Matthew 21–28*, Hermeneia (Minneapolis: Fortress Press, 2005), 59.
2. For a helpful introduction to Jesus' parables, see Arland J. Hultgren, *The Parables of Jesus: A Commentary* (Grand Rapids: Eerdmans, 2000), 1–19.
3. Luz, *Matthew 21–28*, 59.
4. Clearly my interest lies in the illocutionary intent of texts. For more on this see Klyne R. Snodgrass, *Stories with Intent: A Comprehensive Guide to the Parables of Jesus* (Grand Rapids: Eerdmans, 2008), 17. For another helpful introduction (which is somewhat distinct from Hultgren), see ibid., 1–35.
5. An example of this would be considering the wedding garment (v. 11) as a symbol for faith.
6. The change of guests has been variously interpreted throughout the ages: (1) The first guests include the religious establishment, those who have rejected Jesus. (2) The first guests have been understood to be Israel and the second guests, Gentiles. (3) The first guests are the rich and the second, the poor. For further details and concerns regarding these interpretations, see Luz, *Matthew 21–28*, 50–52.
7. Hultgren, *Parables of Jesus*, 346.
8. Snodgrass, *Stories with Intent*, 322.
9. Ibid., 320–21.
10. There are similarities between this parable and the previous two parables (Matt. 21:28-32; 21:33-41). Considering these three parables together, their interpretation may point to Jesus' identity as God's Son. Jesus is surreptitiously responding to the authority question while indicting his hearers.

# October 16, 2011
## Eighteenth Sunday after Pentecost
### Twenty-ninth Sunday in Ordinary Time / Proper 24

| Revised Common Lectionary (RCL) | Lectionary for Mass (LFM) |
|---|---|
| Exodus 33:12-23 or Isaiah 45:1-7 | Isaiah 45:1, 4-6 |
| Psalm 99 or 96:1-9, (10-13) | Psalm 96:1 + 3, 4-5, 7-8, 9-10 |
| 1 Thessalonians 1:1-10 | 1 Thessalonians 1:1-5b |
| Matthew 22:15-22 | Matthew 22:15-21 |

## First Reading
### Exodus 33:12-23 (RCL)
### Isaiah 45:1-7 (RCL alt.)
### Isaiah 45:1, 4-6 (LFM)

Disobedience lurks in the background of Exodus 33. What we have here is a postidolatry exchange between God and Moses. Although Exodus 22:20 states that punishment for idolaters is destruction, here God is speaking to Moses, the one who speaks on behalf of an idolatrous people, face to face, "as one speaks to a friend" (v. 11). Hebrew Bible professor Richard Nysse says, "Given the severity of the covenant breach in making the golden calf, we should linger in astonishment over God's graciousness in continuing a relationship with Israel before rushing to the New Testament inclusion of Gentiles."[1]

Moses makes three requests of the Lord. And, lo and behold, the Lord honors Moses' requests. No doubt this is because God has found favor in Moses, a fact that is repeated five times in verses 12-17. Also repeated five times in these same verses is the acknowledgment that God *knows* Moses *by name*. The Lord is a different kind of god, a real God, unlike the golden one created by the Israelites at Sinai. God is one who establishes a relationship with God's people, who listens to the requests of God's people, who is affected by God's people, who faces God's people (God's *face* or presence is mentioned often in this pericope; see vv. 14-15, 20, 23).

Such a close relationship does not take away from God's authority. God is no pushover. God can and will do what God wants to: "I will be gracious to whom I will be gracious, and will show mercy on whom I will show mercy" (v. 19). The request to see God's face (i.e., God's very self unhindered by a cloud, v. 10) is not granted to Moses. "No one shall see me and live," says the Lord (v. 20).

Hebrew Bible scholar Terence Fretheim highlights how God redirects Moses' question about glory to goodness:

> What will serve as *a more genuine sign* [that God will dwell among the people] to Moses is not some direct view of God but a specific indication of the "good" character of this one who has given the divine name Yahweh to Israel. . . . It is more important to know what kind of God this is than to see that God. Hence Moses must not simply use his eyes, he must use his ears to hear the *proclamation*. It is in fact the proclamation of the very nature of Yahweh that will prove to Moses that God will be gracious in response to what Israel has done.[2]

Relative to today's Gospel reading, Caesar's "face" is readily available on the tax coin, but God's glory is seen in God's goodness (exemplified in God's willingness to be present and maintain a relationship with such a disobedient and idolatrous people). The latter far outweighs the former.

Finally, the Lord does give Moses a way to recognize God (vv. 21-23). While God's own hand (note the anthropomorphic language throughout this section) prevents Moses from seeing God's face, God will remove God's hand while passing by Moses in order that Moses may get a glimpse. This is far more significant than all the jokes about "seeing God's back side" suggest. Seeing God's "back side" affirms that God will be out ahead leading God's people.

Similar themes are present in Isaiah 45. For example, Second Isaiah is concerned with idolatry. In fact, this text is surrounded by such references (see 44:9-20; 46:1-2). Instead of Moses, it is Cyrus with whom God establishes a relationship. Anthropomorphic language is present as God grasps Cyrus's hand. God recounts what God will do so that we will know God is Lord. Very importantly, as in Exodus 33, God knows God's people and calls them by name. God pronounces God's own characteristics in chiastic poetry typical of Isaiah (vv. 5-6). Bookending these two verses is a declaration that recalls the commandments given in Exodus 20:2: "I am the LORD *your* God and there is no other."

A I am the LORD, and there is no other;
  B besides me there is no god.
    C I arm you, though you do not know me,
    C so that they may know, from the rising of the sun and from the west
  B that there is no one besides me;
A I am the LORD, and there is no other.

Truly no one compares to this God.

## Psalmody
### Psalm 99 (RCL)
### Psalm 96:1-9, (10-13) (RCL alt.)
### Psalm 96:1 + 3, 4-5, 7-8, 9-10 (LFM)

Psalm 99 is one of eight "YHWH is King" psalms (93–100). Each of its three sections (1-3, 4-5, 6-9) begins with speaking *of* the Lord in the third person (e.g., 1-2), moves to speaking *to* the Lord (3a), and then switches back to the third person (3b). The connections between this psalm and Isaiah are evident. Essentially this psalm, with its threefold "Holy" (vv. 3b, 5b, 9b), is declaring, "Holy, Holy, Holy is the LORD of hosts; the whole earth is full of his glory" (Isa. 6:3). According to Hebrew Bible scholar Erich Zenger, "YHWH's holiness is shown in his gracious care for his people (and for the world as his royal realm)."[3] The emphasis on God's name is worth noting. We discover that the cries of Moses, Samuel, and Aaron in God's name are answered. This is exemplified in this week's text from Exodus.

Similarly, Psalm 96 (another "YHWH is King" psalm) contains three parts comprised of calls to praise God followed by motivation for praise. Note that God's name is mentioned in verses 2 and 8. The imperatives in the early part of the psalm are verbs of speaking (sing, tell, declare). The verbs in the latter part of the psalm are verbs of worship (ascribe, bring an offering, come into the courts, worship). The psalm concludes with the whole creation declaring praises to and worshiping God.

## Second Reading
### 1 Thessalonians 1:1-10 (RCL)
### 1 Thessalonians 1:1-5b (LFM)

Since 1 Thessalonians will be the epistle for the next five weeks, the preacher is encouraged to take ten minutes to read through the entire letter. This will help one understand the tone of the letter. Overall, one notices that Paul

1. highlights the relationship established in a prior visit;
2. affirms the ongoing work of the Thessalonians, that it is not in vain even when facing opposition;
3. encourages the Thessalonians to stay firm; and
4. emphasizes the Holy Spirit's role in their lives together.

The opening of Paul's letter is typical in its announcement of themes that will appear elsewhere in the letter; for instance, election, imitation of Christ, and Christ's imminent return.[4] Rather than "explaining away" what Paul is saying, note what Paul is doing in this text. Not only is Paul giving thanks to God for the people of Thessalonica; he is telling them that he is thankful for them. He tells the Thessalonians that he remembers their "work of faith," their "labor of love," and their "steadfastness of hope in our Lord Jesus Christ" (v. 3). Paul reminds them what their work has done for the people of Macedonia and Achaia and beyond. Essentially, Paul reports to them what the "word on the street" is about who they are. He does this by reminding them what their beliefs are and by pointing to the power of the Holy Spirit, which helps them.

What would it look like for you to do these things for your congregation? For starters, at no point would your sermon contain a sentence such as this: "As Paul said . . ." The reason is because you will be doing for your hearers what Paul did for the Thessalonian hearers rather than telling them what Paul said Yo his hearers. You would be thanking your congregation for their work and labor of love, reminding them of your common beliefs, and giving them feedback on what others see in them.

# Gospel
## Matthew 22:15-22 (RCL)
## Matthew 22:15-21 (LFM)

Both the opening and the closing of this pericope describe the religious authority figures' movement away from Jesus. Literally, they leave his presence. Figuratively, they walk further away from the truth of who Jesus is.

The religious leaders have been trying to "snare" Jesus for some time (12:14). In the three parables that precede this text, the Pharisees have sensed they are being indicted. (This was evident already after the second parable, 21:45.)

Matthew 22:15-22 is the first of four "controversy stories" that describe how Jesus defeats his opponents in these disputations before launching into the seven "woes" (23:13-39).[5] The center of gravity in these texts is the threat that Jesus' presence poses to some and the ensuing necessity to arrest that threat by arresting Jesus in order to secure their own positions. In other words, this text is just as much about what is behind the exchange and the nature of the exchange as it is about the content of the exchange. Because of this, the following comments will focus on the Pharisees' plan and the way in which Jesus both dodges the entrapment and begins to move into the offense.

### The Plan

Since arresting Jesus would harm the Pharisees' reputation with the crowd, the Pharisees need to devise a plan that will cause Jesus to entrap himself. The plan looks like this. First, flatter him a bit by acknowledging his sincerity, his truthfulness, and his lack of partiality (the latter is clearly hypocritical since the plan is precisely intended to reveal Jesus' partiality). Jesus must be asked a question to which all plausible answers will ensnare him. "Is it lawful to pay taxes to the emperor or not?" The Pharisees' premeditated scheme assumes that if Jesus answers no, the civil authorities would note his disloyalty to the empire. Sedition. If he says yes, the religious authorities would see his disloyalty to God. Blasphemy. In addition, if he says yes, he could lose his popularity among the common people, who always want to do away with taxes.

Curiously, the Pharisees do not actually do the questioning. Instead, after devising the plan, they send others to do the dirty work.[6]

## The Plan Backfires

Jesus' response is the "great nonanswer." Instead of answering the question, he addresses the motives of the questioners: "Why are you putting me to the test, you hypocrites?" Jesus, "the consummate fox," answers a question with a question. Next, he asks them to show him the coin used for the tax. Upon producing a denarius, the religious leaders divulge what they are hoping Jesus will disclose; that is, possessing a coin shows that they themselves pay taxes. Jesus then asks a question of them (though not with malicious intent, it seems, since it is so matter-of-fact). "Whose head is this, and whose title?" They answer as straightforwardly as the question is asked: "The emperor's." The first part of Jesus' next response, "Give therefore to the emperor the things that are the emperor's," says Ulrich Luz, is of no major consequence since it simply confirms what his opponents already have been doing. Note how Jesus has not answered the original question but instead has pointed out that since his questioners pay taxes, it *must* be lawful. Paying taxes was not frivolous; it was something all citizens did. Jesus was no Zealot, so he would agree that taxes have to be paid.

The second part of this response, "[Give] to God the things that are God's," is the response to the original question, even though it does not seem to be. (We are starting to see a pattern: God changes Moses' question about glory to goodness and Jesus changes his questioners' question about paying taxes to obedience to God.) The first part, give to the emperor, was logical. But what does this second part mean? What do we have that is God's? How do we give it? Since this second part is both the surprise and the goal of the text, Luz argues and I agree, the tax issue is not the focus.

Once again Jesus' opponents are amazed and flee the scene. This leave-taking is reminiscent of the demonic tempter leaving Jesus in 4:11. Jesus 1, Jesus' opponents 0.

In trying to prove his disobedience, Jesus' opponents actually reveal their own: (1) They have a coin (Jesus apparently does not); (2) little do they know they are attempting to entrap God; and (3) asking only about Caesar and not about God reveals their focus is not where it should be—that is, on God. Jesus wants to keep the focus on God, and so, too, should we in our sermons on this text.

## Cautions for the Preacher

Since there is such a long history of placing emphasis where it is not in this text, I want explicitly to encourage preachers to avoid the following sermon foci. First, do not miss the intention of the text by focusing on the church/state issue. Though this is an interesting and important topic that could be addressed at some point, doing so from the pulpit using this text as a basis misses the intention of the text. Therefore, the sermon should not aim to provide justification for paying taxes or for fulfilling civic duty. The sermon certainly should not suggest that paying tax as obedience to the state is a special command of God. This text's intent is narrowed when it is read only in light of Romans 13:1-7 in order to provide a basis for a Christian theology of the state.[7] Another misinterpretation along these lines would be to suggest that part of our lives belongs to the state and another part to God. No, everything belongs to God.

The preacher will also want to refrain from casting blame on "those religious authorities" who try to ensnare Jesus. This might take the form of pointing the finger at other preachers as the religious ones. Jeans-wearing, music-stand-using preachers are not necessarily less religious than collar-wearing pulpit preachers. One is not less religious simply by preaching in a makeshift sanctuary in an elementary school gymnasium as opposed to a 150-year-old nave. While Jesus seems to "point the finger" in the text (albeit indirectly), I do not believe this is our role from the pulpit. Not only is blaming others from the pulpit rarely (if ever) effective, since hearers tend to pick up on this quickly, blaming others in this way would only buy into what the Pharisees are doing. Remember, like it or not, we, as pastors, as preachers, are the religious ones in the story who continue to trap Jesus and who are eventually muzzled by Jesus. The first controversy story indicts all who question God's authority by changing the direction to God's questioning our authority to question God's authority.

## Possible Homiletical Trajectories

First, rather than overfocusing on the ever-popular verse, "Give therefore to the emperor the things that are the emperor's, and to God the things that are God's" (v. 21), take seriously the story as a whole in its fuller context. The theological concern then becomes Jesus' identity and authority and the questioning of such identity and authority by humans. The evangelist's interest is "to show how Jesus' Pharisaic opponents in their malice cast a snare around Jesus and how they fail in their efforts."[8] The preacher has an opportunity to jump-start a new perspective on the text; a new history of interpretation can begin.

Second, instead of being interested in adding to the religious commandments a command to pay taxes, Jesus encourages *obedience* to God above all others. (Note the *kai*/"and" in verse 21 is not comparing two equal things.) God's claim on a person has no limits; it embraces all areas of life. We are not being disobedient when we pay taxes. In fact, Jesus says go ahead and give money to the emperor, always remembering who is Lord. Far more than paying what is due to Caesar, disobedience to God's lordship looks like the attempted entrapment of Jesus, whose presence and ways threaten all such agendas. When our obedience is called into question (and it will be), we are encouraged not to walk away from Jesus' presence or true divine identity.

Since another controversy story is the Gospel reading for next week, the preacher can encourage hearers to come back to witness yet another attempt to entrap Jesus. Of course, it can be made clear that this and all such plots against Jesus will backfire.

195

Finally, a common theme running through many of this Sunday's texts is that even when we are disobedient (idolatrous), God remains good, gracious, and present. The Lord, the One who knows our names, who knows us, is our God and there is no other. Yes, other potential gods have their images plastered all over, even on our money. But we cannot see the face of the one true God and still live. Instead, we glimpse the "back side" of this One as he leads us ever closer to the cross and resurrection.

## Notes

1. Richard Nysse, "Exodus 33:19—I Will Be Gracious to Whom I Will Be Gracious," http://www.enterthebible.org/Bible.aspx?rid=891, accessed July 12, 2010.
2. Terence E. Fretheim, *Exodus*, Interpretation: A Bible Commentary for Teaching and Preaching (Louisville: John Knox, 1991), 299.
3. Frank Lothar Hossfeld and Erich Zenger, *Psalms 2*, Hermeneia (Minneapolis: Fortress Press, 2005), 491.
4. Frank J. Matera, *Strategies for Preaching Paul* (Collegeville, Minn.: Liturgical, 2001), 56.
5. All four controversy stories are similar in that the narrator has no interest in the position of Jesus' opponents. In other words, the opponents do not get to speak and defend their view in the texts. Jesus' opponents are simply described as "malicious supernumerary actors." See Ulrich Luz, *Matthew 21–28*, Hermeneia (Minneapolis: Fortress Press, 2005), 61.
6. There is a long history of confusion as to who these disciples and Herodians are. Luz claims that since Pharisees have no disciples, the evangelist is probably thinking of the pupils of the scribes (who are in the same group as Pharisees). Ibid., 62.
7. "Obedience to civil authority is not to be separated from obedience to God" has been a common interpretation of this text dating back to the Reformation.
8. Luz, *Matthew 21–28*, 63.

# October 23, 2011
## Nineteenth Sunday after Pentecost
### Thirtieth Sunday in Ordinary Time / Proper 25

## First Reading
### Deuteronomy 34:1-12 (RCL)
### Leviticus 19:1-2, 15-18 (RCL alt.)
### Exodus 22:20-26 (LFM)

Things happen on mountaintops. In this case, it is Moses' death on Mt. Nebo atop Pisgah. But first, just before his death, Moses looks to the north, to the west, to the south, and to the east. Because the ancient Near East understood that "such viewings amount to a formal act of taking possession," it is clear that this is a fulfillment of what the Lord promised (see Gen. 13:14-17 and Deut. 3:27).[1] Patrick Miller reminds us that one tradition interprets Moses' viewing of the promised land but denial to enter it as an "unfulfillment of the highest order, in that a life is cut short of the goal toward which it has been directed."[2] Moses, in this view, was a tragic figure whose death "at the Lord's command" (v. 5) "is rooted in God's judgment."[3] This view does not seem plausible, however, given that the important element at the close of the Torah is that Moses' accomplishments were not for his own sake, but for the sake of Israel who will see and experience the promised land. Now Israel will be led by Joshua and the Lord himself (Deut. 31:3, 7-8). Miller himself affirms this view:

> Indeed, the primary generation that experienced this story will not receive the land. Theologically, it is not unimportant that Torah is complete without land. Torah opens up the promises of God, explains the intention of God, lays out the way for God's

people, says what is necessary to realize the promise and the land, even looks *beyond* land and disobedience to the future and speaks about the continuing possibility of the promise and land.[4]

These verses, which close the book of Deuteronomy, are eulogistic. "[Moses'] sight was unimpaired and his vigor had not abated" even at the ripe old age of 120. While the significance of this age is uncertain, it may be connected to Genesis 6:3, which refers to the human life span as 120 years. It could also represent the forty-year tenure of a great leader (e.g., Eli, David, Solomon). In Moses' case, he served three such tenures. His greatness is enumerated! Above all, "Never since has there arisen a prophet in Israel like Moses, whom the Lord knew face to face" (v. 10). He was "unequaled" for his signs, wonders, obedience to the Lord, mighty deeds, and terrifying displays of power (vv. 10-12). The strength of these words helps us understand how challenging it was for the Jewish people of Jesus' day to receive him as "the New Moses" as the evangelist Matthew desires to do. New light is shed on today's Gospel when we hear it with these Deuteronomic echoes (as one will do since Jesus is speaking there of the law and refers directly to the *Shema* in Deut. 6:5). Of course, as it turns out, Jesus is actually not precisely "like Moses," for, unlike Moses, Jesus is God.

The alternative RCL reading also has a connection to the Gospel reading. "And a second is like it: 'You shall love your neighbor as yourself'" (Matt. 22:39) is found in the Levitical Holiness Code (Lev. 19:18). This connection sheds light on the question, "Who is the neighbor?" Interestingly, some suggest that Leviticus 19:18 refers to fellow Israelites. However, this is extended to the resident alien already in Leviticus 19:33-34.

The LFM pericope addresses this even more thoroughly. In Exodus 22:20-26, one hears the cries of society's most vulnerable: resident aliens, widows, orphans, the poor. Not caring for _____ (fill in the blank with the most vulnerable in your setting) via wrongdoing, oppression, abuse, "predatory lending," will yield the Lord's wrath, death by sword, and, consequently, one's wife and children becoming similarly vulnerable (v. 24). In other words, this is serious business that sets a high standard of social justice. The Lord heeds the cries of the vulnerable, our neighbors (vv. 23, 27), and we should do the same. While this text seems to be aimed at the male experience, clearly the intention is that the words demand something from us all. As Hebrew Bible scholar Rebecca Alpert writes, "This commandment requires us to 'be open to people, ideas and experiences that seem strange'. . . . We must allow ourselves to consider the possibilities that people who are different from us in their manners, customs and ideas deserve to be listened to and encountered."[5]

# Psalmody
Psalm 90:1-6, 13-17 (RCL)
Psalm 1 (RCL alt.)
Psalm 18:2-3a, 3b-4, 47 + 51 (LFM)

Moses plays a leading role in this week's texts. Psalm 90 is the only one in the psalter that is attributed to him. In it one can hear echoes of Moses' pleading with the Lord to have compassion on the people (vv. 13-17). These petitions follow glorious praise for that which God has done (vv. 1-6). There is an acknowledgment that the disobedient Israelites are vulnerable to God's *justified* wrath (vv. 7-10). The progression is from praise and thanksgiving to confession to supplication. Boldly, there is a call for God to "repent" (v. 13). As Alpert notes, "Only those who know that the wrath of God is their problem will and can pray as the supplicants do."[6]

In a week when a text from the Hebrew Scriptures focuses on Moses' death, it is fitting that we encounter a psalm that is often read at funerals. The limits of time and transience of human life are certainly evident. In this "wisdom lament over mortality," there is a recognition that, according to Alpert, "time is a burden when we have to wait, a scarcity when we are busy. It is the source of anxiety, illusion, remorse. Wisdom, in contrast, sees the time given us as 'the unique opportunity,' the chance to be and do in the fear of the Lord."[7]

Psalm 1 is a beatitude that invites us to read the entire psalter as instruction for right living. Law (*Torah*) is less like a legal rule than it is instruction/guidance. *Torah*, therefore, is not to be kept for self-righteousness or self-justification. Instead, delighting in the law of the Lord is life giving, providing access to water, yielding bounty and prosperity (v. 3). Alpert says, "The fulfillment [of the law] is not so much reward as a result of life's connection with the source of life."[8] There is no gray area between the "happy" ones who delight in the law and the wicked ones who do not. Of course, one will soon discover in the psalter (and in life) that there are times when the wicked prosper and the righteous suffer great affliction.

The verses selected from the lengthy Psalm 18 are those that metaphorically describe God. In one verse alone God is rock, fortress, deliverer, shield, horn, and stronghold. Indeed, God is worthy to be praised. It is significant that each of these predicates (in the longest series of predicates for God in the psalter) is qualified by the possessive pronoun "my." Verse 47 impels one into song (complete with Bible-camp hand motions): "The LORD liveth, and blessed be the rock and may the God of our salvation be exalted."

## Second Reading
### 1 Thessalonians 2:1-8 (RCL)
### 1 Thessalonians 1:5c-10 (LFM)

The preacher is encouraged to refer to comments on Pentecost 18 (above) for the LFM reading and for background for today's RCL reading.

Paul establishes rapport with the Thessalonians by confirming his and his companions' (Silvanus and Timothy) motives for visiting them. The motives were pure and did not have a pretext for greed or praise. One suspects that Paul is either correcting something that was (e.g., complaints that call their motives into question) or preparing them for something to come (e.g., other communities questioning the Thessalonians' motives). Either way Paul has a need to clarify intentions in order to maintain rapport. He appeals to God as the authority who entrusts them with God's message (v. 4). Essentially, Paul reminds the Thessalonians that he cares *for* them and is willing to share himself *with* them. Paul is modeling what it is to be in Christian community.

So how would a preacher do as Paul did (the question proposed last week) with regard to this text? Frankly, this would draw too much attention to the preacher if this were done. In other words, Paul can get away with this, but we cannot. Even so, Paul's words in this section do serve as a model for establishing rapport in an ongoing ministry setting; rapport that encourages ongoing ministry in a challenging situation. Apparently, the Thessalonians needed encouragement. Perhaps you will assess that your hearers do, too.

It is worth noting how Paul compares his role among the Thessalonians to a nurse who tenderly cares for her own children (v. 7). Paul's gentleness is evident in this tender, pastoral letter even as (or perhaps because) he makes demands for his audience to live in a distinctively Christian way.

## Gospel
### Matthew 22:34-46 (RCL)
### Matthew 22:34-40 (LFM)

Jesus has been challenged by those who have been challenged by his display of authority ever since he arrived in Jerusalem. This pericope continues with more of the same. Most recently the Sadducees questioned Jesus about resurrection.[9] Jesus' unconventional response silenced the Sadducees. The Greek word for "silence" means "muzzled." The Sadducees' ability to verbalize was *restrained* by Jesus. Literally, Jesus' wisdom "shut them up." When the Pharisees heard this, they got into the game directly. (Recall that the Pharisees previously "confronted" Jesus indirectly by sending their disciples to ask Jesus about giving taxes to the emperor; see Proper 24, above.)

One Pharisee, a lawyer, attempts (!) to test Jesus. One imagines a series of boxers lined up to have their chance in the ring with this undefeated one, beginning with the possible equal match and proceeding to the defending "champion." The progression of intensity is evident. This will be the last disputation before Jesus moves into the offense (as if he has not been there already). The lawyer asks Jesus which law in the commandments is the greatest. Jesus answers directly by quoting the *Shema* (Deut. 6:5), but with one distinction: he changes "might" to "mind." Essentially, one is to love the Lord with one's whole being. Jesus does not stop with this answer, however; he is not satisfied with answering the question just as it is asked. "Another is like it," he continues. "You shall love your neighbor as yourself" (Lev. 19:18). A Pharisee would know all of this and should know better than to pretend he does not. What is new is the way Jesus links the two commandments.

When preachers highlight the first part, "You shall love the Lord your God with all your heart, and with all your soul, and with all your mind," sermons tend to have a cognitive focus; that is, they address our need to understand and make a decision to love God. This is odd, given that Jesus does not say only, "You shall love the Lord your God with all your mind." What about with our heart and our soul? Indeed, we are to love God with all of who we are. For this week's sermon it is worth exploring such questions as. "What does it mean to love God with our whole beings?" and "What does this look like?"

In my experience, preachers tend to highlight the second of the two greatest commandments; that is, love the neighbor. Such sermons come across as yet one more motivational pep talk (as if this time such a pep talk will "take"). I tell student preachers that chances are good we already know we are supposed to love our neighbors. The struggle is how to do it! Is being reminded all we need? I am doubly frustrated when the preacher says, "It's simple—love the neighbor!" because this means that not only (1) have I failed, but (2) I have failed at something simple.

In addition to exploring the question, "How do we love our neighbor?" (e.g., Is it a feeling or an action?), this is time to ask, "Who is the neighbor?" The latter question has been interpreted in various ways throughout history. Some have argued that "neighbor" is the fellow Israelite or fellow Christian. More commonly the neighbor is anyone and everyone. While this universal understanding of the neighbor is most common, still others believe the biblical command to love the neighbor refers specifically to the most vulnerable in society (see Exodus 22 above). Where do you stand on this question?

In addition to the questions on who the neighbor is and what is meant by love, we have the "as yourself" section with which to grapple. Loving oneself was probably assumed: "Love your neighbor as you (in reality) love yourself." It has been argued that this was disturbed by the "Jesus tradition," which encourages self-denial, love of one's enemy, and martyrdom issues.[10] We live in a society that absolutizes the self, on the one hand, and promotes self-negation, on the other. Ulrich Luz argues Christianity has had a hand in both. Recall Luther's *incurvatus in se*, in which such self-love was considered sinful. Twentieth-century psychology protested against self-denial to the extent that it suggested selfishness could be the result of a lack of self-love.[11] Feminist theologian Elisabeth Moltmann-Wendel agrees that sinfulness is the inability to say yes to self-acceptance.[12] Dorothee Soelle critiques Moltmann-Wendel, arguing that such internal work ought not take precedence over "'external work' that is concerned about the workaday world of one's suffering fellow human beings."[13] While this is likely not a salient issue in the text's horizon, and therefore should not be the main focus of a sermon on this text, it is important that the preacher ponder these concerns.

My challenge for preachers would be to create sermons that interweave these two commandments as Jesus does. A sermon encouraging hearers to love the neighbor without a foundational encouragement to love God with all of one's being is as lacking as a sermon that calls us to love God without addressing that one of the ways we do this is by loving the neighbor. While the two belong together, they are not one and the same. As Luz writes, "One's relationship to God is not merely absorbed into one's human relationships; instead it motivates and carries them."[14] The preacher will want to avoid suggesting that Christian faith can be reduced to ethics (which, some argue, ultimately and dangerously leads to no connection to loving God).

The call to love God, love neighbor, and love self must have more of a foundation. That is where the second part of this pericope becomes crucial. At first blush this may seem like two separate sermons (22:34-40 and 22:41-46). In fact, many sermons on this pericope tend to focus on either part A or part B, with many ending with verse 40 as the LFM encourages. However, the second section provides the theological nuancing, complexity, and motivation for loving God, neighbor, and self. *Everything hinges on the One who is calling us to live in this way.* It is Christ, the Lord, who asks us to love God with our whole being and to love our neighbors as ourselves. Once again we encounter a need to grapple with identity and authority; more specifically, Jesus' identity and authority.[15]

In this pivotal point in the text, Jesus takes the reins by asking the Pharisees who they think the Messiah is. Their answer is given as straightforwardly as their answer to Jesus' question in the first controversy (22:21), "The son of David." This time Jesus questions their response and quotes Psalm 110:1: "The LORD says to my lord, 'Sit at my right hand until I make your enemies your footstool.'" Jesus asks a follow-up question, "If David thus calls [the Messiah] Lord, how can he be his son?" In other words, how could one's descendant call him Lord? No one can answer Jesus' question, for they, the interpreters of the Scriptures, have been stumped in their area of expertise. Of course, the answer is that it could not be. Jesus is talking about his own identity, which, of course, they do not understand. Luz helps us with getting Matthew's broader picture in this regard: "Remember at the beginning of this Gospel we find out that the Son of David was the Son of God (1:18-25), Scripture foretold it (2:15), God revealed it (3:17, 17:5, 16:17), the devil tested it (4:3, 6), Jesus spoke of it to the disciples (11:25-27), and Peter confessed it (16:16)."[16]

Not only was anyone not able to answer this question, but no one dared to ask him any more questions. Muzzled again. This time the silence is not for tactical purposes but simply because they have nothing more to say. Again, Luz: "They who initially have decided to ensnare Jesus 'in a pronouncement' (v. 15: *en logo*) now themselves are caught in a trap and have 'no word' (v. 46: *logon*) with which to answer Jesus."[17]

This text desires for us to recognize Jesus as the true Messiah and, in turn, be motivated to love God and neighbor. Moving hearers beyond cognition to a more comprehensive worship of the true Messiah, Jesus Christ, may be what motivates hearers to serve the neighbor.

## Notes

1. Mark Throntveit, "Deuteronomy 34:1-2—The Death of Moses," http://www.enterthebible.org/Bible.aspx?rid=25, accessed July 15, 2010.
2. Patrick D. Miller, *Deuteronomy,* Interpretation: A Bible Commentary for Teaching and Preaching (Louisville: John Knox, 1990), 243.
3. Ibid.
4. Ibid., 245.
5. Rebecca Alpert, "Exodus," in *The Queer Bible Commentary* (London: SCM, 2006), 75. Alpert quotes Nancy Fuchs-Kreimer, "Mishpatim: What We Must Do," in *The Women's Torah Commentary: New Insights for Women Rabbis on the 53 Weekly Torah Portions,* ed. E. Goldstein (Woodstock: Jewish Lights, 2000), 148–53.
6. Ibid., 293.
7. Ibid., 296.
8. Ibid., 44.
9. Matthew 22:23-33 does not appear at this time in the lectionary.
10. Ulrich Luz, *Matthew 21–28,* Hermeneia (Minneapolis: Fortress Press, 2005), 84.
11. Erich Fromm, *The Art of Loving* (New York: Harper & Row, 1974), 474–76.
12. Elisabeth Moltmann-Wendel, *A Land Flowing with Milk and Honey: Perspectives on Feminist Theology,* trans. John Bowden (New York: Crossroad, 1986), 151–65.
13. Luz, *Matthew 21–28,* 79.
14. Ibid., 86.
15. This has been the concern from the moment Jesus stepped onto the scene, having been asked directly by the chief priests and the elders, "By what authority are you doing these things, and who gave you this authority?" (Matt. 21:23).
16. Luz, *Matthew 21–28,* 90.
17. Ibid., 61.

# October 30, 2011
## Twentieth Sunday after Pentecost
### Thirty-first Sunday in Ordinary Time / Proper 26

**Revised Common Lectionary (RCL)**

Joshua 3:7-17 or Micah 3:5-12
Psalm 107:1-7, 33-37 or Psalm 43
1 Thessalonians 2:9-13
Matthew 23:1-12

**Lectionary for Mass (LFM)**

Malachi 1:14b—2:2b, 8-10
Psalm 131:1, 2, 3
1 Thessalonians 2:7b-9, 13
Matthew 23:1-12

## First Reading
Joshua 3:7-17 (RCL)
Micah 3:5-12 (RCL alt.)
Malachi 1:14b—2:2b, 8-10 (LFM)

At the end of Deuteronomy (last week's RCL reading), we are told that the Israelites would obey their new leader, Joshua son of Nun. Joshua was "full of the spirit of wisdom, because Moses had laid his hands on him" (34:9). In this text, part of Joshua's commissioning by the Lord, similarities with Moses abound. Most clear is the move through the overflowing Jordan just as Moses had led the people through the Red Sea (Exodus 14). "Waters standing in a single heap" (vv. 13, 16) is a profound image. So begins the movement of the Israelites from Moab to Canaan; the beginning of the fulfillment of God's promises to Israel.

There is a clear connection between Micah 3 and Jesus' harangue against the corruption of those in power in Matthew 23. This text is more than a cry exposing such corruption; it is a proclamation that their days will be like night, disgrace and shame shall describe their lives, and their cries to the Lord will be in vain (vv. 6-7). The prophet predicts that the corrupt behavior of leaders will result in the destruction of Jerusalem. These verses depict a battle of the "upright." While the prophet indicts the corrupt rulers, priests, and prophets for their haughty assurance that the Lord is with them and thus will not be harmed (v. 11b), he, too, proclaims his assurance that he is "filled with power, with the spirit of the Lord, and with justice and might" (v. 8). The difference is that Micah represents the *campesinos* of his day. Hebrew Bible scholar Daniel Smith-Christopher says that "Micah, like many other prophets, angrily denounces the abuses suffered by the population of his agriculturally-based village at the hands of elite city dwellers, including rulers, landowners, military leaders and priests."[1] Daniel Simundson highlights the special responsibility of leaders (one of Micah's major themes):

> A whole nation can be dragged down by the actions of those who are supposed to be leaders. Merchants who cheat, political rulers who are more concerned for themselves than their people, religious leaders who cater to the wants of their constituents rather than the word of God—all of these contribute to the downfall of the ordinary citizen and the nation as a whole.[2]

The LFM reading from Malachi is addressed directly and harshly toward corrupt religious leaders. The Lord speaks and will send a curse if they do not take the Lord's commands to heart, fulfilling them in the Lord's name. The text skips ahead to verses 8-10, which point to the corruption that has caused others to stumble and describes that the result will be the disgrace of being made "despised and abased before all the people."

All of these texts highlight the corruption of leaders, which is a common thread in the texts this week. Before one points the finger at others, however, it is well worth our time and energy to look in the mirror at our own leadership.

# Psalmody
## Psalm 107:1-7, 33-37 (RCL)
## Psalm 43 (RCL alt.)
## Psalm 131:1, 2, 3 (LFM)

Psalm 107 begins with thanksgiving to the Lord for gathering the people from far and wide. A major element of this psalm is its repetitive refrain, "Let them thank the LORD for his steadfast love, for his wonderful works to humankind" (vv. 8, 15, 21, and 31). Interestingly, none of these verses is in the pericope. Even so, verse 1 urges us to give thanks for the Lord's steadfast love (*hesed*) that endures forever. The remainder of the psalm provides particular instances of God's loyalty. By the end of the psalm, verse 43, the exhortation is not to an individual, but to a community. There is movement, therefore, from individual salvation to corporate salvation, all the while holding the two together as exemplary of the wonderful work of the Lord's *hesed*. Verses 33-37 are especially poetic as they describe the bounty at the hands of the Steadfast One. The only bases for such steadfastness are the Lord's goodness and the cry to this One in times of trouble.

Psalm 43 is a lament through and through. The psalmist is hoping one day to boast of the Lord's *hesed* ("for I shall again praise him," v. 5). But, for now, all that is present is a great need and a petition for deliverance from the oppression of the enemy. The psalmist is stooped so low that he wonders why God has cast him off (v. 2). Shockingly, this one still sees God as the one who can redeem. Verse 5 finds the psalmist talking to himself, convincing himself to continue hoping in God. This psalm, juxtaposed with Psalm 107, provides a good reminder that while one person in the pew is singing the Lord's praises, the person in the next pew is crying out in need.

Typical of the Songs of Ascent, Psalm 131 is a short three verses. (See Proper 28, below, for a more thorough treatment of the Songs of Ascent.) The connection with the Gospel reading is evident in its admission of humble submission. The metaphor of the weaned child with its mother exhibits a sense of contentedness with this submission. This psalm provides an antidote to Jesus' description of the scribes and Pharisees whose modus operandi is self-exultation.

## Second Reading
1 Thessalonians 2:9-13 (RCL)
1 Thessalonians 2:7b-9, 13 (LFM)

Paul has just described his presence among the Thessalonians as being gentle as a nurse tenderly cares for her own children (v. 7b; see the commentary above on Pentecost 19).[3] Only a few verses later he suggests that he (along with his companions) is like a father is with his children. Paul continues to justify time spent with the Thessalonians. This leads to verse 13, which points to the hearers' wisdom in accepting his words not as human words, but as God's word. The curious thing about this is that it took right action and pure motives, for example, on the part of Paul, Timothy, and Silvanus, in order for the word to be heard as God's. It is worth noting that *euangelion tou theo* ("good news of God") appears three times in this chapter. That the word is not Paul's own but God's word is not to be missed.

Even more, Paul suggests that God's word is in the Thessalonians themselves (v. 13). To what extent do you consider human words delivered to a community of believers (whether from the pulpit or elsewhere) to be God's word? Instead of lifting up oneself as a model to be imitated (something Paul could get away with but we cannot), one might encourage hearers to consider how they are evangelists for God's word and models to be imitated. The tendency toward self-adulation will be tempered by the Gospel reading.

## Gospel
Matthew 23:1-12 (RCL, LFM)

I encourage preachers to base their sermons on Matthew 23 instead of the appointed text for All Saints Sunday since it continues what has begun the past few weeks. At the conclusion of these comments, I will suggest specific ways to connect this text to the celebration of All Saints as well as to the Festival of the Reformation (also celebrated at this time by some).

## Jesus on Offense

Jesus harnesses the opportunity to speak uninterrupted now that his adversaries have been silenced. No one else will "have the word" in all of chapter 23. This pericope precedes the "woes" in which Jesus chastises leaders who fail to follow his teachings. Thus, this pericope serves as a bridge between the controversies and the denunciations. We discover Jesus' (1) unassailability, (2) willingness to accuse his challengers and to expose them publically, and (3) theological and ecclesiological purposes.

## How Are We to Hear?

Are Jesus' words directed toward us? If not, what are we to take from our bird's-eye view of this whole scene? If Jesus' words are directed toward us, are we to hear them as accusations as his challengers might, or as the crowds and the disciples? As onlookers, we glean wisdom regarding the way in which God acts with God's adversaries. Also from this "omniscient" (literally, not epistemologically, speaking) view, we glean wisdom about God's identity in Jesus. Sermons from this perspective are instructive in tone and reflect what may have been Matthew's intent.

A second possibility is that Jesus' words are directed toward us. If so, are we to hear Jesus' words as those who are being accused or as those who have an opportunity to avoid being the brunt of similar accusations? This text certainly might indict those of us who "do not practice what we teach" or "are unwilling to lift a finger" or "do deeds so that others may see them" or "love to have the place of honor at banquets" or "love to be greeted with respect" or . . . if you get the idea that this list is uncomfortably long, then it is working. Chances are that we, as pastors, preachers, and teachers, have claimed too much honor for ourselves at one time or another. While hearing this in the text is a possibility, I do not think a sermon aimed directly at creating this experience for the hearers is appropriate. That is not to say that they may not feel accused by some of these words. If God's word seeks to do and does this, then so be it. But the preacher need not (and, I think, should not) set out to do this.

The other possibility is that Jesus' words are directed at us as those who have an opportunity to learn from the situation about how to be followers of Jesus. The biggest clue for this trajectory comes from verse 1, "Then Jesus said to the crowds and to his disciples . . ." Jesus' adversaries listen in as Jesus speaks to the onlookers. While different from the evangelist's aim, the aim of the sermon is here.

Two caveats are in order. First, it is not wise for the preacher to play the role of an accusatory messiah. In this case, there is wisdom in seeing yourself as one whom Jesus addresses. The pronoun "we" goes a long way. This is especially true since those who are being accused are the religious leaders! You will walk yourself right into a bad situation with your hearers if you take on the role that Jesus is exposing. Since Jesus is the only one who speaks in this section, it would be good to explore ways in which the sermon paves a way for *Jesus'* words to be heard.

While the first caveat safeguards against pointing the accusatory finger toward the hearers, the second caveat safeguards against doing so toward an outside group. Unfortunately, this error is evident in this text's history of interpretation. Matthew 23 has "made a major contribution to the Christian caricature of Judaism" by applying the negative type of Pharisees to all Pharisees, which in turn has been applied to all Jews.[4] This is an abuse of the text. Actually, this text has been used inappropriately to accuse anyone who opposes the church. (Interestingly, and regrettably, such opponents are often labeled "Pharisee.")[5]

Notable in verse 8 is a shift from talking *about* the Pharisees and scribes to talking *to* the crowds and disciples. Because verses 8-12 guide the sermon's trajectory in this way, the following comments will focus on this section.[6]

> [8] But you are not to be *called* rabbi,
> *for* you have *one* teacher,
> and you are all brothers and sisters.[7]
> [9] And *call* no one your father on earth,
> *for* you have *one* Father—
> the *one* in heaven.
> [10] Nor are you to be *called* instructors,
> *for* you have *one* instructor,
> the Messiah.

There is an emphasis in these three parallel prohibitions on God's sovereignty. The three "one" (*eis*) affirmations remind the readers of the *Shema*, Israel's basic confession to the one God. It is significant that as Jesus proclaims there is only one instructor, the Messiah, he is also instructing. Indeed, it is appropriate for him to instruct for he is the Messiah.

Second, hierarchy among brothers and sisters (i.e., anyone who is not Jesus) is challenged. The second prohibition is distinct in its use of active rather than passive voice. In addition, instead of being directed to potential "teachers," it is directed to every member of the community. Following Jesus' admonitions and theological foundations are ecclesiological consequences (see vv. 8c and 11). According to Ulrich Luz, "Before God and the exalted Christ all members of the church are equal servants."[8] There is a subversive call to solidarity. Talk about a controversy.

The double reversals that follow (i.e., of greatness and being a servant, of exaltation and humility) recall important themes of the call to discipleship in the kingdom.[9] Verse 11 does not say, "Those who are servants will be the greatest," or "Go out and be a servant." Instead, those who are the greatest *will be* servants. "The greatest" is not defined but is left up to the hearer (both in Jerusalem and in your church) to decide if he or she is greatest. If so, servanthood is what is expected.

This is the third time we encounter "All who exalt themselves will be humbled, and all who humble themselves will be exalted" in Matthew (see 18:4; 20:26).[10] This wisdom on humility serves as an effective bookend to Jesus' humble entry into Jerusalem the day before (Matt. 21:6-7). Jesus is justified in speaking of humility in this way since he has already exemplified it.

## The Takeaway

God, in Jesus, is the great reverser who seeks to be known as the one, divine Lord by a community of human equals. God does not simply tell us how to be, but, to our surprise, exemplifies it. Preaching this text provides an opportunity to reexamine the ways in which our commitment to God's sovereignty is reflected in our ecclesiological practices. As Luz bluntly states, "A church without higher and lower members, a church of serving, a church of equals, sisters and brothers in solidarity—that is what Matthew has in mind . . . a hierarchical church of the Catholic type or an institutional church of the Protestant type are a fundamental denial of faith."[11] It is on christological grounds, Luz argues, that "Matthew resists the love of titles and the need for worldly prestige in the church as a matter of principle."[12] How might we renounce our own prestige and desire to get our own way for the sake of the community? Responding to this question is a key focus this week for the "reverends" and "doctors" in the house.

Matthew 23 is not dubbed the "unloveliest chapter in the Gospel" for nothing. In some ways we are back where we started: Are Jesus' words blessing or offense to you? As you answer, keep in mind that for those gathered in Jerusalem Jesus had already begun to set the standard for greatness. For us today, we know that the ultimate standard is only a few days, a cross, and an empty tomb away. Trust this standard as you reexamine your role among your hearers and, in turn, encourage them to reexamine their roles in the community.

## This Text in Relation to Festivals

This week's texts have to do with God challenging corrupt leaders in the community. Certainly, there is a connection between leadership and these two festivals.

*All Saints.* At first glance, the introduction to "the woes" in Matthew 23 may not seem as fitting for All Saints as are "the Beatitudes" of Matthew 5. The woes are negative mirror images of the Sermon on the Mount's blessings. Recognizing there are those who believe living lives congruent with these blessings yields sainthood, it can be argued that despite our occasional (or frequent) failure to live as God intends, it is God who sanctifies us. Perhaps this All Saints Day we might point to God's ability to reform our lives even when our ecclesiological ways are not congruent with our theological convictions.

*Festival of the Reformation.* This festival tends to applaud the "advances" in reform made in the sixteenth century. However, even the reformers relied on a certain hierarchical structure that is clearly against the egalitarian structure proposed in Matthew. Perhaps this Reformation Sunday preachers might critique the Reformation for not going far enough in order that we do so now, with God's help.[13]

## Notes

1. Daniel L. Smith-Christopher, "Introduction to Micah," in *The People's Bible,* ed. Curtiss Paul DeYoung et al. (Minneapolis: Fortress Press, 2009), 1070.
2. Daniel Simundson, "Micah: Theological Themes," http://www.enterthebible.org /Bible.aspx?rid=51, accessed July 15, 2010.
3. On maternal imagery in Paul, see Beverly Gaventa, "Our Mother St. Paul: Toward the Recovery of a Neglected Theme," in *A Feminist Companion to Paul,* ed. Amy-Jill Levine (Cleveland: Pilgrim, 2004), 84–97.
4. Ulrich Luz, *Matthew 21–28,* Hermeneia (Minneapolis: Fortress Press, 2005), 94.
5. Even the *Longman Dictionary of Contemporary English* (2nd ed.; Harlow, UK: Longman, 1987) defines a Pharisee as "a person who in a self-satisfied way values too highly the outward form of something." In other dictionaries the word *Pharisee* has become synonymous with "hypocrite." References from Luz, *Matthew 21–28,* 94.
6. There is much to be noted, of course, about Jesus' accusations against the Pharisees and scribes. However, having made the argument for this sermon trajectory, I will not focus on verses 2-7.
7. Translating *adelphoi* as "students" is an error.
8. Luz, *Matthew 21–28,* 107.
9. James Boyce, "Matthew," http://www.enterthebible.org /Bible.aspx?rid=2, accessed July 15, 2010.
10. This saying was well known in early Christianity as well as in Judaism (see 1 Sam. 2:7-8; Job 22:29; Prov. 29:23; Isa. 10:33; Ezek. 17:24; 21:31).
11. Luz, *Matthew 21–28,* 110–11.
12. Ibid., 107.
13. Commentary on the Reformation Day texts by Gail Ramshaw may be found in *New Proclamation Commentary on Feasts, Holy Days, and Other Celebrations,* ed. David B. Lott (Minneapolis: Fortress Press, 2007), 208–13.

# October 30 / November 1 or 6, 2011
## All Saints Sunday / Day

**Revised Common Lectionary (RCL)**

Revelation 7:9-17

Psalm 34:1-10, 22

1 John 3:1-3

Matthew 5:1-12

**Lectionary for Mass (LFM)**

Revelation 7:2-4, 9-14

Psalm 24:1bc-2, 3-4ab, 5-6

1 John 3:1-3

Matthew 5:1-12a

## First Reading
### Revelation 7:9-17 (RCL)
### Revelation 7:2-4, 9-14 (LFM)

Revelation 7 gives us a vision for a possible existence. John of Patmos depicts a scene replete with angels and multitudes of people standing before a king, worshiping, singing, and crying out, "Salvation belongs to our God."

Those who are gathered have made it through "the great ordeal" (v. 14) to this time where there are no more ordeals. "They will hunger no more, and thirst no more . . . the Lamb . . . will be their shepherd . . . and God will wipe away every tear from their eyes" (vv. 16-17). It is no surprise that these words are commonly heard at funerals. On a day when we remember those who have died, we cry out and pray, "Amen! Amen! May it be so for them."

This glimpse of the heavenly banquet is a model for our worship on earth. The hosts of heaven include those from every nation in this great multicultural gathering, as Miguel de la Torre notes:

> The "white man's burden" has historically been to bring civilization, including the gospel message, to the margins of society. But the angel tells John to go back to his center and tell people there *about the margins.* The gospel is already thriving in the margins of society today. The real question facing the Euro-Americans is asked by the people at those margins: Will they join our diversity?![1]

## Psalmody
### Psalm 34:1-10, 22 (RCL)

"The LORD redeems the life of his servants; none of those who take refuge in him will be condemned" (34:22). These words conclude this acrostic psalm. No wonder verses 1-10 depict such dramatic thanksgiving for help received. The psalm begins with an invocation of praise (vv. 1-3), moves to a declaration of deliverance (v. 4), and describes the implications of the deliverance (vv. 5-10). Verse 8 contains a beatitude, which is very appropriate for this All Saints Day: "O taste and see that the LORD is good; happy are those who take refuge in him." "Taste," James L. Mays proposes, suggests that one "find out by experience." That is to say, "taste and see" is a "proposal that one try out the pursuit of peace and the practice of prayer as the way to open living to the Lord's gift of life through his reward and his salvation."[2]

### Psalm 24:1bc-2, 3-4ab, 5-6 (LFM)

Verse 3 of Psalm 24 assumes the response to the questions proposed is, "I would like to ascend the hill of the Lord / stand in his holy place." Prior to the questions, verses 1 and 2 point to the reality of creation and the Lord's ownership of it. This is the necessary foundation for what follows the questions; that is, a description of the blessing and vindication as a result of a relationship with the world and its creator and owner. Two affirmatives—clean hands, pure hearts[3]—and two negatives—do not lift up souls to what is false and do not swear deceitfully—characterize the company of those who seek the creator and owner of all.

## Second Reading
### 1 John 3:1-3 (RCL, LFM)

These three verses declare us children of God and encourage us to live the alternative lives we have been called to live, even when others no longer believe what the author believes is truth about Jesus. All three Johannine epistles call for love-in-action.

While this text is about life in the present, it is also forward looking. We do not know exactly what it will be like when the future is revealed, but we do know we will be like God. Here is where 1 John's high Christology connects to a very present ecclesiology, "unity in the community." We are who we are because of God in Christ.

## Gospel
### Matthew 5:1-12 (RCL)
### Matthew 5:1-12 (LFM)

In my comments on the Gospel reading under Pentecost 20, above, I encouraged preachers to base their Sunday sermons on Matthew 23 instead of these appointed texts for All Saints. Because of this and because specific suggestions for connecting that text to the celebration of All Saints were offered, these comments will assume there is to be a separate worship service on All Saints Day. If the focus of this separate worship service will be on remembering those who have died, I suggest basing the sermon on Revelation 7. If not, 1 John, Psalm 34, and the Beatitudes of Matthew 5 will provide fodder for exploring blessing "God-style."

In the interest of full disclosure, my theological convictions point to God as the One who sanctifies us instead of focusing on our capability to make ourselves holy. And yet, as we live in a certain way, we are blessed. To be sure, this blessing does not resemble what has come to be called "the prosperity gospel," where God rewards signs of faith with wealth, health, and happiness.

Matthew 5 begs our consideration regarding its function as a prescriptive or descriptive word. That is, does it intend to tell us what to do, or does it intend to give us a picture of how things really are? For example, are we to adjust our lives so that we are more merciful? Or is it simply (!) that when we are merciful, we receive mercy? One might be concerned that if Jesus' words in the Sermon on the Mount are prescriptive, people might become peacemakers, for example, not for the sake of those who will benefit from newly found peace, but so that they will be called children of God (v. 9). While this would still generate peace, the goal is not on the peacemaking itself, but on the "heavenly reward." The difference this makes is worth some reflection.

As description, this text would function not to exhort hearers to right action, but to provide assurance that their actions do yield blessing. The descriptive angle is not necessarily a "lazy" perspective. Knowing that persecution for righteousness' sake will yield blessing may be just what a person needs to hear in order to continue in the ways of the Lord despite the persecution in a politically volatile setting.

How wonderful it would be to proclaim to hearers, "You are blessed *when you* are merciful, are peacemakers . . ." instead of having to exhort them to go out and be merciful and make peace. Are you able to do so with any of the Beatitudes in your setting?

Interpreting the text descriptively is to read it from the perspective of those who are marginalized; those who are poor in spirit, who mourn, who are persecuted. In no way does this view endorse persecution or mourning or doing what you can so that people will revile you. When I was a young girl, somehow I got the message that because I was not poor in spirit or meek, because I was not persecuted, because I was a happy, loved child with people around me pointing out my potential, I was not a good candidate to be a Christian. I actually recall trying to act like I was poor in spirit (whatever that might mean to a nine-year-old) with the hope that I would become poor in spirit. Doing so would then ensure that I would be a part of the kingdom. A prescriptive interpretation of Matthew 5 was at work.

It would be a mistake to elevate any kind of oppression in this way. Liberation from oppression is still worth the struggle "because people never get used to being oppressed."[4] The descriptive view of the text acknowledges that this is already reality for some. And when it is, being assured that such experiences are not in vain might be just the motivation for pressing on. If there is an exhortation in the Beatitudes, it is for

213

those who are not living in the margins to hear in them a call to be in solidarity with those who are.

Jesus' words both warn and teach his disciples. They warn that the disciples would be sent out into situations where they would likely experience what the Beatitudes present. They teach that these experiences will not be in vain, for God will bless them with comfort, mercy, the kingdom, and glimpses of God.

Recently I saw a very disturbing bumper sticker. It displayed the peace sign with a caption that read, "Footprint of an American Chicken." Immediately, Matthew 5:9 came to mind. Actually, what came to mind was that the owner of this truck may not be aware of Matthew 5:9. In order for peacemakers to confront the conviction behind the bumper sticker, one would need the assurance of Jesus' teaching in Matthew.

It is worth recalling that at the center of the Sermon on the Mount we find the Lord's Prayer. Indeed, this day we pray that the Lord's kingdom will come, the Lord's will be done—not only in heaven in the future, but on earth . . . now.

## Notes

1. Miguel A. de la Torre, study note in *The People's Bible,* ed. Curtiss Paul DeYoung et al. (Minneapolis: Fortress Press, 2008), 1728.
2. James L. Mays, *Psalms,* Interpretation: A Bible Commentary for Teaching and Preaching (Louisville: John Knox, 1989), 153–54.
3. Here, "clean" and "pure" refer to character and not ritual purification.
4. Michael Joseph Brown, "Matthew," in *True to Our Native Land: An African American New Testament Commentary*, ed. Brian K. Blount et al. (Minneapolis: Fortress Press, 2007), 92. Brown is quoting Theodore Walker.

# November 6, 2011
## Twenty-first Sunday after Pentecost
### Thirty-second Sunday in Ordinary Time / Proper 27

| **Revised Common Lectionary (RCL)** | **Lectionary for Mass (LFM)** |
|---|---|
| Joshua 24:1-3a, 14-25 or Wisdom of Solomon 6:12-16 and Amos 5:18-24 | Wisdom of Solomon 6:12-16 |
| Psalm 78:1-7 or Wisdom of Solomon 6:17-20 and Psalm 70 | Psalm 63:2, 3-4, 5-6, 7-8 |
| 1 Thessalonians 4:13-18 | 1 Thessalonians 4:13-18 or 4:13-14 |
| Matthew 25:1-13 | Matthew 25:1-13 |

## First Reading
### Joshua 24:1-3a, 14-25 (RCL)
### Wisdom of Solomon 6:12-16 (RCL alt., LFM)
### Amos 5:18-24 (RCL alt.)

There are numerous similarities between Joshua and Moses. Instead of Sinai, Joshua and his people are gathered at Shechem. Joshua gathers all the tribes of Israel and recounts all that the Lord has done for them (vv. 2-13). He urges the people to revere the Lord, for, given all that the Lord has done for them, why would they seek the aid of other gods? Firmly, Joshua exhorts, "Put away the gods that your ancestors served beyond the River and in Egypt, and serve the LORD" (v. 14); "Choose this day whom you will serve" (v. 15). (Interestingly, this suggests that membership was not a matter of "lineage" but of "loyalty.") Joshua stands before his people as an example when he proclaims, "As for me and my household, we will serve the LORD" (v. 15). The people affirm they will also serve the Lord. Note the word *also*. Joshua catches this word and warns the people that serving foreign gods alongside the Lord God, who demands full loyalty, will have dire consequences. "Put away the foreign gods," Joshua repeats (v. 23). With this, the people vow to serve and obey the Lord God.

Three notable things arise from this narrative: (1) Do we exhort as boldly as Joshua, "Put away your false gods and serve the LORD"? (2) Joshua's proposal is not an immediate "sell" despite the previously made covenant at Sinai. The people push back a bit. However, Joshua's persistence leads to the renewed covenant. (3) There are times when we need to be held accountable, to revisit our commitments we have made in response to God's goodness, and to renew them. The "allure of foreign gods" is a danger even for us. Homecoming Sunday takes place annually in the fall (perhaps right around this time) in southern churches. This is a time when former members return to the church, the history of the congregation is recounted, and, together, all look toward the congregation's future. This is a perfect time to proclaim, "Put away your false gods and serve the Lord," with the hope that it might lead to a renewed covenant.

Amos 5:24 is a well-known biblical proclamation that focuses on a commitment. "Let justice roll down like waters, and righteousness like an ever-flowing stream" is at the heart of Amos's preaching. If you want to delight the Lord, Amos argues, bypass the festivals, skip the solemn assemblies, and get right to justice and righteousness. Actually, Amos places these words in the Lord's mouth: "I hate, I despise your festivals, and I take no delight in your solemn assembles." Amos was a city man who saw firsthand the market vendors' schemes to cheat the customer but could speak the agrarian lingo. In both settings he saw the "plight of the poor" and bravely spoke out on their behalf. Amos was likely not against worship, but against empty piety that fails to connect liturgy and justice for all people.

Wisdom of Solomon is a collection of sayings attributed to Solomon (but not written by Solomon). Like Psalm 78, a key theme in chapter 6 is transparency. Wisdom personified is discernible, locatable, and available. She (!) even goes out of her way to be these things. The interesting sorites (from the Greek word meaning "to heap"—a form of logic that proceeds little by little), found in verses 17-20, suggest that desiring wisdom will lead one to God's eternal kingdom.

## Psalmody
Psalm 78:1-7 (RCL)
Psalm 70 (RCL alt.)
Wisdom of Solomon 6:17-20 (RCL alt.)
Psalm 63:2, 3-4, 5-6, 7-8 (LFM)

Psalm 78, the second-longest psalm in the psalter, collects various events and stages in Israel's history and presents a continuous interpretation of the whole. The first seven verses present a curious interplay between "I" and "we." The speaker is clearly one who has established authority with the people and has been invited to instruct, as the first four verses demonstrate. The psalmist gives a sneak preview of the role of the Lord's instruction (vv. 6-7): upon teaching the next generation so that they might know the decrees, that generation will rise up and teach their children, and so on, so that "they should set their hope in God, and not forget the works of God, but keep his commandments" (continue this through v. 8). The psalmist then proceeds to do as the Lord commands; he teaches the things they hear and know. Transparency is key in this psalm.

In Psalm 70, the psalmist seeks revenge and petitions the Lord to help. The situation must be dire, given the psalmist's threefold plea for *quick* aid, "Make haste to help me!" (v. 1), "Hasten to help me," and "do not delay" (both v. 5). This individual cry for help points to the psalmist's situational need and dependence on the Lord. While one's cry for the Lord's help is generally urgent, it is unusual for such urgency to be this exposed.

There is an emphasis on "soul" (Hebrew *nefesh*, which implies one's whole being) in Psalm 63 that begins each of its three sections: "My soul thirsts for you" (v. 2), "My soul shall savor the rich banquet of praise" (v. 6), and "My soul clings fast to you" (v. 9). While the need might be just as great as the need of the psalmist in Psalm 70, the poetic character of the language slows the sense of urgency. Even more, this one who longs for God has time to move from location to location, from the sanctuary (v. 3) to "my bed" (v. 7). Also evident is the involvement of the psalmist's whole being: the body burns, the eyes look, the lips offer worship, hands are lifted up, and the voice calls out the Lord's name, the mouth honors with joyful lips.

*(For commentary on Wisdom of Solomon 6:17-20, see the first reading above.)*

## Second Reading
### 1 Thessalonians 4:13-18 (RCL, LFM)
### 1 Thessalonians 4:13-14 (LFM alt.)

This verse seems to be a non sequitur to what comes before. After acknowledging the Thessalonians' love for one another and encouraging them in their faithful behavior, Paul switches his focus to death and resurrection (this is not the first time resurrection appears in the letter; see 1:10). Has there been an argument regarding resurrection? What is this about? Are people wondering when the resurrection will happen? There seems to be a concern that those who have already died will not rise again with the Lord. Verse 15 is a solid proclamation: "We declare to you . . ." Paul assures the Thessalonians that all will be "caught up in the clouds together" to "meet the Lord in the air." Paul encourages his hearers to encourage one another with this assurance.

Preaching on this text has likely looked like explaining death and resurrection to folks. However, considering our desire to "do what Paul does as opposed to say what Paul says" (see the introduction, above), the timing of resurrection and what will happen to those who are still living if the Lord comes again may not be the most pressing theological concerns on people's minds. Some may be curious about this (and then this section of the letter will helpfully guide your responses), but most do not have a sense that Christ's return is imminent. So what are the primary theological questions on people's minds in your congregation? This pericope and Gross's homiletical question may be just what are needed to jump-start a solid theological discussion.

Consider how Paul addresses a complicated theological issue. He responds both theologically and pastorally. In this instance, he repeats a formula that is likely already well known, "Jesus died and rose again," in order for this proclamation to be one's primary consolation. Paul acknowledges grief and comforts those who grieve by (1) helping the Thessalonians reframe their grief by seeing it in "relationship to the future God intends" and (2) placing "responsibility for a ministry of consolation squarely within the community."[1]

# Gospel
## Matthew 25:1-13 (RCL, LFM)

A typical but imprudent interpretation of this parable is an allegorical one in which Christ is the bridegroom, we are the bridesmaids, oil is good works or love, the closed door is eschatological judgment, and the marriage is the time of God's salvation. Jesus tells this parable, Matthew recounts it, and the preacher interprets it so that we can ensure that we do not experience the same disastrous results of the foolish bridesmaids, whose irresponsibility and lack of preparation lead to a lost opportunity to enter God's kingdom. Instead, we are to strive to be like the "wise" bridesmaids, prepared for the unknown time when the bridegroom, Christ, returns. There you have it, another "earn your salvation" sermon. Unfortunately, this kind of allegorizing, which is used to define how we should live now and who will be in the kingdom, has reigned for centuries. However, this interpretation simply does not correspond with what we know to be true about why God sent Jesus and the truth that, in Jesus, God overcame sin, death, and the power of evil.[2] Not only is this reading misguided, but it misses out on a possible transformation. Let's explore why the interpretation outlined above is misguided in order to offer some possible interpretations that might guide your sermon trajectory.

First, regarding the behavior of the bridesmaids, how is it that the behavior of the wise bridesmaids is commended? First, they fail to share. Vicky Balabanski "sees the refusal of the clever women as complicity in patriarchy/kyriarchy."[3] Their lack of solidarity with other women does not correspond with the broader picture of the gospel. Second, they, too, fall asleep when the bridegroom is delayed. If wisdom as resourcefulness is what this text promotes, I'd put my money on the foolish bridesmaids, since they are somehow able to find oil even when (1) they are dismissed by their peers and (2) the shops are closed at midnight. Yes, some suggest looking for oil at midnight shows just how foolish these bridesmaids are. But talk about tenacity. If having enough oil, or enough of anything, is what is key to getting into the banquet, then this is simply unfair to all of those who simply do not have access like others do.

A second issue with the common interpretation has to do with the bridegroom's delay. Obviously, the delay in the bridegroom's (as Christ's) return is much longer for us. It is so delayed that most of us no longer live in anticipation of Christ's return. So we must either reinvigorate our sense of anticipation or move on from it. If we choose the former (as does the common interpretation described above), for what purpose would we do so? If we choose the latter, what would that look like? This text (including v. 13) does not support the former since the wise also fell asleep when the bridegroom was delayed and they still made it into the banquet. (Even more, the parable just before this one was about Christ coming early.) The text does support the latter interpretation, as I explain below.

This brings us to the big issue, the bridegroom. While Scripture does depict Jesus or God as the bridegroom, that is not necessarily the intent here.[4] Hearers may not have associated the bridegroom with Jesus. Even more, since the bride is not mentioned, it is not likely that the narrator had in mind the allegory of the bridegroom and the church.[5] Luise Schottroff says boldly, "The traditional allegorical interpretation of this parable makes the representative of social injustice, the bridegroom, a divine figure and thus corrupts the gospel."[6]

When the bridegroom is not Christ, the foolish bridesmaids do not miss out by being on this side of the closed door. The bridegroom is with those who do not share, those who have access to the goods and materials that are required. Might it not be the case, then, that Christ is on the side of those who are shut out? Of course, Jesus stands with the excluded. We know that! Even more, since Jesus has been attempting to encourage his disciples not to be led astray by false messiahs (Matthew 24), could not the bridegroom be one of those? That is, could the bridegroom in the story be one who tries to convince us to work harder and harder, to claim what we have earned for ourselves without the need to care for the other, to revel in our own accomplishments? If the bridegroom is a false prophet, then when he says to the "foolish" bridesmaids, "I do not know you," what's keeping the bridesmaids from responding, "We do not know you"?[7]

This is not an innocent text, argues Schottroff, and no allegorical interpretation can make it so. It is a story that speaks of social oppression, indeed of violence. It may be that in social reality people laughed at ugly or naïve girls, but in fact that laughter was something like a social death sentence. That tradition of interpretation has made the clever girls a metaphor for right behavior before God, at the expense of the naïve girls, and found this to be "Good News."[8]

## The Proposal

Schottroff proposes that all depends on the interpretation of the word *then*, which begins this parable. In order to understand this, it is important to look at the broader textual context. The whole fifth discourse (24:1—25:46) is precipitated by the disciples' question, "Tell us, when will this be, and what will be the sign of your coming and of the end of the age?" (24:3). Jesus first encourages his disciples not to be led astray by false prophets (24:5). All the present suffering, Jesus says, will not be the end, but the beginning of the birth pangs (24:8). Those who endure all of this to the end will be saved (24:13). The sign of the end will not be destruction or closed doors, but a pronouncement of good news (24:14). "Then if anyone says to you [upon seeing the 'desolating sacrilege standing in the holy place,' 24:15], 'Look! Here is the Messiah!' or 'There he is!'—do not believe it" (24:23). In other words, suffering will not be the sign of the end. Only after the suffering will Jesus come (24:29-30).

The common interpretation has assumed the "then" refers to the coming of Jesus, but that just does not correlate with the text's context. Rather, the "then" (which occurs seventeen times in the whole discourse) could refer either to the beginning of the birth pangs (the destruction) or to the postdestruction when the Messiah has come.[9] The parable at hand, argues Schottroff, refers to the beginning of the birth pangs, the present.[10] This proposal is a rhetorical possibility, given that "Then the kingdom of heaven will be like this" does not mean that what follows will be a description of what the kingdom of heaven is like. Instead, the hearers are invited to compare the story to the kingdom of heaven, in which case, this story is opposite. The closed door describes the destruction, the beginning of birth pangs, but keep awake, foolish bridesmaids, keep hope; despite being shut out now, there is another one coming.

### Time

Time plays an important role in this text ("then," "bridegroom is delayed," "midnight," "later," "you know neither the day nor the hour"). But it is not linear time as we know it. Schottroff writes, "The idea of time in this eschatology is not intended to present a coherent scenario for the end-time but to help listeners to understand their own present in relation to the coming of God. These listeners are to be strengthened to maintain their hope that injustice will have an end and justice alone will rule on earth."[11]

The last line is the homiletical key. Enduring, keeping awake, is trusting that the Savior will come after the suffering, trusting that there will be something better, trusting that that one is truly Lord and not a false prophet. Then God alone, who is more powerful than all horrors, will be king.

### Homiletical Possibilities

Two things to avoid: the traditional allegorical interpretation and unnecessary explanations of ancient wedding customs. The three parables (Matt. 24:45-52; 25:1-13; 25:14-30) "make the catastrophes of the present transparent to God's righteousness, which will make the last to be first."[12] Schottroff argues that 25:1 prepares one to hear with new ears and see with new eyes that this bad scenario is not the end. "The hearers are to compare their world with God's kingdom and derive hope that God will renew the world. Those who can hear and see will be transformed; they awaken; they remain awake, they recognize Jesus in their suffering brothers and sisters."[13]

Consider the next three weeks as a unit. This week and next we get the "then," which describes the penultimate destruction. From this we learn what God is *not* like. Then (!) on Christ the King Sunday we get the "then" of the end (fitting on the last day of the church year), which is really a new beginning—"then," when the Son of Man comes in his glory.

So help us be a listening community that is aware of the signs of the times. Describe for us the present birth pangs. Help us compare our present world to God's kingdom. Help us to pray that God's kingdom come. Awaken us to the hope that God will renew the world, that the door will be closed on this age. Note that this is not a proposal to preach universal salvation, for

> this general message of Jesus' love cannot reach those who suffer from violence and injustice, the majority of people in today's world. It is no help to them when God's undistinguishing love is preached. It remains grace to those who are already sitting at the table, at the wedding feast, who have access to nourishment, medical care and education. The message of judgment and of God's justice, which is able to distinguish between the perpetrators and the victim, is fundamental to the Jesus tradition.[14]

This is also not a proposal that will tolerate complacency. The parable, like all parables, is intended to alter the lives of the addressees. But instead of endorsing the individualized, self-focused, and, perhaps, smug behavior of the so-called wise bridesmaids, this parable endorses the present as a "time of longing, of standing fast in resistance, and of testing."[15] Wisdom is knowing what God has done for us (see Joshua, above) and, because of that, not seeing destruction as a sign of God's presence. Wisdom is trusting and living into justice that rolls down like waters (Amos).

## Notes

1. Beverly R. Gaventa, *First and Second Thessalonians,* Interpretation: A Bible Commentary for Teaching and Preaching (Louisville: John Knox, 1998), 68.
2. Two questions the preacher might ponder include: Is it appropriate to uphold an interpretation of a text even though it does not square with what I understand to be true about God? When might such interpretation challenge what I understand to be true about God?
3. Luise Schottroff, *The Parables of Jesus* (Minneapolis: Fortress Press, 2006), 33. Quoting from Vicky Balabanski, "Opening the Closed Door: A Feminist Reading of the Wise and Foolish Virgins (Mt. 25:1-13)," in *The Lost Coin: Parables of Women, Work and Wisdom,* ed. Mary Ann Beavis (London: Sheffield Academic Press, 2002), 71–97.
4. "J. Jeremias, among others, argued that the metaphor of the Messiah as a bridegroom is foreign to the OT and the literature of late Judaism." From Klyne R. Snodgrass, *Stories with Intent: A Comprehensive Guide to the Parables of Jesus* (Grand Rapids: Eerdmanns, 2008), 513.
5. Snodgrass (757) references Eta Linnemann's assessment in *Parables of Jesus: Introduction and Exposition,* trans. John Sturdy (London: SPCK, 1966).
6. Schottroff, *Parables of Jesus,* 33.
7. Balabanski, "Opening the Closed Door," 78.
8. Schottroff, *Parables of Jesus,* 33.
9. Ibid., 35.
10. Ibid., 36.
11. Schottroff, *Parables of Jesus,* 35.
12. Ibid., 36.
13. Ibid., 37.
14. Ibid., 33.
15. Ibid., 35.

# November 13, 2011
## Twenty-second Sunday after Pentecost
### Thirty-third Sunday in Ordinary Time / Proper 28

**Revised Common Lectionary (RCL)**

Judges 4:1-7 or Zephaniah 1:7, 12-18
Psalm 123 or 90:1-8, (9-11), 12
1 Thessalonians 5:1-11
Matthew 25:14-30

**Lectionary for Mass (LFM)**

Proverbs 31:10-13, 19-20, 30-31
Psalm 128:1-2, 3, 4-5
1 Thessalonians 5:1-6
Matthew 25:14-30 or 25:14-15, 19-21

## First Reading
### Judges 4:1-7 (RCL)
### Zephaniah 1:7, 12-18 (RCL alt.)
### Proverbs 31:10-13, 19-20, 30-31 (LFM)

"The Israelites again did what was evil in the sight of the Lord, after Ehud died."
Israel's disobedience was a common occurrence. This time the result is being handed
over to the king of Canaan, Jabin, who oppressed them for twenty years until they
cried out to the Lord. Mark Throntveit notes that it seems that "as long as the people
obeyed God there was progress toward the consolidation of the promised land. But
when they disobeyed, that progress was stopped and Israel was subjected to tyranny."[1]

Deborah, one of the many female key players in Judges, led the way out of the
oppression. Speaking on behalf of the Lord, she sends Barak to lead the war against
Jabin's army. Deborah's fidelity as a judge of Israel is presented in contrast to Israel's
lack of fidelity. Chapter 5 reiterates this story (with some variation) in poetic form.

Zephaniah begins with judgment and ends in salvation. These verses depict the
Lord's judgment of the complacent people—and it "ain't pretty." The people's labor
will be in vain, their days will be full of distress, anguish, and darkness, they will
be aimless like the blind. All the money in the world cannot buy them out of this
one; all this because they have sinned against the Lord. Zephaniah's "on that day" is
reminiscent of but very different from the one in Isaiah (4:2-3). That is, until the end
of Zephaniah (3:11) when the "on that day" points to hope and redemption. Although
we do not hear these verses in the lectionary, it is important to read the judgment
through this lens.

This reading from Proverbs is the final one in the collection of sayings. In these words taught to King Lemuel by his mother (31:1), a good woman is described. Ultimately, a woman ("woman" and "wife" are the same word in Hebrew) who fears the Lord is most valuable; that is, at the height of capacity. She labors much, shows compassion to the poor, and deserves a "share in the fruit of her hands." She "is the living embodiment of Woman Wisdom's teaching and attributes and does not rely on simple appearances (vv. 25-26, 30)," according to Carole Fontaine.[2] This proverb affirms the work and recognition of women in the public sphere, "in the very gates of the city where Woman Wisdom first raised her cry."[3]

## Psalmody
**Psalm 123 (RCL)**
**Psalm 90:1-8, (9-11), 12 (RCL alt.)**
**Psalm 128:1-2, 3, 4-5 (LFM)**

Psalm 123 is one of fifteen Songs of Ascent that make up a special collection in the psalter (Psalms 120–134). All Songs of Ascent refer to journeys of the pilgrim. These hymns reveal a true pilgrim piety; dependence on God for salvation, acknowledgement of God's work in the past, and hope for the same in the future.

This short psalm is voiced while looking up to the heavens where God is enthroned. This gesture is one of both "entreaty and dependence." In it there is an acknowledgment of the Lord's ability to provide help, just as servants look to the hand of their master and as a maid to the hand of her mistress (v. 2). James L. Mays suggests that "embedded in the notion of 'servant' is the responsibility of master and mistress to and for their servants."[4]

The Roman Catholic lectionary attends to another Song of Ascent, Psalm 128. Production and reproduction yield fruitfulness. Fearing the Lord and walking in the ways of the Lord (which, in one sense, are a "receptivity to the blessing of the Lord") yield happiness. Mays says, "There is a concurrence between the way life is lived and the way life is enhanced."[5] This psalm connects nicely with the Gospel in its conviction that "mortals work, but it is the blessing of God that brings work to completion and makes the labor satisfying."[6] It concludes with a benediction (part of which is curiously and unfortunately not included in the lectionary) that blesses the people with the elements mentioned in the first part of the song.

*(For commentary on Psalm 90, see the Psalmody for Pentecost 19, above.)*

## Second Reading
**1 Thessalonians 5:1-11 (RCL)**
**1 Thessalonians 5:1-6 (LFM)**

Paul says to the Thessalonians, "You do not need anyone to tell you that . . ." before proceeding to tell them. This apophasis draws attention to his proclamation, "You, brothers and sisters, are not in darkness." This is not just a reminder; it is made so in its declaration.

Essentially Paul encourages his hearers to live into who they already are (that is, those who live in the light). Living into that state is to clothe oneself, surround oneself in faith, love, hope, and salvation, and to encourage one another in these things. Concerning encouraging one another, Paul tells them yet one more time that they already know this for they are already doing it. They do so because God has destined them for something great—not wrath, but salvation. It may be just the right time to remind your hearers of the same.

## Gospel
### Matthew 25:14-30 (RCL, LFM)
### Matthew 25:14-15, 19-21 (LFM alt.)

This parable is yet another story that contrasts a picture of reality with the kingdom of God. This is the third parable in a row that Jesus tells as part of the response to the disciples' question, "Tell us, when will this be, and what will be the sign of your coming and of the end of the age?" (24:3). One of these parables was considered last week (see Proper 27, above), and the contrasting picture of the kingdom of God will be addressed next week (see Christ the King, below).

Because these comments may vary sharply from most common interpretations, a summary of the latter will be helpful. First, this parable has been the basis of stewardship sermons in which the hearers are encouraged to use their God-given talents (that is, skills and abilities). Those who do will yield greater abilities. A second common interpretation is an allegorical one in which the master is Jesus, the delay is the time between Jesus' death/resurrection and the parousia, and the *doulous* (slaves/servants), "faithful" and "unfaithful," represent Jesus' followers. This interpretation calls us to faithfulness by presenting the actions of the third *doule* as a warning. The sermon exhorts hearers to act a certain way as they wait for Jesus' coming again.

Both interpretations above are focused on us and not God. All we find out about God is that God entrusts us with responsibilities, rewards those who fulfill them, and punishes those who do not. Since Scripture is primarily about God, especially so in this section of Matthew in which the people wonder who Jesus is, the primary focus is God's identity in Jesus Christ. Of course, God has chosen to involve us, so, yes, we do find out the implications of God's identity for our own lives. Even so, the primary focus is God. With anthropocentric interpretations, there tends to be an obsession with what *we* will get out of this; that is, salvation. This, even though the parable itself suggests the results will give the *doulous* greater responsibilities (vv. 21, 23) and the joy will belong to the master into whose service the *doulous* can enter.

Beyond this primary problem of anthropocentrism, there are three other overarching concerns with these interpretations: misinterpretation of basic definitions, lack of attention to textual context, and inconsistency with overall Scripture.

## Basic Definitions

While our word *talent* likely came from this text, this parable is not about our poetic prowess, endurance on the track, or vocal virtuosity. Even if "talent" stood for our unique skill set, the parable does not suggest *how* we are to use this. The "hide-it-under-the-bushel-NO! sermon" simply is not a faithful homiletical trajectory. A talent is an amount of money, equivalent to over fifteen years' wages (a daily wage = one denarius; six thousand denarii = one talent). Yes, it's a lot. The *doulous* in Matthew 25 are entrusted with the master's estate.

Some have suggested "talent" represents the word of God that is not to be restrained. Take a risk, invest God's word by . . . well, by doing what? We are stuck here because the parable simply does not address this. Others say, "The talents do not stand for anything other than the great value of the kingdom and the significant responsibility it brings."[7] Each of these allegorical interpretations is unsupported by the text and yields a random, moralistic message focusing on our responsibility to take a risk and lacking connection to God.

Another term that needs clarification is the Greek word *kyrios*. This same word is used in Scripture to identify both a human master (lord) and God as master (Lord). Most interpretations assume the parable desires for us to see in this human lord our eternal Lord. I will propose otherwise.

## Textual Context

The interpretations above do not consider a possible function of the story and its place in Jesus' fifth discourse. The "it" in "For it is as if a man . . ." (v. 14) does not represent the kingdom of God. Nor is this necessarily a further explication of what comes immediately before (v. 13). Instead, this parable desires that we compare this story with the kingdom of God. What we will soon discover is that it is actually a contrast. Luise Schottroff suggests that the opening line is to be read as a "challenge to critical comparison, not as an invitation to equation (e.g., not: God is like a king, who . . .). I ask: Where is the God of the Torah, and the Torah itself, to be seen—alongside, behind, and/or in the parable?"[8]

This point alone opens the possibility that the master in the story does not represent a divine figure. Another justification of this view is the consideration of the parable within the whole fifth discourse. As mentioned above, Jesus is still responding to the disciples' question about what things will look like when he returns. One of the ways he responds is by warning his hearers against false prophets. What if we were to understand the master in this story as representing a false prophet? The difficulty in viewing the text in this new way points to the enticing and longstanding power of the allegorical interpretation. Schottroff says, "This tradition is so powerful that I continually fall back into it if I do not stay alert to social history—and to the internal contradictions between the message of Jesus, in this case according to the Gospel of Matthew, and the behavior of the kings and masters in the parables."[9]

The unknowns in the parable (e.g., no guidelines for what to do with the talents) push us beyond itself. The parable alone is not intended to answer our questions. The disciples had to continue listening to Jesus and we have to read on (to Matt. 25:31-46) in order to see that the behaviors in this parable eventually will be confronted with divine judgment.

Jesus' humble entry into Jerusalem, which precedes this text, gives us a glimpse of his identity and provides a lens through which to see Matthew's entire fifth discourse, and this parable within it. The picture of a master who crassly demands interest on his investments does not coincide with Jesus' arrival.

## Scripture Overall

"For to all those who have, more will be given, and they will have an abundance; but from those who have nothing, even what they have will be taken away" (v. 29). This verse alone would have alerted Jesus' hearers and should alert us to the fact that this is not God's way. Jesus' entire ministry has flipped everything upside down: "Blessed are the poor in spirit, for theirs is the kingdom of heaven" (5:3); "It is not the will of your Father in heaven that one of these little ones should be lost" (18:14); "The last will be first, and the first will be last" (19:30; 20:16); "All who exalt themselves will be humbled, and all who humble themselves will be exalted" (23:12). The "law of increase" (a form of positive thinking that endorses the idea that "thoughts and attitudes based on abundance and success attract and produce more abundance and success"[10]) is not at work in Jesus' ministry. The interpretations above buy into this.

Did the master obtain many lifetimes' worth of income in one lifetime via "the law of increase"? Are the *doulous* to be faithful to this economic principle? Since there is no guidance in the story regarding precisely what faithfulness is, one is left to assume that the *doulous* will mirror what the master has done; that is, turn around and make two and a half lifetimes of wages. The delay would have to be mighty long. Having that much money (the master calls even these amounts "little") smells of excessive greed. It is the opposite of what Jesus will promote in the subsequent text. Two imitated these means (according to their abilities, as the master sees it) and one refused to do so because of the master's behavior. In his view, the master's ways are not to be reiterated. Are we to think the third assessment of the third *doule* is accurate? According to the interpretations above, we are not. But why not? Perhaps his role is to prompt us to consider that the master's behavior and economic system encouraged by this parable do not reflect God and the ways of the kingdom of God. Schottroff writes, "Those who have something will be given more, and those who have nothing will be squeezed. . . . The narrative is absolutely clear. It describes the economic and political structure of an exploitative kingship."[11] The excessiveness in the parable is absurd. In fact, absurdity is the point. It is absurd to think God would be at the center of such a system.

If faithful servants are those who get returns on their gifts, then we all would be in trouble in a bad economy. Those of us who were able to squeeze out a commission would likely have taken something from others. How would this be faithful (see Pentecost 21, above, regarding the "wise" virgins' refusal to share oil)? As Ulrich Luz writes, "It is too bad the parable does not tell of an additional slave who invested his capital, failed, and then declared bankruptcy. Would the master have invited him to 'enter his joy'? One hopes so!"[12]

If Jesus is speaking to his disciples about how they are to live their lives in his absence, this does not pertain to us, for although we do live in the already-not-yet era, we are not without God; not ever. God is not one whose disappearance promotes gain through self-sufficiency. No, God wants a relationship with us and is always present. In other words, this parable cannot be interpreted through the lens of an absent God. When it is, we are left to our own devices much like the slaves in the *doulous* who were given no direction. This is not an accurate depiction of the kingdom of God. Even Matthew bookends his account with an emphasis on God's presence (throughout history—represented in the genealogy—and into the future—"I am with you always until the end of the age," Matt. 28:1).

Finally, do we know God to dole out grace "according to our abilities"? No, God distributes God's grace according to God's graciousness. God does not settle accounts via a simple faithfulness/reward or unfaithfulness/punishment system. God settles accounts on the cross toward which Jesus is heading in this parable.

## Homiletical Trajectories

I suggest a sermon that does one or more of the following:

1. *Contrasts the parable's ways and God's ways.* When this text is allowed to tell us about God, we discover the master is nothing like God. Help us distinguish between the system in the parable and the way of God in Jesus. The sermon will function like a tail wind causing us to lean forward into next week's depiction of God's kingdom.

Since this is a part of a long discourse, it does not make sense to carve out this story and preach solely on it. You will not find good news in it. As the preacher, you help us interpret it in light of the whole story. In that case the good news for the day is that there is more. You are the new Matthew who takes what you have and directs it for a particular people in a particular time in a particular place.

2. *Addresses judgment appropriate to the text.* That this parable alone does not point to God's judgment surely does not suggest God does not judge. Suggesting the latter would be to mislead your hearers.[13] "Weeping and gnashing of teeth" (denoting extreme sorrow and emotion) certainly does point to judgment. Indeed, this is key in Matthew. Of the seven times this appears in the New Testament, six are in Matthew

and five times it is used to conclude parables.[14] There will be judgment; it's just that this is not yet a picture of God's judgment. (That is next week.)

While this text does not provide a thorough description of judgment, the text does "arrest, warn, and force consideration."[15] The sermon might do the same as long as its warning is not to avoid the behavior of the *doulous*, but to beware false masters.[16] The point of this parable of judgment is not to put fear into hearers so that they avoid judgment, but to encourage and solidify their trust that God will not deal with them as this master did with his *doulous*. This is what the third servant did not understand. Schottroff explains, "God will be a just judge. What is at stake now is to draw the conclusion from that. Parables are also to be understood by those who, up to this point, have obstinately refused. They are texts of eschatological hope, and telling them is practical love of neighbor."[17]

It is possible here to draw upon judgment themes in the other lectionary texts. Rather than interpreting Matthew 25 in light of them, consider interpreting them in light of this view of Matthew 25.

3. *Convinces us that faithfulness to God is not a risk.* This text does not support an interpretation whereby the preacher uses it as a proof text for launching a congregational capital campaign. In fact, any encouragement of risk is a misuse. Again, this parable is a depiction of what God is not. God is not a risky investment. Proclaim that there is no risk in trusting God, for it is the surest thing. The parable may cause us to enter into the joy of a master, but not the master in the parable. Entice us to consider what it is to enter into the joy of Jesus Christ.

4. *Provides a sneak preview of God's kingdom.* Don't leave us hanging. Give us a sneak preview of what the kingdom of God looks like and what it looks like for us to be faithful. This will require reading Matthew 25:31-46 as an application of this parable.

## Notes

1. Mark Throntveit, "Judges 4:1—5:31—Deborah and Barak," http://www.enterthebible.org/Bible. aspx?rid=27, accessed July 16, 2010.
2. Carole R. Fontaine, "Proverbs," in *The Women's Bible Commentary*, ed. Carol A. Newsom and Sharon H. Ringe (Louisville: Westminster John Knox, 1992), 152.
3. Ibid.
4. James L. Mays, *Psalms*, Interpretation: A Bible Commentary for Teaching and Preaching (Louisville: John Knox, 1989), 395.
5. Ibid., 404.
6. Klyne R. Snodgrass, *Stories with Intent: A Comprehensive Guide to the Parables of Jesus* (Grand Rapids: Eerdmans, 2008), 535.
7. Luise Schottroff, *The Parables of Jesus* (Minneapolis: Fortress Press, 2006), 225.
8. Ibid., 223.
9. Snodgrass, *Stories with Intent*, 542.
10. Schottroff, *Parables of Jesus*, 185. While Schottroff is speaking about the Lukan version of the parable, she suggests this applies to Matthew as well.
11. Ulrich Luz, *Matthew 21–28*, Hermeneia (Minneapolis: Fortress Press, 2005), 255 n. 74.

12. Though he does not agree with this interpretation, Snodgrass rightfully warns against interpreters who try to "bring Jesus' teachings into line with ideas of justification by grace and to avoid moralism" (Snodgrass, *Stories with Intent,* 536). That is not the intent here.

13. See Matt. 8:12; 13:42, 50; 22:13; 24:51; 25:30; Luke 13:28; Ps. 111:10; Job 16:9; Ps. 34:16; 36:12; Lam. 2:16.

14. Snodgrass, *Stories with Intent,* 536.

15. My view of "warn" is certainly different from that of Snodgrass (see n. 14).

16. Schottroff, *Parables of Jesus,* 224.

17. Ibid.

# November 20, 2011
## Christ the King / Reign of Christ
### Thirty-fourth or Last Sunday in Ordinary Time / Proper 29

| **Revised Common Lectionary (RCL)** | **Lectionary for Mass (LFM)** |
|---|---|
| Ezekiel 34:11-16, 20-24 | Ezekiel 34:11-12, 15-17 |
| Psalm 100 or 95:1-7a | Psalm 23:1-3a, 3b-4, 5-6 |
| Ephesians 1:15-23 | 1 Corinthians 15:20-26, 28 |
| Matthew 25:31-46 | Matthew 25:31-46 |

## First Reading
### Ezekiel 34:11-16, 20-24 (RCL)
### Ezekiel 34:11-12, 15-17 (LFM)

God's reign is unique. It is as a shepherd with his flock. The first part of this pericope comforts us by proclaiming that the shepherd himself will seek us out, rescue us, gather us, feed us, heal us, strengthen us. Just when we are thoroughly wallowing in this grace, there is an unfortunate "but." While some (e.g., Israel's leaders who have "ruled harshly, enriching themselves at the expense of the people and failing to safeguard the interests of those who depend on them"[1]) may wish the "but" were not there, it is. And, ultimately, even the "but" is good news for all: "But the fat and the strong I will destroy, I will feed them with justice" (v. 16). Clark Pinnock reminds us:

> We are rather like fat sheep in Ezekiel's pathetic picture, which 'push and thrust at the weak until they are scattered abroad' (Ezek 34:21). We, the wealthy six percent of the world's population, cluster around the well of the earth's resources and drink deeply from it, while the vast majority of people are shunted aside lapping up the trickles that spill from our cups.[2]

The "but" is good news because God's judgment on the "fat" gives an opportunity to the majority of people (whom some might call the minority). It also is good news to the potentially "fat" who have an opportunity to stop "pushing" and "butting at all the weak animals." As Carolyn J. Sharp has put it, "Justice means that God holds bullies accountable."[3] This is good news for both the bullied and the bullies. For us all, God will be Shepherd and King.

## Psalmody
Psalm 100 (RCL)
Psalm 95:1-7a (RCL alt.)
Psalm 23:1-3a, 3b-4, 5-6 (LFM)

It is no surprise that a "YHWH is King" psalm appears on Christ the King Sunday. Psalm 100 is the culmination and pinnacle of this group of psalms (see Proper 24, above, for commentary on the other two). Overall, this is a description of and call for exuberant worship. The presence of God, a faithful and steadfast One who is for us, makes for enthusiastic and authentic worship. James L. Mays says that Psalm 100 "creates a worship that knows who God is and why he is praised."[4] Coming into God's presence singing conjures images both of worship now and of the future heavenly banquet. The utterance of this psalm actually moves us into the presence of the Lord praising and thanking God for steadfast love.

One can envision the King on the throne upon hearing "enter his gates," "enter his courts," "come into his presence." These imperatives confirm that we are entering into the presence of royalty. Mays suggests the assembly's symbols and rituals come from political life convening to recognize the locus of the power that rules. Worshiping points to our "opting" for God's "power structure." Ultimately, the invitation is out for all the earth to join the people of God in worship and confession. Let the exuberance of this psalm shine in worship and in your preaching this day.

Psalm 95 is another "YHWH is King" psalm, in which two theological claims stand out; God reigns and he is our God. This psalm invites us to worship the Lord who reigns and gives the reasons for doing so. The "hand" imagery throughout this psalm is significant: "In his hand are the depths of the earth" (v. 4); "The sea is his . . . which his hands have formed" (v. 5); we are the "sheep of his hand" (v. 7b). Verse 3 is curious since it might suggest there is more than one God over which God reigns. But the pair of royal titles, "Great God" and "Great King," leaves no doubt as to who reigns.

*(For commentary on Psalm 23, see the Psalmody for Pentecost 17, above.)*

## Second Reading
Ephesians 1:15-23 (RCL)
1 Corinthians 15:20-26, 28 (LFM)

These two texts provide variations on similar themes; Christ reigns, we are his subjects, and yet, as the church, we are his body. There are, of course, significant differences between the two. This is not surprising since Paul is writing to two very different audiences (and since only 1 Corinthians is certainly written by Paul). The issue in Corinthians, a dispute over whether or not there is a resurrection of the dead, is not at play with the Ephesians. Paul uses the conviction that Christ was raised from the dead (over which there seems to be no dispute) in order to convince the Corinthians of the former.

How might the preacher let these texts speak in the sermon? Certainly not by providing an excursus on the resurrection of the body or a lecture on the resurrection of Christ. What we have here, says Mary Hinkle Shore, is a "window on a congregation and preacher trying to sort out the real-life implications of the gospel."[5] Therefore, it is worth asking what you, as the pastor of a congregation, might learn from the way Paul addresses these communities. First, there are real-life implications of your congregation gathering on this day to declare and celebrate the reign of One who died what was seen as a shameful death on the cross. Even more, this One, sent by God, was fully human, and yet was God. This is no easy pill to swallow, so there may be some explanation that needs to take place. Second, Paul uses strong, declarative language. Could this be effective for you? Third, note how Paul's teaching is embedded in affirmation and thanksgiving, especially in the Ephesians text. This thanksgiving is offered to God in prayer. Perhaps your prayer is that God would give your hearers *a spirit of wisdom and of revelation in knowledge of him,* that so enlightened, they know the hope, rich inheritance, and power God has for those who believe.

The aspects of God that were given glory and praise are now requested for the Ephesians. That is, as wisdom is God's (v. 8), the author prays that God "may give you a spirit of wisdom" (v. 17); as hope is set on Christ (v. 12), the prayer is for knowing "the hope to which he has called you" (v. 18); as he chose us in Christ (v. 4), so also may we know that it is hope to which we are called (v. 18); as we are destined for adoption (v. 5), the prayer is that we see with the eyes of our hearts "the riches of the inheritance" (v. 18) given to Christ.[6]

Significant for this day is the last verse of each pericope: "And he has put all things under his feet and has made him the head over all things for the church, which is his body, the fullness of him who fills all in all" (Eph. 1:22-23); "When all things are subjected to him, then the Son himself will also be subjected to the one who put all things in subjection under him, so that God may be all in all" (1 Cor. 15:28). The distinctions are worth exploring. But, essentially, this is a day to celebrate the One who *is* all in all and *fills* all in all. One would think the resurrection would be enough, but God's reign continues through it and beyond to its *telos* (as purpose and end).

The Gospel text also calls us to seeing with the eyes of the heart. Create a sermon that enlightens the eyes of our hearts that we may know the hope to which God has called us, the riches and benefits of God's glorious inheritance, and the immeasurable greatness of God's power.

## Gospel
### Matthew 25:31-46 (RCL, LFM)

We made it! For a couple of Sundays Jesus' parables have invited us to consider alternatives to the kingdom of God. Finally, on this last day of the church year, we are presented with a depiction of God's reign. Indeed, as Dolores Dufner declares in a hymn text, Jesus is "a different kind of king"![7] It is this claim we celebrate this day. Even as we celebrate, however, the claim brings us to our knees: "Forgive us for what we have done and for what we have failed to do."

Imagine you are a theater director who must stage this scene. What do you see? What does the throne look like upon which the Son of Man sits? What does the Son of Man look like? Who are "all the nations" gathered around the throne? Picture Jesus separating the nations—putting some on the right and some on the left. Who is on the right? Who is on the left? What do their faces reveal when they ask, "When was it that we saw you hungry . . . ?" Is Jesus' tone different when he responds to each group? Who are and where are the "least of these"? Do you picture a celebration or a fearful reckoning? This exercise will help you ascertain what convictions you have brought into your encounter with this text.

### Who Are "All the Nations" Gathered around the Throne?

The phrase *panta ta ethne* ("all nations") has been at the center of debate for centuries. Does it refer to everyone, Christian and otherwise ("universal" interpretation), Christians only ("classic" interpretation), non-Christians only ("exclusive" interpretation)? The majority of interpreters throughout the ages have claimed the universal interpretation. I will do the same here since (1) this seems to be in line with the entire account (both the disciples and those who persecute the disciples are held accountable by Jesus), and (2) it is very important that the church/ourselves be included in the judgment.

### Who Is on the Right? Who Is on the Left?

Because "goats" did not carry a negative interpretation in ancient Palestine, the sheep/goat distinction is not the key element here. Right/left is. (See, for example, 20:21, 23; 27:38.) Jesus speaks first to those on the right and then to those on the left. The movement of the speeches is the same with slight but evocative differences.

| Right | Left |
|---|---|
| Come | Go |
| Blessed ones | Accursed ones |
| Inherit the kingdom | Depart from me into the eternal fire |
| Prepared for you from the foundation | Prepared for the devil |
| You gave me . . . | You did *not* give me . . . |
| When did we . . . ? | When did we . . . ? |
| Brothers (*sic*), | (no salutation) |
| You did it to the least of these | You did *not* do it to the least of these |
| You did it to me | You did *not* do it to me |

233

A few interesting details are worth highlighting. First, we find out that the kingdom given to those on the right was intended for all from the beginning. Contrast this with the "eternal fire" that was prepared for the devil and his angels. In other words, the accursed are not where they belong. This was not the divine intent. Second, the "ignorance motif" is key. Neither group knew that Jesus was connected to the "least of these" in such a way. Both sheep and goats share a common bewilderment at Jesus' claim that they either did or did not care for him. As Klyne Snodgrass writes, "If people had known the identity of the king, they would have acted differently. Kings we treat nicely; the little people we ignore, which only shows that we act from selfish motives. But compassion has no other motive than meeting a need."[8] While the unrighteous responded in indignation, the righteous do not claim to be righteous. Their service rendered was not done for a reward—that is the surprise in the text.

It is worth noting that "the accursed" shortened the list (in its fourth repetition) to simply listing the "who" and not the "how." They still did not understand that actions toward the "least of these" are not a superficial add-on.

The question of who is on the right and who is on the left is not to be predetermined by the preacher. Only Jesus as the world judge can do this. It could be the case, however, that congregation members hear themselves into one side or the other. In fact, this text elicits just this type of response.

### Who and Where Are the "Least of These"?

Jesus is shown to be a just judge (on God's behalf) who wants justice for his people; in fact, he will see to it that there is justice. Those who are listed are the people alongside whom Jesus has stood, for whom Jesus has fought, and to whom Jesus has shown mercy throughout his ministry; the hungry, the thirsty, the stranger, the naked, the sick, and the imprisoned. Jesus deflects the glory for the sake of these; he is a different kind of king, indeed!

Another hotly debated question is who these people are. Are they all those who are oppressed? Jews? All Christians? Christian missionaries? Your response to this question affects the function of the sermon. For example, if "brothers" (*sic*) means only Christian brothers, then Jesus is likely judging non-Christians who are not treating his followers well. This does not seem plausible since the point is not to console threatened Christians, but to motivate faithful discipleship marked by mercy and love. Just as all nations suggests all people, it is likely that "least of these" means all people who find themselves in a situation where they are hungry, thirsty, unwelcomed, naked, sick, or imprisoned.

This litany is recited four times in this text; it is not to be missed. The list corresponds with what Matthew has told us about Jesus' deeds (see Matt. 11:2-6). Even so, there is nothing particularly Christian about the list since attention to the poor and needy is paid in ancient Near Eastern texts, Greco-Roman writings, and early and later Jewish writings.[9] What is particular to Jesus' kingship is that the world judge is on the side of society's lowliest ones.

Where were the "least of these" in your staging of the scene? Were they a part of "all nations" being judged? I understand "all nations" to mean "all," therefore suggesting that no one is outside Jesus' judgment. I do, however, as you may have noted, suggest that the "least of these" could be any one of us at any time. *All* are to be on high alert to care for *anyone* in need. That is Jesus' call to which we will be held accountable.

## Do You Picture a Celebration or a Fearful Reckoning?

"God will be a just judge. What is at stake now is to draw the conclusion from that," says Luise Schottroff.[10] Given our actions as "the nations," this judgment is a fearful reckoning. However, given Jesus' identity as a humble, merciful, and just judge, this event is a celebration.

The text never addresses us as individuals giving an account for our deeds. Because the second person, "you," is always plural here, the intention is to address the systemic treatment of the "least of these." In this arena, we have not fared well. For this we fall to our knees in corporate confession. Beyond such confession is a call to action; a need to address issues such as health care, immigration, world hunger (to name only three of many). Naming such concerns on this Sunday is unavoidable, for not doing so would surely equate us with those who asked, "Lord, when was it that we saw you hungry or thirsty or a stranger or naked or sick or in prison, and did not take care of you?" (v. 44).

It would be good to let marginalized voices speak on this day. Robert McAfee Brown explains:

> One important aspect of justice, José Miranda reminds us, involves the restoration of what has been stolen. Giving food to the hungry or clothing to the naked is not a charitable handout but an exercise in simple justice—restoring to the poor what is rightfully theirs, what has been taken from them unjustly. So Jesus' vision is not a plea for tax-deductible donations but a fervent cry for justice, for setting right what has gone wrong.[11]

Miranda is speaking not of individual charity, but "collectivized charity" that "challenges social structures of injustice and replaces them with structures that benefit all people." Jesus places a high premium on corporate accountability. What we do to one another matters. Matthew's depiction of the kingdom of God insists that our relationship with God is inseparable from our relationships with people.

It is important that when naming the circumstances for which we are held accountable, we do so in light of the One who is holding us accountable.

Identity of Jesus

These past few weeks we have been moving toward clarity regarding Jesus' true identity. The people in Jesus' day wanted to know and we want to know. What we discover is that Jesus' judgment of the people "based on the treatment of the oppressed, stems from his own solidarity with the oppressed."[12] Matthew 26:2 announces Jesus' own crucifixion. Therefore, the king who identifies with the poor and oppressed does so out of his own experience.

We also discover the following about Jesus' identity:

1. Jesus is the Son of Man who has authority to summon all the nations.
2. Jesus has authority to pass judgment.
3. Jesus is accompanied by angels.
4. Jesus, as judge, is the one who performs the desires of the Father.
5. Jesus will become (is!) his challengers' "least of these".

Again, McAfee Brown:

The judge who directs attention to the poor and outcast is numbered among the poor and outcast. The judge is not an abstract or aloof—or terrifying—deity. Rather the judge is Christ himself, one whose own life was actively identified with the poor and outcast, which is the surest possible sign we could have that love for God (represented by such a one) and love for the poor (represented by such a one) are inseparable.[13]

On this day, help your hearers see others with the eyes of their hearts (Ephesians 1). When they do, they see Christ, the King. Jesus does not just hold us accountable; he offers his solidarity with the oppressed and his own experience of oppression as a lens through which to view the least of these. Emphasize that Jesus, as Christ and King, gives us these new lenses so that we might see and experience the "least of these" anew. And through the "least of these," we see and experience God anew. This calls for a celebration, as Dufner declares:

But still, beyond the span of years, our glad hosannas ring,
For now at God's right hand you reign, a different kind of king.[14]

## Notes

1. Carolyn J. Sharp, commentary on first lesson, http://www.workingpreacher.org/preaching.aspx?lect_date=11/23/2008&tab=1, accessed July 3, 2010.
2. From *The People's Bible,* ed. Curtiss Paul DeYoung et al. (Minneapolis: Fortress Press, 2009), 997. Quoting "A Call for Liberation for North American Christians," *Sojourners* (September 1976): 23–24.
3. Sharp, commentary on first lesson (see n. 1).

4. James L. Mays, *Psalms,* Interpretation: A Bible Commentary for Teaching and Preaching (Louisville: John Knox, 1989), 320.

5. Mary Hinkle Shore, "1 Corinthians: Summary," http://www.enterthebible.org /Bible.aspx?rid=7, accessed July 16, 2010.

6. Insights in this section come from Jennifer Krushas and David Drysdale, students in a preaching course at Lutheran Theological Southern Seminary (Columbia, South Carolina).

7. Dolores Dufner, "O Christ, What Can It Mean for Us," in *Evangelical Lutheran Worship* (Minneapolis: Fortress Press, 2006), #431.

8. Klyne R. Snodgrass, *Stories with Intent: A Comprehensive Guide to the Parables of Jesus* (Grand Rapids: Eerdmans, 2008), 562.

9. For example, see ibid., 544–48.

10. Luise Schottroff, *The Parables of Jesus* (Minneapolis: Fortress Press, 2006), 224.

11. Robert McAfee Brown, *Unexpected News: Reading the Bible Through Third World Eyes* (Philadelphia: Westminster, 1984), 134.

12. Snodgrass, *Stories with Intent,* 550.

13. McAfee Brown, *Unexpected News,* 133–34.

14. Dufner, "O Christ, What Can It Mean for Us."

# November 24, 2011 (U.S.A.) /
# October 11, 2011 (Canada)
## Thanksgiving Day

| **Revised Common Lectionary (RCL)** | **Lectionary for Mass (LFM)** |
|---|---|
| Deuteronomy 8:7-18 | Deuteronomy 8:7-18 or Sirach 50:22-24 or 1 Kings 8:55-61 |
| Psalm 65 | Psalm 113:1-8 or 138:1-5 |
| 2 Corinthians 9:6-15 | 1 Corinthians 1:3-9 or Colossians 3:12-17 or 1 Timothy 6:6-11, 17-19 |
| Luke 17:11-19 | Luke 17:11-19 or Mark 5:18-20 or Luke 12:15-21 |

## First Reading
### Deuteronomy 8:7-18 (RCL, LFM)

The texts assigned for Thanksgiving Day encourage us to be God directed and not self directed. This focus begins right away with the first reading. "Do not say to yourself, 'My power and the might of my own hand have gotten me this wealth.' But remember the LORD your God, for it is he who gives you power to get wealth, so that he may confirm his covenant that he swore to your ancestors, as he is doing today" (Deut. 8:17-18). The emphasis on God's ability to create abundance for all is very evident throughout this sermon delivered by Moses to the Israelites. You may consider creating a responsive reading with this text using verse 18 as a refrain.

The verb "remember" (*zakar* in Hebrew) appears fourteen times in Deuteronomy alone. One cannot help but recall the commandments given to the Israelites: "Remember that you were a slave in the land of Egypt, and the LORD your God brought you out of there with a mighty hand and an outstretched arm" (Deut. 5:15). Without a collective memory, especially in times of prosperous abundance as the Israelites experienced in the promised land, we might be tempted to forget our dependence on God and become self directed. Essentially, this is what thanksgiving is about. Remember what God has done, know what God is doing, and be assured of what God will do for you. For God's followers, remembering and giving thanks go hand in hand.

Sirach 50:22-24 (LFM alt.)
1 Kings 8:55-61 (LFM alt.)

This great blessing from the lips of King Solomon recorded in 1 Kings 8 follows a long prayer (vv. 22-53) at the dedication of the newly constructed temple. The prayer is actually bookended by the king's blessing of the people (vv. 14-21 and 54-61). The second blessing announces the Lord as one who keeps promises, who is present (as the Lord was with the ancestors), and who commands that ordinances and statutes are kept. The pericope concludes with an exhortation to devote oneself completely to the Lord. This text, which may not be the focus of the sermon, might be appropriated (perhaps in an amended form) as the closing benediction of the Thanksgiving worship. Sirach 50:22-24 may also serve as the closing benediction.

# Psalmody
## Psalm 65 (RCL)

The theme of God's abundance is detectable in this song of joyful praise. Verse 9 especially ("You visit the earth and water it, you greatly enrich it") reminds me of the exuberant praises sung by Zimbabweans in long when the rains ended the long drought. This psalm is an unabashed song of thanksgiving that God answers prayer, forgives transgressions, combats chaos, visits the earth and softens its ridges with showers, and stirs the fruitfulness of the land. The poetic description of how God is active in the world is stunning and worth highlighting. In the end, all parts of creation are praising God in their own particular way (vv. 12-13).

The psalm's three sections highlight God's reign over the temple (vv. 1-4), the world (vv. 5-8), and the earth (vv. 9-13). The conclusion of each section describes the effect of God's works on the members of the congregation (v. 4), on the whole cosmos (v. 8), and on the earth (vv. 12-13). This may serve as the movement of a sermon based on this psalm.

## Psalm 113:1-8 (LFM)
## Psalm 138:1-5 (LFM)

Both Psalm 113 and Psalm 138 are hymns of praise and thanksgiving and are thus fitting for this occasion. Psalm 113 is typical in its form. That is, the call to "Praise the Lord!" bookends the entire psalm. Between the calls to praise the Lord is an impressive list of why such praise is justified. No one is like the Lord our God, who is high above all nations, who unpredictably raises the poor from the dust and gives the barren woman a home. Curiously, and unfortunately, the lectionary leaves off the last verse of the psalm, which not only serves to aid the poetic form, but notes God's care for the barren woman. The preacher is encouraged to utilize Psalm 113 in its entirety.

Psalm 138 is an individual hymn of thanksgiving sung by one who, having been in need of "strength of soul," has been answered by the Lord. This one praises the Lord and gives thanks with his whole heart, before the gods, in reverent prostration.

This individual hymn of thanksgiving models for us what it looks like to "sing of the ways of the Lord."

# Second Reading
## 2 Corinthians 9:6-15 (RCL)

This text provides a different twist on generosity compared with the other Thanksgiving texts. Instead of God being glorified through God's generosity (though that is certainly assumed here), Paul is asserting that God is glorified through the generosity of the Corinthians ("You glorify God . . . by the generosity of your sharing with them and with all others"). This pericope is the conclusion of a larger section (chaps. 8 and 9) in which Paul is concerned with the collection for the churches in Jerusalem.

In addition to our generosity having the potential to glorify God, there are a few other salient observations about generosity in this text. First, God, as the one who "supplies seed to the sower and bread for food will supply and multiply your seed for sowing and increase the harvest of your righteousness" (v. 10), is the reason we can be generous in the first place. Second, generosity cannot be forced. "Each of you must give as you have made up your mind, not reluctantly or under compulsion" (v. 7). This is followed by one of the most popular phrases heard on stewardship Sunday: "God loves a cheerful giver." The Greek word for "cheerful" is *hilaron*, which, of course, is the Greek word from which we get *hilarious*. God loves a hilarious giver. In other words, encourage your hearers to laugh all the way up to the offering plate. For God's abundance, worthy of exuberant laughter, allows us to be generous, which in turn glorifies God.

## 1 Corinthians 1:3-9 (LFM)
## Colossians 3:12-17 (LFM alt.)
## 1 Timothy 6:6-11, 17-19 (LFM alt.)

The opening of 1 Corinthians highlights Paul as an encourager as he rhetorically establishes rapport with his addressees. This is probably necessary since he is preparing to address the quarreling and interpersonal conflicts that have arisen in the church he founded.

The Colossians and 1 Timothy pericopes address directly the ways of Christian discipleship. Colossians 3:15 and 17 specifically encourage thankfulness as a mark of discipleship. Living in this way points to Christ's lordship over our lives, which is a major theme in Colossians. The 1 Timothy and 1 Corinthians texts offer the preacher an opportunity to connect thanksgiving and stewardship. Indeed, the way we care for one another and creation and share our resources has the potential to reflect our gratefulness for the abundance God has first given and continues to give us.

# Gospel
## Luke 17:11-19 (RCL, LFM)

The danger of encountering this story every Thanksgiving is the pressure to preach a fresh perspective. The joy of encountering this story every Thanksgiving is the opportunity to preach a fresh perspective. In order both to avoid the danger and to harness the joy, consider setting aside the occasion for a moment. Since this holiday tends to govern how the story is heard, the most common perspective of the text focuses on the one leper who returns to Jesus after perceiving that he has been cleansed, resulting in a sermon that encourages the hearers to be thankful in the same way. While the story might indeed suggest this, it suggests a lot more. Therefore, resist the temptation, at least for starters, to allow the context to trump the text.[1]

Above all, this story is about Jesus more than it is about the lepers. Even more, it is a healing story more than it is a story about giving thanks. Its intrigue is in its cast of characters, kinesthetic movement (e.g., approach, "Go!" and prostration), attention to and yet disregard of boundaries, and its building from something unexpectedly great to something unimaginably greater.

### The Ten

Ten lepers have found company in their misery. We know nothing about them as individuals, for in the beginning of the story they function as a group, accepting their social identity as outcasts by "keeping their distance." And yet, boldly, the group approaches Jesus and asks for mercy. In other words, the group did not accept its status quo enough not to desire to be made clean. And so they approach Jesus but keep their distance. Although their request was probably common, the response they receive this day is not. Without delay, without further inquiry, without any requirements, Jesus sees, really sees, their plight. Without pomp and circumstance, Jesus tells them to go and show themselves to the priest. The text assumes we will know what this means. According to Levitical law (Leviticus 13–14), the temple priests must examine and provide the cleanliness approval before one with leprosy can be reinstated into the community. The ten lepers would have known this even though they are not told they are or will be made clean. As a group, again, they follow Jesus' instruction and head to the temple priests. On their way, all are made clean (*ekastharistheson*).

A few things are clear at this point: (1) The group mentality is strong. (2) Jesus, too, treats the ten as a group by "making clean" all of them. In other words, Jesus did not consider some to be worthy to be made clean and others not. (3) Beyond approaching (yet keeping their distance) and asking for mercy, there is nothing the individuals of the group had to do in order to be made clean. (4) All ten obeyed Jesus' command to go to the priest.

### The Ten Shall Become Nine

Group identity breaks down even before they reach the priests. The cause? Accurate and thorough perception. There is one leper who makes a break from the group when he sees, really sees, that something life changing has happened. (Note that this is the same verb "to see" that is used when Jesus sees the ten in verse 14.) The text is not clear about whether "the nine" (Jesus' words in v. 17) recognized yet that they were clean. We know nothing more about them (their ethnicity, their motivation, their health), except that they followed Jesus' instruction, which was in line with societal expectations. In other words, "the nine" have done nothing wrong. Even so, as we discover in Jesus' words, they have fallen short of doing everything right. Since we never find out what happened to them, the text clearly wants us to focus elsewhere; that is, on "the one" and Jesus.

### The One

What we do know is that the one leper sees that he was "healed." Upon this recognition, the verb changes from "being made clean" to "being healed" (*iathe*). The one sees more clearly what has happened to him; what he experienced is more than a cleansing—it is a healing. When he sees this, he embarks on a liturgical journey. He turns around, raises his voice to praise God, prostrates himself before Jesus, and thanks him. As worship should be, the actions of the one are God directed and not self directed.[2]

Then comes the shocking part: the one was a foreigner, a Samaritan. In other words, the one who had been doubly outcast as both a leper and a foreigner is now triply blessed. Not only was he cleansed, but he was healed. Even more, Jesus declares him thoroughly well: "Your faith has saved you" (*sesoken* is from the root word meaning "saved," v. 19).

### God Who Cleans, Heals, and Makes Well

The focus of this text really is on God in Jesus Christ. What do we discover about who God is and how God is at work in the world? First, we see that Jesus is differently affected (clearly not unaffected) by society's placement of the outcast. He is willing to be in relationship with those who are cast out by others. Jesus requires nothing from them in order to cleanse them from their leprosy. Well, it is true that the ten lepers recognize their need and recognize that Jesus can do something about it and pray to Jesus to have mercy on them. We also find out that God cleanses and then sets the cleansed free. Jesus did not say, "There will be a surprise, and once you realize it, come back and tell me about it. You can thank me at that time." There is no command to give thanks or even a clear protocol about how to respond. God cleanses because God is a gracious God.

The one leper's distinctiveness is not only in his being a double outcast (both as leper and as Samaritan). It is this doubly outcast one who helps us see that there is a different priest to go to in order to experience reintegration into society, wholeness. The one leper sees Jesus as the new high priest.

The message here is that God is the one who cleans, heals, and saves and that God does this through Jesus. That Jesus is en route to Jerusalem when he encounters the ten lepers provides some clarity with regard to the interplay between these three verbs.

## The Context

So . . . what about preaching this healing text on Thanksgiving? Let me give you a summary of a common thanksgiving sermon on the text. In short, we are told we should remember always to give thanks like the one leper. Apparently, Jesus berates the nine for not taking time to give thanks where it is due. We should not be like those nine. Even more, if we are like the one who gives thanks for God's great gifts in our lives (which is usually analogous to a sign of faith), we will be made well also.

The problems with this interpretation are numerous: (1) There are so many other themes in the text worth exploring besides thanksgiving. For example, Jesus' power to heal, Jesus cleans all without much pomp and circumstance on the individuals' part, the cultural customs that are followed (regarding the unclean and the outcast, going to the priests to be certifiably clean), and recognizing that the work of God in our lives might separate us from others who want to follow the local customs. (2) We've heard it all before. Might not this Thanksgiving offer something new for us? (3) Since there is no command in the text to give thanks, it does not seem appropriate to command this of our hearers. (4) Jesus' tone when he asks, "Were there not nine others who were made clean?" is unclear. Instead of being angry or disappointed, perhaps Jesus is concerned or confused or simply trying to make sense of the whole situation. In other words, we do not know that Jesus berates the nine. (5) There is no place in the text that suggests that our cleaning is conditional; that is, *if* we turn to God and give thanks, then we will certainly be all the more blessed. (6) The interpretation above says nothing about God as the active agent when, really, God is indeed the primary agent.

Since the whole Thanksgiving worship service can be shaped so that it *does* the text (as pointed out above), my suggestion is for preachers to help their hearers see, really see, what God has done for them. Point out the cleansing, the crossing of boundaries, the reintegration into community, the abundant wholeness God in Jesus has given them. Your hearers will be sent on their way and, even without being told the protocol, will come back and give thanks when they realize how they have been affected by such abundance. If they do not do this, they are still cleansed by God's word and work. When they do this, God will be glorified.

## Mark 5:18-20 (LFM alt.)
## Luke 12:15-21 (LFM alt.)

Mark 5 is a small section in the broader story of Jesus' healing ministry. Jesus is in the land of the Gerasenes and has just healed the man possessed by unclean spirits. In these three verses we find the healed man begging to go with Jesus. However, Jesus does not allow this. Instead, Jesus encourages the man to go to his friends and family and tell them all what the Lord has done for him. The man's evangelism leads to the amazement of many.

The parable recorded in Luke 12 confuses those of us immersed in a capitalist society. Those rewarded by Wall Street standards are called fools by Jesus. Once again, we are called to live lives that are God directed (that is, that point to God and are led by God) and not self directed. Not even our possessions are beyond the purview of Christian discipleship. This parable's focus on money is not unlike other texts for Thanksgiving Day in the LFM. The discernible connection between thanksgiving and stewardship is a possible common thread to be addressed when attending to the LFM texts.

## Notes

1. Thanks to the Luther Seminary Doctor of Ministry in Biblical Preaching cohort (especially Joel Hoogheem and Rhoda Preston) and my colleague Fred Gaiser for their insights on this text. For more on healing texts, see Fred Gaiser, *Healing in the Bible: Theological Insight for Christian Ministry* (Grand Rapids: Baker Academic, 2010).
2. Fred Gaiser, "Your Faith Has Made You Well": Healing and Salvation in Luke 17:12-19, *Word and World* 16, no. 3 (Summer 1996): 291–301.[